Teenage intimacies

Manchester University Press

GENDER IN HISTORY

Series editors:

Lynn Abrams, Cordelia Beattie, Julie Hardwick

The expansion of research into the history of women and gender since the 1970s has changed the face of history. Using the insights of feminist theory and of historians of women, gender historians have explored the configuration in the past of gender identities and relations between the sexes. They have also investigated the history of sexuality and family relations, and analysed ideas and ideals of masculinity and femininity. Yet gender history has not abandoned the original, inspirational project of women's history: to recover and reveal the lived experience of women in the past and the present.

The series Gender in History provides a forum for these developments. Its historical coverage extends from the medieval to the modern periods, and its geographical scope encompasses not only Europe and North America but all corners of the globe. The series aims to investigate the social and cultural constructions of gender in historical sources, as well as the gendering of historical discourse itself. It embraces both detailed case studies of specific regions or periods, and broader treatments of major themes. Gender in History titles are designed to meet the needs of both scholars and students working in this dynamic area of historical research.

To buy or to find out more about the books currently available in this series, please go to: https://manchesteruniversitypress.co.uk/series/gender-in-history/

Teenage intimacies

Young women, sex and social life in England, 1950–80

Hannah Charnock

MANCHESTER UNIVERSITY PRESS

Copyright © Hannah Charnock 2025

The right of Hannah Charnock to be identified as the author of this work has been asserted in accordance with the Copyright, Designs and Patents Act 1988.

Published by Manchester University Press
Oxford Road, Manchester, M13 9PL

www.manchesteruniversitypress.co.uk

British Library Cataloguing-in-Publication Data
A catalogue record for this book is available from the British Library

ISBN 978 1 5261 7315 7 hardback

First published 2025

The publisher has no responsibility for the persistence or accuracy of URLs for any external or third-party internet websites referred to in this book, and does not guarantee that any content on such websites is, or will remain, accurate or appropriate.

EU authorised representative for GPSR:
Easy Access System Europe - Mustamäe tee 50, 10621
Tallinn, Estonia.
gpsr.requests@easproject.com

Typeset by Newgen Publishing UK

Contents

Acknowledgements *page* vi

Introduction: sexual histories 1

Part I: Growing up

1 Becoming sexual 41
2 Sexual presents and imagined futures 85

Part II: Relationships

3 Boyfriends and sexual partners 131
4 Friends and peers 172
5 Parents and family 204

Conclusion 248

Bibliography 268
Index 289

Acknowledgements

First and foremost, I would like to acknowledge the women around whose lives this research revolves. I am grateful to the Mass Observers who so diligently told their stories to the Project and to the Mass Observation Trust for allowing me to use and reproduce their testimonies here. I am particularly thankful to the men and women who participated in oral history interviews. I had a wonderful time listening to their stories and I hope they found the experience similarly enjoyable! When recruiting oral history participants, I was especially lucky to have the support of the Exeter branch of the University of the Third Age, the Exeter and Ottery St Mary branches of the National Women's Register, and the University of Exeter Alumni Association; I cannot thank Maggie Teuten, Carol McCullough, Bertram Brockington, and Sheila Bushell enough for their enthusiasm and support.

I thank the Economic and Social Research Council for funding core elements of this research. This research would not have been possible without additional support from the University of Exeter's College of Humanities, the University of Bristol Faculty of Arts research fund, the Royal Historical Society, and the Social History Society.

Over the last ten years this project has evolved significantly and I am deeply grateful to the colleagues, friends, and mentors whose insights and reflections have informed the work. A particular debt is owed to Kate Fisher and Claire Langhamer whose guidance and feedback have been invaluable. Ben Mechen has been an excellent conference companion and research pal since year one and he changed the trajectory of my research by suggesting that I look

Acknowledgements

at Mass Observation material. My colleagues at the University of Bristol have been extremely generous with their time and support. Special thanks go to Josie McLellan, Will Pooley, Grace Huxford, Vivian Kong, and Andy Flack who read various chapter and article drafts and whose comments and reflections have coloured this work in myriad ways.

For their company and friendship, I thank the residents of 71 Cotham Hill. Sarah Jones and Amy Edwards deserve special mentions in these acknowledgements. They are the best of colleagues but, more importantly, the greatest of friends.

Finally, I want to share my heartfelt gratitude to my family. This would not have been possible without the love and support of my parents and siblings or Carol and David Freeman's endless generosity. Last but so far from least, I am forever grateful to James Freeman for all the wisdom he has brought to this research and for the joy he has brought to my life beyond it.

I dedicate this book to my grandmother, Pat Charnock, a woman born before her time and the smartest person I know.

Mass Observation material reproduced with permission of Curtis Brown, London on behalf of the Trustees of the Mass Observation Archive © The Trustees of the Mass Observation Archive.

Introduction: sexual histories

'Okay, so you're going to want to know how I felt about boys, sex, all that sort of thing really aren't you?'[1] Tracy was born in 1963 and grew up in the south west of England in the 1970s. Being interviewed as part of an oral history project in 2014, this was Tracy's response when I asked her to discuss 'being a teenager'. Over the next couple of hours Tracy candidly recalled the sexual experiences of her youth. She discussed her teenage sexual practice, describing not only the first time she had penetrative intercourse but also her earlier experiences of getting 'poked' and having her breasts fondled at youth club discos. For Tracy, 'boys, sex, all that sort of thing' were synonymous with her adolescence. Thinking about, talking about, spending time with, and eventually having sex with, boys all played a central role in being a teenager.

That heterosexuality was a structuring influence upon the lives of young women was not new in the post-war period. Yet while a preoccupation with boys, romance, and marriage was no revelation, Tracy's reference to sex did reflect a significant departure from previous generations. Although Tracy and her friends were interested in boyfriends and romance, they were also interested in the physical aspects of heterosexuality. Contrary to their romance story counterparts, girls like Tracy actively engaged in, and at times sought out, 'snogging', 'fumbling', 'heavy petting', and penetrative sex. Compared to their mothers and grandmothers, girls of Tracy's generation were increasingly likely to have sex before marriage and to engage in a number of sexual relationships before getting married.[2]

As these changes in sexual practice became apparent, post-war teenagers became symbolic of a new 'permissive' culture. In so far as they were more openly sexually active, Tracy and her friends embodied modern sexual values. But listening to Tracy tell the story of her teenage years, existing caricatures of the 1960s 'sexual revolution' appear wildly out of touch. In contrast to the image of the Dolly Bird, clothed in '[t]opless dresses, miniskirts … edible knickers [and] seethrough blouses', strictly regulated school uniform and parent-approved ensembles were the wardrobe staples of Tracy and her classmates.[3] In 1965, an American journalist asserted that '[y]oung English girls take to sex as if it is candy and it's delicious'.[4] Tracy, like many of her generation, engaged in a range of sexual activities as a teenager but this was not a universally 'delicious' experience. Having sex for the first time on her mother's dining room floor with the family dog sniffing around, Tracy's experience was far from the supposedly glamorous orgies of 'Swinging London'.

While 'Swinging London' has a place in histories of mid-twentieth-century sexual culture, this book tells the story of girls like Tracy who grew up in England in the 1950s, 1960s, and 1970s to offer a new perspective on the history of sexual change in post-war Britain.[5] Drawing on 280 personal testimonies, *Teenage Intimacies* traces the everyday experiences and relationships of teenage girls and the ways in which matters of sex and intimacy shaped their young lives. Rather than seeing sex as an isolated or discreet element of individual experience, the book shows how sex and intimate relationships influenced the broader experience of being a teenager at this time. It demonstrates the centrality of sexuality to ideas of development and discourses of 'growing up' before going on to illustrate how matters of sex figured within girls' relationships not only with their boyfriends but also with their friends, classmates, peers, parents, and families.

In telling these stories, *Teenage Intimacies* puts young women's experiences 'on the record', offering a new vantage point from which to consider histories of English sexuality in this period. Doing so matters not only because it adds texture to existing accounts but because it reveals new explanations as to why sexual mores shifted in this period. The book shows that understandings of what sex meant and what it was for changed significantly in the post-war period and that young women and their sexual lives were instrumental in determining the trajectory of these changes. As we will see, adult society and its values certainly influenced young people's lives but, particularly when it came to matters of sex, young people navigated the changes of post-war society in their own ways. Teenage girls were not necessarily subscribing to radical new ideologies but the subtly different responses they had to the conversations, interactions, and experiences that made up their day-to-day lives came to constitute seismic shifts in English sexual culture.

Schoolgirl revolutionaries

While women of the post-war generation have witnessed many profound social transformations in their lifetimes, three stand out as having shaped their adolescent heterosexuality. These were the 'rise of the teenager' associated with the 1950s and 1960s, the 'sexual revolution' of the 1960s and 1970s, and the longer-term reconfiguration of the rights and place of women in society. Writing the history of teenage sexuality allows us to bring scholarship on these separate strands of British social history into conversation with one another for the first time and, in so doing, this book casts these fields and the social changes associated with each in a new light.

Teenage revolution

The 1950s are often characterised as having witnessed the 'birth' of the teenager. In part, this describes demographic change as there were simply more teenagers in the 1950s and 1960s than there had been previously. The high birth rate in the years immediately following the Second World War meant that the number of people within the British population under the age of twenty rose from approximately three million in 1951 to over four million by 1966.[6] Beyond sheer numbers, however, what it meant to be young also changed in this period. The post-war generation grew up alongside the expansion of the 'Welfare State' and were the first generation to benefit from free universal healthcare, universal education to the age of fifteen (to sixteen from 1972) and a national Youth Service. These provisions created new opportunities for teenagers and young people, setting them apart from generations who had come before them.[7] At the same time that young people were becoming some of the key beneficiaries of new forms of state support, from the mid-1950s they also became the face of the new 'affluent society'. As one oral history interviewee put it: 'I was young, I was free ... I had plenty of money, there were plenty of jobs ... I could grow with what was happening around me and change with it.'[8] Studying the teenage consumer in the late 1950s, social researcher Mark Abrams found that teenagers of the post-war period were 'newly enfranchised, in an economic sense', with twice the spending power of teenagers in 1939.[9] Crucially, Abrams noted that teenagers had very distinctive spending patterns; they spent their money 'mainly on dressing up in order to impress other teenagers and on goods which form the nexus of teenage gregariousness outside the home'.[10] While young people had been spending hard-earned wages for decades, it was in the post-war period that the 'young consumer' became an economic force and a raft of new products and services emerged to capture their wealth.[11]

The affluence of youth not only created new markets for consumer goods and leisure providers but also contributed to shifting understandings of the life cycle. In 1969, the age of majority was lowered from twenty-one to eighteen. Tasked with investigating the legal status of young people in English society, the Latey Committee reported that 'the historical causes for 21 [being the age of majority] are not relevant to contemporary society ... most young people today mature earlier than in that past'.[12] Across the twentieth century, marriage was perhaps the most profound threshold in the transition from childhood to adulthood. In the first half of the century, most people left school and entered work in their early to mid-teens and continued to live at home until marriage (although military service and domestic service formed significant exceptions to this). The act of getting married was an important moment of transition: it not only saw the legal union of the couple but also usually prompted young people to move out of the family home. In many women's cases, it also meant leaving employment, and opening oneself up to the possibility of becoming a parent in their own right.[13] As *Teenage Intimacies* demonstrates, however, in the second half of century the dynamic between marriage and adulthood shifted. In the post-war period, affluence gave many young couples the financial security they needed to establish their household earlier and contributed to a lowering of the average age at marriage;

between 1950 and 1970 the average age of marriage for young men fell from 29.5 to 27.2, and for young women fell from 26.4 to 24.7.[14] At the same time, opportunities to stay in education longer, expanded work prospects, greater geographical mobility, and gradually shifting gender norms meant that, while marriage remained a hugely important step in the life cycle for many, its status as the *key* marker of 'growing up' and becoming adult began to diminish.

These changes prompted much social research into the shifting status and experience of youth. In particular, the distinctive approach to youth subcultures pioneered at the Centre for Contemporary Cultural Studies (CCCS) at the University of Birmingham in the 1970s has provided scholars with critical apparatus that has been deployed in many youth studies over the last fifty years.[15] Although the work of the CCCS and other subcultural theorists has been highly influential – not least in demonstrating the importance of taking youth cultures on their own terms – the emphasis on 'spectacular' subcultures, style, and particular forms of working-class culture meant that other experiences were not well accounted for in its approach.[16] In the mid-1970s, Angela McRobbie and Jenny Garber offered a pointed critique of existing subcultural studies which had almost entirely ignored the lives of young women and neglected to consider the role of gender in shaping youth cultures.[17] The focus on working-class boys' cultures, McRobbie argued, had led to a preoccupation with youth cultures of the street and had not adequately considered the domestic and home lives of subcultural members.[18] To a certain extent, this dynamic persists. While historians such as Claire Langhamer and Selina Todd have written pioneering studies of girls' work and leisure lives before the Second World War and Penny Tinkler has offered important insights into experiences of young women during and immediately after the Second World War, the experiences of young women in the post-war period remain relatively unexplored.[19] At the same time, scholars have also highlighted the somewhat fraught status of class in writing about youth. Michael Clarke, for example, has questioned the relationship between subculture and 'mainstream' culture.[20] Although studies within the CCCS model have been premised on the importance of taking youth cultures seriously, this ethos has been applied unevenly, often uncritically dismissing, if not caricaturing, 'mainstream' youth.[21] Later studies of youth have been less unkind to young people in the mainstream and middle classes but their experiences remain obscured within histories of twentieth-century youth, leading some to identify a 'missing middle' in youth studies.[22]

Teenage Intimacies sheds new light on 'mainstream' and middle-class cultures while highlighting how affluence, new educational opportunities, and mobility blurred many of the boundaries between working- and middle-class girlhood identities. Through its use of personal testimonies and a focus on the lives of middle-class youth, this study offers an important new perspective on what it meant to be a teenage girl in post-war England. Teenage girls were not simply being swept along by a current set in motion by politicians, educators, marketing executives, or indeed their male peers. As we will see, young women were certainly engaging with new opportunities for education and employment and the vastly expanded popular culture of the time, but they were not passive dupes, simply taking what they were given or directed towards. They did not see their experiences as peripheral to more 'authentic' subcultures. Instead, they spent a great deal of time wanting to be 'normal'.[23] Girls had their own tastes, values, and agendas that were certainly informed by broader cultural influences but which often evolved in response to teenagers' specific cultures and contexts.

Sexual revolution

As the 1950s turned into the 1960s, public anxiety about youth was reinforced by emerging concerns about the rise of the so-called 'permissive society' and the onset of a potential 'sexual revolution'. Even a brief glance at the newspapers and social commentary of the period indicates that those living through it believed themselves to be witnessing great change.[24] In the final few weeks of 1958, for example, the *Sunday Pictorial* ran a major feature entitled 'While Parents Sleep'. It claimed to offer 'a blunt, candid-camera close-up of a revolution which is taking place'.[25] Drawing upon the casebooks of four 'wise doctors', the report asserted that a 'disturbingly huge' revolution was in train and that young people across the country (not just those in major cities) were caught up in it. This series and others like it were undoubtedly hyperbolic but we should not dismiss mid-century commentators' anxieties about social change as mere tabloid fear-mongering and exaggeration. Historians may now have moved beyond understanding the (long) 1960s as having witnessed a singular, instantaneous 'revolution' in sexual mores but it is undeniable that sexual attitudes and practices did change significantly over the post-war period. The term 'sexual revolution', when understood as a process rather than an event, can serve as a useful shorthand for describing these developments.[26]

To borrow Jeffrey Week's phrase, there was certainly 'a decisive ... escalation of the volume' of sexual discourse in mid-century Britain.[27] In its most traditional mode of reporting on politics, government, and legal cases, the press and media covered and editorialised on legislative changes that altered the legal status of sex in the 1950s and 1960s.[28] There was extensive coverage, for example, of the 1957 Wolfenden Report which reflected on the legal status of sex work and homosexuality, as well as the 1961 Lady Chatterley trial.[29] The press took a particular interest in 'permissive' legislation such as the Obscene Publications Act in 1959, the partial decriminalisation of abortion and male homosexuality (both 1967), the liberalisation of divorce law (1969), and the provision to make contraception available for free on the National Health Service (1974).[30] A series of sexual scandals only added to the culture of political sex talk.[31] Yet, perhaps the greatest evidence of the shifts in sexual culture lay in the extent to which matters of sex and sexuality pervaded popular consciousness in the periods between the frenzied moments of political intrigue. The tabloid and the broadsheet press as well as broadcast media persistently covered news with sexual overtones, such as the exploits of celebrities, features on contemporary fashions and social behaviour, and reports of studies into sexual attitudes, sexual practices, and pregnancy rates.[32] Sexual imagery was also increasingly prevalent. Advertisements on billboards, in print publications, and on screen commonly featured scantily clad women. Moving into the 1970s, cultures of sexual suggestion were joined by more explicit depictions of sexuality. In 1970, *The Sun* printed its first 'Page Three' featuring a topless woman and the following year an advert for Fisons slimming biscuits printed in *The Times* featured an image of model Vivien Neves completely nude.[33] As Marcus Collins has shown, the underground press revelled in sexual excess and soft-core pornography became a common feature in newsagents across the country.[34] While the film classification system (at least in theory) continued to limit the public's exposure to graphic sexual content at the cinema, the 1970s became the era of the 'sexploitation' film and marginally more highbrow soft-core pornography.[35] In contrast to the 1950s, when the British Board of Film Censors had warned against filmic depictions of women having pre-marital sex, which they worried would become 'a living advertisement for a shiftless and promiscuous way of life', popular culture of the 1960s and 1970s openly played with ideas and depictions of sex for both drama and comedy.[36]

Mid-century commentators were convinced that they were witnessing change and although social surveys indicated that many individuals continued to hold 'traditional' values (when interviewed by Michael Schofield in the mid-1960s, 61 per cent of girls agreed with the statement 'Sex before marriage is wrong', for example), retrospective quantitative data indicate that behaviours were changing.[37] Post-war teenagers were more likely to engage in sex outside of marriage and the average age at first intercourse fell from twenty-one among those born in the early 1930s to eighteen for women born between 1951 and 1955. Explaining how or why this had come about proved difficult, however; a challenge that has similarly been faced by historians in the intervening decades.[38]

Perhaps the cause most often attributed to – or blamed for – the 'sexual revolution' is the invention of the oral contraceptive pill (often referred to as the Pill). The first oral contraceptive pills were made available to married women in England in 1960. In July 1962, 150,000 women were taking the Pill and this had risen to half a million women by 1964.[39] As Hera Cook has indicated, there is little doubt that the Pill 'propelled the cultural transformation of attitudes to sexual behaviour forwards',[40] but we should be wary of overly deterministic accounts of sexual change that simply assert that the Pill unilaterally transformed sexual culture.[41] There have long been practical issues with this narrative – not least that the Family Planning Association refused to distribute contraceptives to unmarried women until 1968 and that contraceptives were not made freely available until 1974, long after the 'revolution' is deemed to have begun. More fundamentally, however, this model of social change assumes that the only thing that had stopped young couples from having penetrative sex in earlier periods was the threat of getting pregnant. As Kate Fisher and Simon Szreter have shown, that simply was not the case. They have demonstrated that cultures of courtship, chastity, and respectability encouraged many young couples to refrain from penetrative intercourse prior to marriage.[42] Fisher's research has also revealed that in the mid-twentieth century, it was men, rather than women, who took the lead in contraceptive practice. What occurred in the 1960s was, in Fisher's words, 'an extremely significant break in social practice' and the arrival of a new technology cannot solely account for this change.[43] Explaining sexual change requires us to focus less on the *supply* of contraceptives and more upon the changing contexts that increased women's *demand* for the capacity to engage in penetrative intercourse but avoid pregnancy. Rather than assuming that young women's sexual desire was an innate impulse that was 'freed' by the Pill, therefore, we need to explore the different emotional regimes and cultures that informed young people's sexual relationships in order to explain why increasing numbers of teenagers were willing to engage in (penetrative) sexual activity in this period.

Changing understandings of what forms of behaviour were morally 'right' and 'good' may have contributed to this. For many commentators in the mid-century, the 'permissive society' could not be separated from a decline in Christian morality. Sam Brewitt-Taylor has indicated that Christian commentators were themselves responsible for a so-called 'Sexual Revolution' in so far as they 'shaped the narrative' that post-war sexual change was 'widespread, unstoppable' and constituted a 'post-religious "revolution"'.[44] Analysing survey data from the 1950s, 1960s, and 1970s, Callum Brown has argued that 'high religiosity may have restrained sexual liberalization in the 1950s' and that 'sexual liberalization, once started in the 1960s and 1970s, rapidly undermined religiosity'. However, it has proven more difficult to attribute declining religious observance and faith as a cause of shifting sexual practice.[45] Indeed, scholarship has challenged traditional stereotypes of British churches as 'essentially backward looking' and 'against all challenges and changes to traditional morality', noting instead the complex and often ambiguous ways that the churches responded to modern sexual cultures and practices as well as how church bodies and leading figures contributed to policy debates.[46]

What *Teenage Intimacies* shows is that transformations at a national level (such as legislation and health policy) and at a cultural level (religious doctrine and changing emotional landscapes) and individuals' sexual behaviour were often mediated through local communities and social networks. Brewitt-Taylor has highlighted the importance of discourse in shaping people's understandings of themselves and how the stories that a society tells about itself matter.[47] Undoubtedly, young people in the 1950s, 1960s, and 1970s were aware of and were influenced by what they saw on television and film as well as what they read in newspapers, magazines, and books. All this informed how they thought about themselves and how they interpreted their feelings and actions. Crucially, though, this book argues that much of the potency of these ideas and the reason they had so much influence was because they were often being repeated, shared, and translated by people that girls cared about. Rather than being abstract ideas articulated by distant figures, young people were hearing about sex from their parents, teachers, romantic partners, friends, and peers.[48] As we will see, young people lived within the broader sexual culture but they did not just passively accept all the ideas that were shared with them. They formed their own opinions based upon their own feelings and experiences and often acted accordingly. Young people's sexual culture was therefore characterised by this interplay between broad culture-wide discourse and local interpersonal dialogue, as well as their own individual sense of sexual selfhood. In this way, young women were responding to changes going on around them and, in finding ways to navigate this, were also driving changes themselves.

Liberating women

The final context essential for understanding the history of teenage girls' sexuality explored here is the shifting status of women in English society. Indeed, much of the trajectory of the teenage and sexual revolutions was shaped by changing understandings of gender and material shifts in young women's lives. New expectations and opportunities for women's work and education challenged traditional notions of the feminine life cycle, which in turn fed into new ideas about the role and function of youth, adolescence, and sexuality.

Across the twentieth century, it was commonplace for girls to go in to paid work upon leaving school. For many women growing up before the Second World War, this period of employment was seen as a stopgap between school and marriage.[49] Leaving school at fourteen, most girls in the interwar period expected to live in their parents' home while going out to work, before finding a suitable husband in their late teens or early twenties. Upon marriage many women would start their own home and family and stop working. This life stage of 'youth' (distinct from childhood), characterised by paid labour, came to be marked by distinct leisure cultures and patterns of consumption facilitated by girls' disposable income. These leisure cultures often underpinned the courtship rituals that would lead to marriage.[50] This trajectory was reinforced by formal marriage bars within a number of professions, which prevented married women from staying in work, as well as by a welfare system that revolved around models of the patriarchal family, the male breadwinner, and wifely dependence.[51]

For many of those born in the wake of the Second World War, work came to occupy a different role in their lives. The 1944 Education Act raised the school leaving age to fifteen and reconfigured the structure of secondary education in England through a new tripartite system of grammar, comprehensive, and technical schools.[52] This legislation had a particularly transformative effect for young women.[53] Under the new system, academically gifted girls of all social backgrounds were given the opportunity to attend grammar schools (although due to limited provision girls had to attain higher examination marks than boys to secure a place).[54] By the mid-1950s, approximately 2.5 per cent of girls entered university. As Carol Dyhouse has explored, the expansion of higher education in the 1960s played an important role in extending degree-level study to girls.[55] In 1950, just under 4,000 women obtained university degrees; in 1970, degrees were awarded to more than 15,600 women.[56]

Of course, not all girls were able or wanted to go to university and/or into professional training.[57] Across the post-war period there remained scepticism about the value of educating young women when many would cease paid employment upon marrying or having children. For many women, however, new educational opportunities radically altered the trajectory of their lives. As Julia Pascal put it, her grammar school was 'a place where I saw that women could hold positions of power and authority, where the pleasures of learning, particularly languages, could offer me a freedom'.[58] Growing numbers of women went into professional and skilled work and this generation adopted an alternative view of 'careers' in which they did often move from paid employment to a period of domesticity upon the birth of their children, but also anticipated that they would eventually go back to work.[59] In 1956, the sociologists Alva Myrdal and Viola Klein described this dynamic in terms of adult women having a 'dual role' as both workers and as wives and mothers, highlighting that these were not mutually exclusive but that women moved in and out of paid employment as their domestic situation required.[60] Rather than employment functioning as a stopgap between childhood and wifely domesticity, in the postwar period full-time domesticity was increasingly perceived as a temporary pause from work and career. Seeing work as a long-term investment, there was more incentive for girls to commit to professions that required training, and, growing up with an expanded welfare state, in a period of affluence, there were more opportunities to pursue this.

Changing opportunities for work and education did not entirely transform the status of women in society.[61] Many inequalities persisted and these became the focus of 'second-wave' feminism and the Women's Liberation Movement in the 1970s. Emerging, in many cases, from broader leftist politics, feminists sought to draw attention to the ongoing oppression of women in British society and abroad, and campaigned for structural change to secure equal rights. Feminists succeeded in attaining a certain degree of institutional and legislative reform, such as the Sex Discrimination Act (1975), the 1975 Employment Protection Act, and the 1976 Domestic Violence and Matrimonial Proceedings Act, and the Women's Liberation Movement was highly influential in providing key social services to women in their communities. The total number of women who considered themselves to be 'members' of the movement was small as a proportion of the population and many women were deeply ambivalent about feminism and its desire to disrupt the existing gender order.[62] Yet while individual women may not have been entirely sympathetic to the 'project' of feminism and did not necessarily consider themselves 'feminists', women were increasingly articulating their rights and expectations of fair treatment.[63] They may not have felt a need or desire to organise around the politics of gender but many women were increasingly empowered to stake a claim to social, cultural, and economic opportunity. They had a new language and, critically, growing financial resources, which enabled them to more powerfully assert their worth.[64]

All of this is to say that women growing up in the 1950s, 1960s, and 1970s were encountering and shaping a social landscape that was quite different from that experienced by their mothers and grandmothers. We should, of course, be careful not to overstate claims of difference – discrimination, inequality, and misogyny did not disappear, and, as the following chapters explore, young women's lives were still highly gendered. What it meant to 'grow up' and the expectations and experiences that characterised this life stage were different depending on whether you were a boy or a girl. The changes taking place in this period were significant, however, and led many women of this generation to think of themselves as a distinct group. Women born in the 1940s and 1950s have been named a 'breakthrough generation': their experiences of youth marked the transition from post-war domesticity to Women's Liberation and second-wave feminism in the 1970s.[65] Contrasting their experiences of education, professional life, and marriage with those of their mothers, women of this generation perceive themselves to have been gifted with opportunities for freedom, self-expression, and individual fulfilment that were not available to previous generations;[66] in Lynn Abrams' words, 'they saw the world through a different lens'.[67] These changes directly informed how young women in the 1950s, 1960s, and 1970s understood their sexuality, and, as I show in the following chapters, through their choices and actions teenage girls of the post-war generation were change-makers in their own right.

Understanding social change in post-war Britain

In its study of young women's adolescent lives and relationships, *Teenage Intimacies* suggests new ways of thinking about each of these strands of post-war British history. It prompts a re-evaluation of how and why the experience of being a young person shifted in the second half of the twentieth century. The following chapters nuance our understanding of intergenerational relations, challenge the assumption that young people in the past passively absorbed and subscribed to the rules and discourses of adult society, and encourage more sensitive analyses of how notions of 'growing up' change over time. In relation to changing sexual mores, this research not only offers a uniquely detailed account of how sexual practice was evolving in post-war England but in situating sexual experiences in the broader context of girls' social lives it also offers a number of new explanations as to why sexual practice was changing.

More broadly, this research offers three key interventions into how historians think about change in the past and the role of ordinary people within this. First, it recognises individual experience as multifaceted and adaptive and demonstrates the importance of considering it holistically. In contrast to historians who (for good reason) tend to divide the past into neat strands such as specific policy areas (housing, education, healthcare) or individual elements of social or cultural life (religious practice, spending patterns, media representations), for historical actors these phenomena co-existed in their experience; developments in one aspect of life often had consequences for others by virtue of the fact that they were experienced simultaneously. Instead of seeing mass consumerism and new expectations for women's work and education as a mere backdrop for understanding girls' sexual lives, the testimonies presented here indicate that these were all inextricably connected within girls' worldviews. Recognising this interconnectedness in experience is helpful, I argue, in challenging overly simplistic accounts of 'agency' in the past. It prompts us to move away from understandings of behaviour rooted in rational action and binaries such as resistance versus compliance. As the following discussions show, changes in social practice and the specific form these took were often the result of individuals attempting to navigate myriad (often competing) influences, structures, and power dynamics.

Second, this research develops a much fuller concept of intimacy as both a subject of inquiry and an analytical tool for historians.[68] This book takes people's relationships as its core subject, exploring how young women's relationships with various figures in their lives influenced and informed their adolescent sexual lives. Though sexuality is subjective, the feelings evoked by matters of sex, be they lust, obligation, joy, fear, security, frustration, or others, were often relational and young women's behaviour reflected not simply individual desire but negotiations of other people's hopes and expectations (or at least what girls perceived these to be). Boyfriends and sexual partners played a key role, but so too did parents, teachers, friends, and peers. Beyond simply identifying that these interpersonal dynamics existed, however, thinking about intimacy and asking about how it functioned within these relationships helps to illuminate elements of experience that may otherwise be overlooked. It reveals emotional registers and affective dynamics that may be obscured if we only consider sexuality in terms of romantic love or desire, for example, and in turn these can suggest new ways of thinking about power within interpersonal relationships.

Where previous studies have interrogated the nature and form of relationships in the past, this study goes further in demonstrating that intimate relations (broadly defined) were powerful motors of social change in their own right. In contrast to historians that have looked to social structures and institutions or individual psychology to explain why mores and worldviews evolved in the past, the account of teenage sexuality presented here revolves around more gradual incremental change, brought about through an accumulation of individual choices. Crucially, the testimonies repeatedly highlight the importance of interpersonal relationships in shaping women's lives: individuals' choices were not made in isolation or necessarily in deference to abstract 'rules' but were made in reference to other people and specific relationship dynamics. This is not to say that legal systems or cultural norms were insignificant – these certainly did impinge on individuals' understandings of the choices before them – but it is to suggest that these structures and discourses acquired potency and meaning through the 'local' intermediaries that voiced them. As *Teenage Intimacies* demonstrates, foregrounding the relationships and interpersonal dynamics that made up individuals' social worlds in our analyses allows us to better understand the motivations and logics that underpinned subtle shifts in behaviour which, when repeated at scale, amounted to significant social change. In these ways, this social history of post-war Britain does not put women's experiences on the record for the sake of adding colour to existing historical narratives but to demonstrate the vital role that young women played in shaping English society and culture.

Sexual storytelling

Teenage Intimacies draws upon a wide range of source material to tell the story of young women's sexual lives. To get a sense of how adults were trying to guide girls through adolescence it considers the advice offered in mid-century magazines such as *Jackie, Honey, Petticoat,* and *Cosmopolitan* as well as the guidance set out in post-war 'facts of life' literature. It also uses post-war social science, government documents, and the popular press to trace how adult society was attempting to make sense of shifting sexual mores. At the heart of the book and its analysis, however, are 280 reflective personal testimonies of women who were teenagers between 1950 and 1980. Focusing its analysis on these testimonies enables this study to move beyond looking at the *ideals* of heterosexual intimacy outlined in guidance texts and the *representation* of sexuality offered by novels, plays, film, and television, to focus on the *lived sexual experiences* of individuals. People in the past rarely kept written records of their sexual lives, especially the seemingly mundane and ordinary components of their relationships or the details of specific sexual encounters. This archival gap is even greater when it comes to recording the experiences of young people whose letters, diaries, and stories are rarely kept into adulthood and are only very occasionally preserved in institutional archives.[69] As Elizabeth Roberts, Kate Fisher, Simon Szreter, David Geiringer, and others have demonstrated, personal testimonies offer unique perspectives on intimate life that would otherwise be obscured.[70]

Building on a rich tradition of using oral history to explore aspects of intimate life in the twentieth century, this research draws upon thirty-three original oral history interviews that I recorded in 2014/15 as part of an oral history project on 'Romance, sex and youth culture in the 1960s and 1970s'. Based in Exeter, participants were recruited through local organisations such as south-west branches of the University of the Third Age and the National Women's Register as well as the University of Exeter alumni association and history groups in the Exeter area.[71] Interviews on projects such as this have to strike a balance between using the limited time with an interviewee to capture accounts of the relevant themes and topics (in this case intimate life and sexuality) while incorporating enough of the broader context of an individual's life to be able to make sense of specific experiences. As such I used a semi-structured interview technique. I often opened interviews with a broad question such as 'What does the term "the Swinging Sixties" mean to you?' and would then ask interviewees to describe their living situation growing up. Following this, there was no set order to the questions asked or topics raised. Interviews often opened with broad conversations regarding childhood home life, schooling, and youthful social life before moving on to more specific discussions of sexual cultures and practice.

Alongside its oral history material, *Teenage Intimacies* also draws upon testimonies contributed to the Mass Observation Project (MOP). The MOP is a life-writing and social research organisation dedicated to 'capturing the experiences, thoughts and opinions of everyday people'.[72] It was established in 1981, building on the earlier work of the Mass Observation movement founded in 1937. The post-1981 MOP moved away from the ethnographic and diary-based model that characterised Mass Observation in the 1930s and 1940s. Three times a year it sends broad-form questionnaires called 'Directives' to a panel of several hundred volunteer writers (known as 'Observers') from across the country. Directives are usually made up of two or three parts, each of which asks Observers to reflect and comment on a particular theme. *Teenage Intimacies* draws on four Directives: the summer 1990 Directive on 'Close Relationships', the spring 1993 Directive on 'Growing Up', the summer 2001 Directive on 'Courting and Dating', and the autumn 2005 Directive on 'Sex'.[73] In total 187 women of the right demographic (born between 1940 and 1965 and who grew up in England) responded to these Directives. Forty-two of these women responded to more than one of these Directives, meaning that in total 247 individual Mass Observation testimonies were consulted.

Mass Observation material is not, by default, retrospective; different Directives ask Observers to take on different roles and write in specific styles. Since 2019, for example, Observers have been asked to describe their experiences of current events such as the COVID-19 pandemic, to offer their opinions of social issues and campaigns such as Brexit and the Black Lives Matter movement, and to keep day diaries on specific dates such as election days.[74] Fortunately for this historical study, the Directives on 'Courting and Dating' and 'Sex' explicitly asked Observers to respond autobiographically, with many prompts directly encouraging Observers to record their own experiences. The 2005 'Sex' Directive prompted Observers to record their sexual life history in chronological order from 'Early Years', through 'School and Adolescent Years' to their 'Adult Years' before asking separate questions about their opinions and feelings about specific aspects of sex and sexuality. Other Directives were less explicitly reflective and therefore had to be used more selectively. For example, when asked to give their thoughts on sex education as part of the 1990 Directive on 'Close Relationships', the boundary between past experience and contemporary opinion in the responses was often slippery. Observers such as Andrea moved between the two modes of writing in their response:

> I believe that sex education is extremely important. I didn't have it at school, except for a brief explanation of human reproduction in O level biology lessons, and several films which I happened to miss because I was away ill. To my mind this is not proper sex education.[75]

Such responses contain much valuable material for historians, though this is needs to be carefully distilled.

Primarily using each set of testimonies in their 'reflective' modes, this book uses oral history and Mass Observation material interchangeably. Interested in what these retrospective testimonies can tell us about sexual practices, feelings, and experiences in the past, the perspectives offered by each of these approaches sit comfortably alongside one another. There are, however, some important differences between these two approaches to collecting personal testimonies. Unlike oral history participants, who usually agree to participate in a single, specific research project on a particular theme, Observers sign up to the broader MOP and they have no prior knowledge of the Directives they will be sent. Of course, Mass Observers are not obliged to respond to Directives but as Dorothy Sheridan, former director of the MOP, has discussed, Observers' desire to be 'good' and fulfil a perceived duty to the project and future researchers compels many to respond to Directives.[76] We might expect that individuals would be reticent or reluctant to share information about their sexual and intimate lives to a research organisation, particularly one such as Mass Observation, which makes its material available to the public. Certainly, a number of individuals did refuse to participate in the 2005 Directive on 'Sex'.

A fifty-eight-year-old male Observer wrote: 'This is one of the subjects I indicated in joining the mass observation [sic] scheme that I preferred not to answer, and I am still of this opinion. Accordingly this question will remain unanswered.'[77] Other Observers did respond to the Directive but articulated their discomfort. Pamela joined MOP in 1991 and had previously submitted responses to the 'Close Relationships' and 'Courting and Dating' Directives as part of her contributions to the Project. She was fifty-eight years old at the time of responding to the 'Sex' Directive. Pamela handwrote a four-page response to the 'Sex' prompts but she noted in the middle of her contribution that '[t]his is really quite difficult to do and I'm feeling quite uncomfortable'. At the end of her response she wrote: 'This was quite a difficult area.'[78] Though some Observers appear to have enjoyed reflecting on their past sex lives, others were clearly uneasy and perhaps would not have offered testimonies had they not been prompted and had they not already made a commitment to MOP. In total, 235 Observers responded to the 2005 Directive on 'Sex', a response level similar to that of all the Directives issues between 2004 and 2006. The response to this early twenty-first-century survey mirrors the experience of other sexual surveys (including Mass Observation's own 'Little Kinsey' survey of the late 1940s) which suggest that the British public are more willing to discuss sex with researchers than may be anticipated.[79] It is worth noting, for example, that more responses were submitted to the 'Sex' Directive than to the 'Public Library Buildings' Directive sent at the same time![80]

Perhaps one factor shaping individuals' willingness to contribute was the fact that responses were written and anonymous. Observers provide some basic demographic information (age, occupation, marital status, location) when they sign up to the Project and are asked to include this at the beginning of each of their responses but their names are not made public and they are instead given a unique ID number which is used to catalogue their submissions. Observers are asked not to name individuals or use identifying details in their responses in order to ensure the anonymity of both themselves and those they are writing about. Several Observers indicated that it was not just their anonymity that they valued but that of the future readers too. Mandy framed her response with the caveat: 'I'm quite happy about an anonymous researcher reading what I write but

I don't like the feeling of this personal information being on my hard disc.'[81] Unlike in oral history interviews, which are based on face-to-face conversations between the interviewer and interviewee, the interviewer behind Mass Observation Directives is invisible, allowing Observers to negotiate the Directives on their own terms.

The other major difference in format between Mass Observation and oral history testimonies relates to the time over which they are compiled. For this project, each of the oral history testimonies was collected in a single interview, which usually lasted between ninety minutes and three hours. In contrast, Mass Observation testimonies often represent a much longer process of deliberation and consideration; responses are commonly written months after the Directive was initially circulated and are sometimes written in multiple instalments. Irene described how her feelings towards to the 'Sex' Directive changed in the time between initially seeing the Directive topic and coming to write about it: 'I was very excited initially when I saw the title of this directive thinking that it would be a very interesting exercise. Three months later I think it may be a chore. The nature of sex and my relationship to it/with it? Possibly.'[82] For memory scholars invested in the spontaneous truthfulness of oral history interviews, Mass Observation material might seem more contrived as participants take time to craft their answers. At the same time, however, the level of deliberation and the ability of Mass Observers to 'fill in' their testimonies over a longer period of time can sometimes render them more 'complete'. Rather than seeing these differences in form and construction as rendering Mass Observation and oral history incompatible, for research such as this, whose primary aim is to uncover lived experience in the past and its shifting meaning, I see these as complementary, with the differences adding depth to the material.

As these discussions suggest, though at times 'knotty', oral history and Mass Observation testimonies are exceptionally rich sources that allow for different layers of analysis. In this research life histories are used primarily to excavate sexual experiences of the past and explore the activities and behaviours that made up teenage sexuality in this period. Jason Ruiz has highlighted that silences remain around questions of sexual practice in the past, in part because these histories have previously been considered 'too vulgar and too personal' for investigation.[83] If we want to explain shifting sexual cultures, it is essential to have a grasp on the reality of people's sexual practice. The problem is not necessarily one related to the squeamishness of historians either. Broader societal taboos and reservations relating to how we talk about bodies and their functions mean that discussions of intimacy and sexuality often fall into the territory of euphemism and fudged terminology. Phrases such as 'love-making' and 'having sex' are slippery and can be used to describe a wide array of sexual practices. They can both describe penetrative intercourse but can also be used to denote a variety of other forms of sexual behaviour including myriad forms of 'petting'. As shown in Chapter 1, distinguishing between these acts matters greatly when discussing teenage sexuality. As such, using oral history interviews and Mass Observation Directives to explicitly ask individuals about the details of their sexual practice is a form of recovery that allows us to put these aspects of individual experience 'on the record'. Rather than assuming that sexual practice is universal and that all people in the past engaged in the same types of sexual activity, using personal stories allows us to trace the specific sexual cultures of specific groups at a specific moment in time.[84]

Beyond simply recovering the 'fact' of teenage girls' sexual experiences, using personal testimonies also allows us to get a clearer sense of how and why sexual cultures and practices were changing. In the same way that personal testimonies enable us to recover sexual experiences from the past, they also make it possible to explore the emotions and understandings that shaped such experiences and informed what they meant to individuals. As Lynn Abrams has discussed, the post-war generation of women are uniquely invested in this kind of emotional memory work, viewing their emotions (both in the present and the past) as 'things to think, work and act with, rather than to suppress'.[85] The Mass Observation testimonies and the flexible nature of oral history interviews created opportunities to directly ask women about how they felt about their sexual experiences, what was motivating their choices, and how sex fit into their adolescence more broadly. Reflective testimonies represent a dialogue between past and present and it is impossible to tease apart the 'reality' of past experience from its memory.[86] Emotions and mindsets can be tricky to pin down and define in the present and accounts of these offered in testimonies are mediated through time and individuals' later experiences. There is, therefore, a delicate balancing act to manage in letting participants 'speak for themselves' and taking testimonies on their own terms while not ignoring the fact that accounts of past feelings may not fully articulate experience as it was lived and understood at the time. By exploring accounts at scale – in this case considering 280 testimonies and relating these to attitudes and experiences that were articulated in the post-war decades themselves – it is, however, possible to identify emotional regimes shared across the cohort and analyse commonalities in how women describe their teenage selves' sexual lives.

As with all participatory research, there are legitimate questions to be asked about the potential for self-selection bias within oral history projects and MOP. Although concerns about the self-selecting nature of participants and the truthfulness of reflective testimonies may seem heightened when studying an apparently 'sensitive' topic such as sex, my experience echoes that of the historian Kate Fisher, who has made the case that these concerns are perhaps overstated.[87] Undoubtedly, it is impossible to entirely negate self-selection bias within projects such as these and neither the oral histories nor the MOP claim to be representative of all experiences. As the variety of testimonies discussed in the rest of this book demonstrates, however, people have different reasons for wishing to contribute to such projects and we should be wary of assuming that only the most gregarious and sexually-adventurous individuals are prepared to share their sexual life histories. Although Observers could be hesitant in their responses, they did, nevertheless, respond to the Directives. Mabel's initial response to the 'Sex' Directive was panic: 'My first thought when I read this directive was "Oh no". I can't think of probably a less informed candidate in many ways.' This initial anxiety appears to have dissipated, however, as she went on to write a twelve-page response to the Directive![88] Elsewhere, the Directive and interview prompts appear to have evoked a genuine curiosity among participants. Several participants asserted that they had never been asked to discuss their intimate or sexual lives before and had not thought about this aspect of their teenage lives in some time. In concluding her response to the 'Sex' Directive, Rita noted: 'I will say that this has been quite an interesting exercise, and has brought back to me all sorts of things I had almost forgotten about.'[89]

Popular memory and stereotypes undoubtedly informed many women's accounts but women were not dupes to these. Oral history participants often framed their life histories in reference to dominant images of the period but women used these reference points for different purposes. For women like Jacqueline, their interview was an opportunity to showcase their participation in 'Swinging London'.[90] Others, like Daphne, had the opposite intent, indicating that they had participated in the project as they wanted to puncture glamorised and sexualised images of the period and shine a light on other experiences that are less well captured in popular memory.[91] Different agendas and worldviews could motivate individuals to offer their life histories to these projects and this is reflected in the diversity of experiences captured. Although some participants did share stories of having been 'promiscuous', recalling their youth as a time of sexual freedom and experimentation, there are many testimonies from women who saw themselves as 'late bloomers', as well as others who only ever engaged in penetrative sex with their husbands.

Just as the attitudes and agendas of those participating in Mass Observation and my oral history project varied, the demographic backgrounds of the women whose experiences are explored here are also heterogeneous. As far as it is possible to know (Mass Observation does not record Observers' ethnicity or designated sex at birth), all of the testimonies explored here belong to white cisgender women. There remains a need for historical research into the sexual cultures and experiences of trans women, women of colour, and migrants in twentieth-century Britain, though these are beyond the scope of this current study. This research is concerned with young women's experiences of heterosexuality and relationships with men although neither the oral history project nor any of the Mass Observation Directives specified this directly and all were open to individuals of all sexual orientations and several women described having also had sexual relationships, encounters, or experiences with other girls or women. The nature of the source material also means that this research focuses solely on England. A rich seam of scholarship already exists on post-war sexual cultures in Scotland and further work on Welsh and Northern Irish experience will be essential before fuller narratives of 'British' experience can be offered.[92] Having recruited oral history participants in Exeter, and given the over-representation of individuals based within the south east among Mass Observers, accounts of post-war life in the south of England are perhaps slightly over-represented in this study, although the hometowns of participants range from Cleethorpes and Middlesbrough in the north, to Birmingham and Wolverhampton in the Midlands, and Chard and Poole in the south. As such, while the research is not quantitatively representative, it does chart a wide range of regional experiences extending far beyond the common focus on London and Manchester.[93]

By far the thorniest demographic characteristic to unpack is that of class. Mass Observation has long acknowledged the over-representation of the middle classes among its Observers and at first glance many of my oral history participants possess key markers of middle-class identity in so far as many of them owned their own homes, had higher degrees, and/or worked in 'elite' professions at the time of interview. Of the thirty-three women interviewed for this project, only three did not have any qualifications beyond O levels. However, the testimonies of interviewees and Observers reveal a more complex negotiation of economic status than traditional frameworks of social class suggest. Echoing Eve Worth's work on women's social mobility, for example, several of my interviewees had not gone to university in their youth but had achieved degrees by returning to study later in life.[94] Although some participants self-identified as middle class, others described changing status and social positions. Diana, for example, had just moved into a new house when I interviewed her in 2015. She was a company director and had an MSc in sociology and politics, having gone to university immediately after finishing grammar school. As she explained, however, she had a working-class background. Her father was a coal tipper and her mother worked in a food packing factory (where Diana herself worked during school and university vacations). She recalled her feelings of alienation as a teenager: 'Once I got to grammar school, I wouldn't say I felt poor … I felt socially inferior once I got to grammar school.'[95]

In many ways, Diana is an example of how educational opportunity facilitated social mobility for the post-war generation. Elsewhere, however, the life histories of the women here showcase the limitations of existing frameworks of class and socio-economic status. For example, definitions of class have often been tied to the nature of an individuals' employment, but young women's work complicated categories of 'professional', 'skilled', and 'unskilled' labour. Many of the testimonies tell of young women undertaking secretarial training and going on to work in offices across the country. This required its own skillset (most commonly shorthand and typing) and was a popular form of work for young women of all social backgrounds.[96] Though they were raised in middle-class homes and had the opportunity to go to university, for example, girls such as Sally and Hazel who had grown up in small towns and rural areas chose to pursue secretarial work, believing it to be a passport to a more cosmopolitan life in the city.[97] Although secretarial and administrative work has never been particularly prestigious, it facilitated both physical and social mobility for lots of young women.[98] While many young women set themselves on a path to greater economic security than their parents through higher education and/or work, for many this was cemented through marriage. Working in offices, for example, young women were often in the company of businessmen and professionals; Pauline worked as a cashier in a building society and met her future husband at the office.[99] As these examples suggest, trying to apply generic labels of social class on women of this generation is difficult and not necessarily analytically constructive.

Teenage Intimacies, led by the testimonies at its heart, focuses primarily on the sexual cultures of the middle classes, very broadly defined. As explored throughout the book, there was no singular 'middle-class' experience. To name just a few areas of diversity within the testimonies, women grew up in different family arrangements (some had siblings while others were only children; where some lived with both of their parents, others lived with just one parent, or with aunts and uncles or grandparents); they belonged to different religions; they experienced different levels of financial security (where some families became more affluent as adults climbed the career ladder or inherited wealth, others faced periods of substantial financial hardship); women had profoundly different experiences of schooling (ranging from elite private schools to state grammar schools, convent schools, secondary modern schools, and comprehensives); women also grew up in distinct communities, with what it meant to be 'middle class' in large cities or suburbs looking quite different to that in villages, market towns, rural areas, and coastal communities. Moreover, we should be wary of assuming that class cultures of this period were entirely insular. In the era of mass culture and at a time when young people encountered and interacted with peers from a range of backgrounds through school, work, and training and in leisure spaces such as dance halls, cinemas, and youth clubs, there was a certain porousness to young people's cultures.

For the sake of brevity, *Teenage Intimacies* uses 'girls' and 'young women' as a shorthand. The analyses here are not based upon an entirely representative sample of experience and cannot claim to offer a universal account of youth sexuality in this period. Though my instinct is that the core arguments put forward here similarly informed the experiences of working-class girls' experiences at this time, further work (especially that which can speak to the intersections of class, race, migration, and region) will be needed to test this.[100] Taking its source material on its own terms, this study offers a new perspective on the mid-twentieth century, demonstrating the importance of acknowledging not only young women's experiences of social change but also their role in having brought much of this change about.

Self and social life

Teenage Intimacies argues that understandings of what sex meant and what it was for changed significantly in the post-war period. Two dynamics underpinned these changes and the book uses a two-part structure to consider these in turn. Part I illustrates how ideas about the life cycle, 'growing up', and reaching adulthood informed understandings of sexuality in this period and how these set adolescent sexuality apart from that of adults. These dynamics are considered across two chapters. Chapter 1 explores how the idea of 'becoming sexual' was increasingly central to adolescence and notions of 'growing up' in the 1950s, 1960s, and 1970s. Examining women's accounts of sex education, specific forms of sexual practice during adolescence, and their experiences of having penetrative sex for the first time, the chapter illustrates how girls of the post-war generation conducted their sexual lives in relation to their own sense of maturity. Where Chapter 1 shows how girls used having sex and engaging in sexual activity as a measure of maturity and a means of claiming adult status, Chapter 2 explores the extent to which girls pushed back against neat binaries of 'adult' and 'child', positioning themselves as young adults, eager for the freedom that came with age, though not necessarily desiring the burdens or responsibilities that they associated with adult femininity. The chapter considers the future-facing elements of women's youthful sexual lives, in particular their practices of abstinence and birth control and their responses to pregnancy, to investigate how adolescent sexuality was understood to function within broader models of the life course. Taken together, these chapters demonstrate how middle-class girls of the post-war generation understood sexuality as an essential part of their development and progress to adulthood. The emergence of sexual feelings and pursuit of sexual activity were seen to be essential to the process of growing up. This process was not without danger, however, and girls had to carefully navigate this landscape in which their developing sexuality potentially threatened the futures they wanted for themselves as much as it offered opportunities to transform their intimate relationships and successfully achieve adult status.

Where Part I is orientated around individually framed sexual subjectivities, Part II broadens the frame to offer a more overtly relational history of teenage sexuality. It illustrates the extent to which teenage girls' understandings and experiences of sexuality were embedded in their social lives and relationships. Examining elements of sexuality that existed between the macro levels of culture and legislation and the micro level of individual psychology, these chapters explore how sexual feelings and discourses came to life through young women's interactions and relationships with people around them.

Chapter 3 interrogates girls' relationships with boys and young men, considering the complicated ways in which sexual activity was bound up with ideas of intimacy. While intimacy was sometimes framed as a prerequisite for engaging in sex acts, sex was simultaneously understood to have the potential of establishing and enhancing intimacy. This interplay helps to explain the heightened emotions associated with sex and why sex could be so enmeshed in feelings of romantic love and joy while also being the cause of anxiety and trauma. Chapter 4 turns its attention to girls' relationships with the young people, particularly other girls, that made up their friendship groups and peer networks. It offers a bridge between histories of early twentieth-century cultures of chastity and studies of late twentieth-century sexual cultures concerned with 'peer pressure', demonstrating how young people of the post-war generation increasingly viewed sexual knowledge and experience as a source of social currency. Though sanctions still existed for girls deemed to have gone 'too far', new cultures of display came to characterise young women's heterosexual practice as they sought to benefit from the heightened social status associated with sexual experience. The final chapter considers what these shifting understandings and experiences meant for girls' home lives. Many girls' 'modern' sexual values had the potential to create conflict with their parents. Wanting to have relationships with boys and engage in sexual activity, but unwilling to threaten familial peace, many young women's sexual lives were defined by a politics of evasion. For the post-war generation, teenage sex was synonymous with sneaking around and their contributions to changing sexual mores were often hidden from (adult) sight. In all of these ways, girls' sex lives were innately social. Their interpersonal relationships were central to how they came to view and experience sexuality and their feelings about sexuality in turn altered how they related to and engaged with their loved ones and broader social network.

Overall, *Teenage Intimacies* shows that young women of the post-war generation were key to the changes in sexual values, cultures, and practices witnessed in the 1950s, 1960s, and 1970s. Their importance was rooted not necessarily in the uptake of radical new ideologies of sexual liberation but rather in subtle shifts in everyday life and ordinary relationships. Far beyond 'Swinging London', a quieter, more mundane transformation in intimate life was taking place. It was doing so in school playgrounds, church youth clubs, local cinemas, and suburban bedrooms, and teenage girls were its vanguard.

Notes

1 Tracy (1963), OH-14-02-01. All names are pseudonyms.
2 Kay Wellings, Julia Field, Anne M. Johnson, and Jane Wadsworth, *Sexual Behaviour in Britain: The National Survey of Sexual Attitudes and Lifestyles* (London: Penguin Books, 1994), pp. 37–41.

3 Linda Grant, *Sexing the Millenium: Women and the Sexual Revolution* (New York: Grove Press, 1993), p. 86.
4 John Crosby, 'London, The Most Exciting City in the World', *Weekend Telegraph*, 16 April 1965.
5 Frank Mort, *Capital Affairs: London and the Making of the Permissive Society* (New Haven: Yale University Press, 2010).
6 Department of Employment, *British Labour Statistics Historical Abstract 1886–1968* (London: Her Majesty's Stationery Office, 1971), pp. 206–7.
7 Eve Worth, *The Welfare State Generation: Women, Agency and Class in Britain since 1945* (London: Bloomsbury Academic, 2022). For an overview of the British welfare state see Rodney Lowe, *The Welfare State in Britain since 1945*, 3rd ed. (Basingstoke: Palgrave, 2004); Derek Fraser, *The Evolution of the British Welfare State: A History of Social Policy since the Industrial Revolution*, 5th ed. (London: Palgrave, 2017).
8 Jacqueline (1945), OH-15-04-03.
9 Mark Abrams, *The Teenage Consumer* (London: The London Press Exchange, 1959), p. 3.
10 Abrams, *Teenage Consumer*, p. 10.
11 On youth consumerism in the interwar period see David Fowler, *The First Teenagers: The Lifestyle of Young Wage-Earners in Interwar Britain* (London: Woburn Press, 1995); Katherine Milcoy, *When the Girls Come out to Play: Teenage Working-Class Girls' Leisure between the Wars* (London and New York: Bloomsbury Academic, 2017). On post-war youth consumerism see Bill Osgerby, '"Well, It's Saturday Night an' I Just Got Paid": Youth, Consumerism and Hegemony in Post-War Britain', *Contemporary Record* 6, no. 2 (1992); Christian Bugge, '"Selling Youth in the Age of Affluence": Marketing to Youth in Britain since 1959', in *An Affluent Society: Britain's Post-War 'Golden Age' Revisited*, ed. Lawrence Black and Hugh Pemberton (Aldershot: Ashgate, 2004); Daniel O'Neill, '"People Love Player's": Cigarette Advertising and the Teenage Consumer in Post-War Britain', *Twentieth Century British History* 28, no. 3 (2017).
12 *Report of the Committee on the Age of Majority*, Cmd. 3342 (London: Her Majesty's Stationery Office, 1967), p. 42. In 1969, a separate law was passed that allowed 18–20-year-olds to vote in elections; Thomas Loughran, Andrew Mycock, and Jonathan Tonge, 'A Coming of Age: How and Why the UK Became the First Democracy to Allow Votes for 18-Year-Olds', *Contemporary British History* 35, no. 2 (2021), https://doi.org/10.1080/13619462.2021.1890589.

13 Selina Todd, *Young Women, Work, and Family in England, 1918–1950* (Oxford: Oxford University Press, 2005).
14 Office for National Statistics (ONS), *Marriages in England and Wales: 2017* (London: ONS, 2021), www.ons.gov.uk/peoplepopulationandcommunity/birthsdeathsandmarriages/marriagecohabitationandcivilpartnerships/bulletins/marriagesinenglandandwalesprovisional/2017 [accessed: 15 May 2024].
15 On the continuing influence of this approach to youth studies see works within the 'Palgrave Studies in the History of Subcultures and Popular Music' book series, edited by The Subcultures Network.
16 Andy Bennett, 'Situating "Subculture": On the Origins and Limits of the Term for Understanding Youth Cultures', in *Researching Subcultures, Myth and Memory* ed. Bart van der Steen and Thierry P. F. Verburgh (Basingstoke: Palgrave Macmillan, 2020).
17 Angela McRobbie and Jenny Garber, 'Girls and Subculture: An Exploration', in *Resistance Through Rituals: Youth Subcultures in Post-war Britain*, ed. Stuart Hall and Tony Jefferson (London: Hutchinson, 1976).
18 Angela McRobbie, 'Settling Accounts with Subcultures: A Feminist Critique', in *On Record: Rock Pop and the Written Word*, ed. Simon Frith and A. Goodwin (London: Routledge, 1990).
19 Claire Langhamer, *Women's Leisure in England, 1920–60* (Manchester: Manchester University Press, 2000); Todd, *Young Women, Work, and Family*; Milcoy, *When the Girls Come out to Play*; Penny Tinkler, 'Cause for Concern: Young Women and Leisure, 1930–50', *Women's History Review* 12, no. 2 (2003).
20 Michael Clarke, 'On the Concept of "Sub-Culture"', *The British Journal of Sociology* 25, no. 4 (1974). See also John Clarke, 'Defending Ski-Jumpers: A Critique of Theories of Youth Subcultures', in *On Record: Rock Pop and the Written Word*, ed. Simon Frith and A. Goodwin (London: Routledge, 1990).
21 For example, Paul Willis, 'How Working Class Kids Get Working Class Jobs', CCCS Stencilled Occasional Paper (Birmingham: University of Birmingham, 1975).
22 Dan Woodman, 'Researching "Ordinary" Young People in a Changing World: The Sociology of Generations and the "Missing Middle" in Youth Research', *Sociological Research Online* 18, no. 1 (2013), www.socresonline.org.uk/18/1/7.html [accessed: 25 September 2024]; John Goodwin and Henrietta O'Connor, 'Ordinary Lives: "Typical Stories" of Girls' Transitions in the 1960s and the 1980s', *Sociological Research Online* 18, no. 1 (2013), www.socresonline.org.uk/18/1/4.html [accessed: 25 September 2024]. Important exceptions include David Fowler, *Youth Culture in Modern Britain, c.1920–c.1970*

(Basingstoke: Palgrave Macmillan, 2008); Sian Edwards, *Youth Movements, Citizenship and the English Countryside: Creating Good Citizens, 1930–1960* (Basingstoke: Palgrave Macmillan, 2017).
23 As Claire Langhamer has shown, notions of ordinariness are themselves constructed: Claire Langhamer, '"Who the Hell Are Ordinary People?": Ordinariness as a Category of Historical Analysis', *Transactions of the Royal Historical Society* 28 (2018).
24 Jeffrey Weeks, *Sexuality and Its Discontents* (London: Routledge and Kegan Paul, 1986), p. 20.
25 'While Parents Sleep', *Sunday Pictorial*, 23 November 1958.
26 Angus McLaren, *Twentieth-Century Sexuality: A History* (Oxford: Blackwell, 1999); Hera Cook, *The Long Sexual Revolution: English Women, Sex and Contraception 1800–1975* (Oxford: Oxford University Press, 2004); Jeffrey Weeks, *The World We Have Won: The Remaking of Erotic and Intimate Life* (London and New York: Routledge, 2007); Matt Cook, 'Sexual Revolution(s) in Britain', in *Sexual Revolutions*, ed. Gert Hekma and Alain Giami (Basingstoke: Palgrave Macmillan, 2014).
27 Weeks, *Sexuality and Its Discontents*, p. 20.
28 Frank Mort, 'The Ben Pimlott Memorial Lecture 2010: The Permissive Society Revisited', *Twentieth Century British History* 22, no. 2 (2011).
29 Nick Thomas, '"To-Night's Big Talking Point Is Still That Book": Popular Responses to the Lady Chatterley Trial', *Cultural and Social History* 10, no. 4 (2013); Adrian Bingham, *Family Newspapers? Sex, Private Life, and the British Popular Press 1918–1978* (Oxford: Oxford University Press, 2009).
30 On the politics of this legislation see Stephen Brooke, *Sexual Politics: Sexuality, Family Planning, and the British Left from the 1880s to the Present Day* (Oxford: Oxford University Press, 2011); Lesley Hoggart, *Feminist Campaigns for Birth Control and Abortion Rights in Britain* (Lewiston: Edwin Mellen Press, 2003). On political sex scandals see John Preston, *A Very English Scandal: Sex, Lies and a Murder Plot at the Heart of the Establishment* (London: Viking, 2016); Gillian Swanson, *Drunk with the Glitter: Space, Consumption and Sexual Instability in Modern Urban Culture* (London: Routledge, 2007); Richard Farmer, 'The Profumo Affair in Popular Culture: *The Keeler Affair* (1963) and "the Commercial Exploitation of a Public Scandal"', *Contemporary British History* 31, no. 3 (2017); Mort, 'Permissive Society Revisited'.
31 Mort, 'Permissive Society Revisited'.
32 Bingham, *Family Newspapers?*

33 *The Times*, 17 March 1971. Adrian Bingham, 'Pin-Up Culture and Page 3 in the Popular Press', in *Women and the Media: Feminism and Femininity in Britain, 1900 to Present*, ed. Maggie Andrews and Sallie McNamara (London: Routledge, 2014); Rebecca Lonchraine, 'Bosom of the Nation: Page Three in the 1970s and 1980s', in *Rude Britannia*, ed. Mina Gorji (London and New York: Routledge, 2007).

34 Marcus Collins, *Modern Love: An Intimate History of Men and Women in Twentieth-Century Britain* (London: Atlantic Books, 2003).

35 I. Q. Hunter, 'Take an Easy Ride: Sexploitation in the 1970s', in *Seventies British Cinema*, ed. Robert Shail (Basingstoke: Palgrave Macmillan, 2008).

36 Tony Aldgate, '"I Am a Camera": Film and Theatre Censorship in 1950s Britain', *Contemporary European History* 8, no. 3 (1999).

37 Michael Schofield, *The Sexual Behaviour of Young People* (London: Longmans, 1965), p. 131. See also the finding of Mass Observation's 'Little Kinsey' survey reported in 'British Men and Women Reveal What They Think about Marriage: "Free Love": Divorce', *Sunday Pictorial*, 20 July 1949.

38 Karen Dunnell, *Family Formation 1976* (London: Her Majesty's Stationery Office, 1979), pp. 6–7; Wellings et al., *Sexual Behaviour in Britain*, pp. 37–40.

39 Cook, *The Long Sexual Revolution*, pp. 279–81.

40 Cook, *The Long Sexual Revolution*, p. 339.

41 Emma Dickens, *Immaculate Contraception: The Extraordinary Story of Birth Control from the First Fumblings to the Present Day* (London: Robson Books, 2000), p. 116; Cate Haste, *Rules of Desire: Sex in Britain World War I to the Present* (London: Chatto & Windus, 1992), p. 186.

42 Simon Szreter and Kate Fisher, *Sex before the Sexual Revolution: Intimate Life in England 1918–1963* (Cambridge: Cambridge University Press, 2010).

43 Kate Fisher, *Birth Control, Sex, and Marriage in Britain 1918–1960* (Oxford: Oxford University Press, 2006). On the contraceptive market prior to the Pill see Jessica Borge, *Protective Practices: A History of the London Rubber Company and the Condom Business* (Montreal: McGill-Queen's University Press, 2020); Claire L. Jones, *The Business of Birth Control: Contraception and Commerce in Britain before the Sexual Revolution* (Manchester: Manchester University Press, 2020).

44 Sam Brewitt-Taylor, 'Christianity and the Invention of the Sexual Revolution in Britain, 1963–1967', *The Historical Journal* 60, no. 2 (2017).

45 Callum G. Brown, 'Sex, Religion, and the Single Woman c.1950–75: The Importance of a "Short" Sexual Revolution to the English Religious Crisis of the Sixties', *Twentieth Century British History* 22, no. 2 (2011): 214.
46 Quote from Laura Monica Ramsay, 'The Ambiguities of Christian Sexual Discourse in Post-War Britain: The British Council of Churches and Its Early Moral Welfare Work', *Journal of Religious History* 40, no. 1 (2016): 83. See also David Geiringer, *The Pope and the Pill: Sex, Catholicism and Women in Post-War England* (Manchester: Manchester University Press, 2019); Alana Harris, '"The Writings of Querulous Women": Contraception, Conscience and Clerical Authority in 1960s Britain', *British Catholic History* 32, no. 4 (2015); Matthew Grimley, 'Law, Morality and Secularisation: The Church of England and the Wolfenden Report, 1954–1967', *The Journal of Ecclesiastical History* 60, no. 4 (2009).
47 Brewitt-Taylor, 'Christianity and the Invention of the Sexual Revolution in Britain'.
48 Hannah Charnock, 'Teenage Girls, Female Friendship and the Making of the "Sexual Revolution" in England, 1950–1980', *The Historical Journal* 63, no. 4 (2020).
49 Todd, *Young Women, Work, and Family*.
50 Langhamer, *Women's Leisure*; Milcoy, *When the Girls Come out to Play*; Selina Todd, 'Young Women, Work, and Leisure in Interwar England', *The Historical Journal* 48, no. 3 (2005).
51 Jane Lewis, *Women in England, 1870–1950: Sexual Divisions and Social Change* (Bloomington: Indiana University Press, 1984); Helen Jones, *Women in British Public Life 1914–1950* (Harlow: Longman, 2000); Kate Murphy, 'A Marriage Bar of Convenience? The BBC and Married Women's Work 1923–39', *Twentieth Century British History* 25, no. 4 (2014); Helen Glew, *Gender, Rhetoric and Regulation: Women's Work in the Civil Service and London County Council, 1900–55* (Manchester: Manchester University Press, 2016).
52 Peter Mandler, *The Crisis of Meritocracy: Britain's Transition to Mass Education since the Second World War* (Oxford: Oxford University Press, 2020).
53 Phillida Bunkle, 'The 1944 Education Act and Second Wave Feminism', *Women's History Review* 25, no. 5 (2016).
54 Stephanie Spencer, *Gender, Work and Education in Britain in the 1950s* (Basingstoke: Palgrave Macmillan, 2005); Deborah Thom, 'Better a Teacher than a Hairdresser? "A Mad Passion for Equality" or, Keeping Molly and Betty Down', in *Lessons for Life: The Schooling of Girls and Women, 1850–1950*, ed. Felicity Hunt (Oxford: Blackwell, 1987).

55 Carol Dyhouse, *Students: A Gendered History* (London: Routledge, 2005), 100–3.
56 Paul Bolton, 'Education: Historical Statistics', House of Commons Library (27 November 2012), SN/SG/4252, https://researchbriefings.files.parliament.uk/documents/SN04252/SN04252.pdf [last accessed: 25 September 2024].
57 On the ambitions of girls at secondary modern schools see Laura Carter, 'The Hairdresser Blues: British Women and the Secondary Modern School, 1946–72', *Twentieth Century British History* 34, no. 4 (2023). See also Worth, *Welfare State Generation*.
58 Julia Pascal, 'Prima Ballerina Absoluta', in *Truth, Dare or Promise: Girls Growing Up in the Fifties*, ed. Liz Heron (London: Virago, 1985), p. 41.
59 Eve Worth, 'Women, Education and Social Mobility in Britain during the Long 1970s', *Cultural and Social History* 16, no. 1 (2019).
60 Alva Myrdal and Viola Klein, *Women's Two Roles: Home and Work* (London: Routledge, 1998 [1956]). On the study of women's lives see Helen McCarthy, 'Social Science and Married Women's Employment in Post-War Britain', *Past & Present* 233, no. 1 (2016).
61 Helen McCarthy, *Double Lives: A History of Working Motherhood* (London: Bloomsbury, 2020); Lewis, *Women in England*.
62 Lynn Abrams, 'Talking about Feminism: Reconciling Fragmented Narratives with the Feminist Research Frame', in *Beyond Women's Words: Feminisms and the Practices of Oral History in the Twenty-First Century*, ed. Katrina Srigley, Stacey Zembrzycki, and Franca Iacovetta (London: Routledge, 2018).
63 Emily Robinson et al., 'Telling Stories about Post-War Britain: Popular Individualism and the "Crisis" of the 1970s', *Twentieth Century British History* 28, no. 2 (2017); Florence Sutcliffe-Braithwaite and Natalie Thomlinson, 'Vernacular Discourses of Gender Equality in the Post-War British Working Class', *Past & Present* 254, no. 1 (2022).
64 Lynn Abrams, *Feminist Lives: Women, Feelings and the Self in Post-War Britain* (Oxford: Oxford University Press, 2023), 27–32.
65 Mary Ingham, *Now We Are Thirty: Women of the Breakthrough Generation* (London: Eyre Methuen, 1981). On this generation as 'transitional' see Betty Jerman, *The Lively-Minded Women: The First Twenty Years of the National Housewives Register* (London: Heinemann, 1981).
66 Helena Mills, 'Using the Personal to Critique the Popular: Women's Memories of 1960s Youth', *Contemporary British History* 30, no. 4 (2016), 463–83; Lynn Abrams, 'Mothers and Daughters: Negotiating

the Discourse on the "Good Woman" in 1950s and 1960s Britain', in *The Sixties and Beyond: Dechristianisation in North America and Western Europe, 1945–2000*, ed. Nancy Christie and Michael Gauvreau (Toronto: University of Toronto Press, 2013).
67 Abrams, *Feminist Lives*, p. 12.
68 For an overview of existing approaches see George Morris, 'Intimacy in Modern British History', *The Historical Journal* 64, no. 3 (2021).
69 Louise Jackson, 'Childhood and Youth', in *Palgrave Advances in the Modern History of Sexuality*, ed. H. G. Cocks and Matt Houlbrook (Basingstoke: Palgrave Macmillan, 2005), p. 231.
70 Elizabeth Roberts, *Women and Families: An Oral History, 1940–1970* (Oxford: Blackwell, 1995); Fisher, *Birth Control, Sex, and Marriage*; Szreter and Fisher, *Sex before the Sexual Revolution*; Geiringer, *The Pope and the Pill*.
71 The project's remit was wider than the topic of this book, recruiting both men and women born between 1940 and 1980 who lived in all areas of the United Kingdom. Only interviews with women born between 1940 and 1965 who grew up in England are drawn upon in this book.
72 Mass Observation Archive website, https://massobs.org.uk/about-mass-observation/ [accessed: 1 October 2024].
73 For copies of the Directives see https://www.massobs.org.uk/past directives/ [accessed: 1 October 2024].
74 On different styles of writing within Mass Observation see Dorothy Sheridan, '"Damned Anecdotes and Dangerous Confabulations": Mass-Observation as Life History', *Mass Observation Occasional Papers* 7 (1996), https://www.massobs.org.uk/research [accessed: 3 October 2024]; Anne-Marie Kramer, 'The Observers and the Observed: The "Dual Vision" of the Mass Observation Project', *Sociological Research Online* 19, no. 3 (2014).
75 Andrea (1957), Mass Observation Project (MOP), 'Close Relationships' Directive, Summer 1990, A2212.
76 Dorothy Sheridan, 'Writing to the Archive: Mass-Observation as Autobiography', *Sociology* 27, no. 1 (1993).
77 S3035 (1947), MOP, 'Sex' Directive, Autumn 2005. See also B3111 (1971), MOP, 'Sex'.
78 Pamela (1947), MOP, 'Sex', R860.
79 L. R. England, 'Little Kinsey: An Outline of Sex Attitudes in Britain', *The Public Opinion Quarterly* 13, no. 4 (1949–50): 589–90.
80 The Mass Observation database indicates that 229 responses were submitted to the 'Public Library Buildings' Directive while 235 responses were submitted to the 'Sex' Directive.

81 Mandy (1938), MOP, 'Sex', M1979.
82 Irene (1952), MOP, 'Sex', H2418.
83 Jason Ruiz, 'Private Lives and Public History: On Excavating the Sexual Past in Queer Oral History Practice', in *Bodies of Evidence: The Practice of Queer Oral History*, ed. Nan Alamilla Boyd and Horacio N. Roque Ramirez (Oxford: Oxford University Press, 2012).
84 On the social construction of sex acts see Will Fisher, '"Wantoning with the Thighs": The Socialization of Thigh Sex in England, 1590–1730', *Journal of the History of Sexuality* 24, no. 1 (2015); T. Hitchcock, 'Sex and Gender: Redefining Sex in Eighteenth-Century England', *History Workshop Journal* 41, no. 1 (1996); Mark McLelland, '"Kissing is a Symbol of Democracy!" Dating, Democracy, and Romance in Occupied Japan, 1945–1952', *Journal of the History of Sexuality* 19, no. 3 (2010).
85 Abrams, *Feminist Lives*, p. 30.
86 Penny Tinkler, Laura Fenton, and Resto Cruz, 'Introducing "Resonance": Revisioning the Relationship between Youth and Later Life in Women Born 1939–52', *The Sociological Review* (2022); Penny Summerfield, 'Culture and Composure: Creating Narratives of the Gendered Self in Oral History Interviews', *Cultural and Social History* 1, no. 1 (2004).
87 Fisher, *Birth Control, Sex, and Marriage*, pp. 12–25.
88 Mabel (1946), MOP, 'Sex', M3408.
89 Rita (1944), MOP, 'Sex', R1227.
90 Jacqueline (1945), OH-14-04-03.
91 Daphne (1941), OH-15-03-05. On this tendency amongst oral history participants see Szreter and Fisher, *Sex before the Sexual Revolution*, pp. 11–14. On the difference between popular and individual memory of the 1960s see Helena Mills, 'Using the Personal to Critique the Popular'.
92 Charlie Lynch, 'Moral Panic in the Industrial Town: Teenage "Deviancy" and Religious Crisis in Central Scotland c. 1968–9', *Twentieth Century British History* 32, no. 3 (2021); Roger Davidson, *Illicit and Unnatural Practices: The Law, Sex and Society in Scotland since 1900* (Edinburgh: Edinburgh University Press, 2019); Roger Davidson and Gayle Davis, *The Sexual State: Sexuality and Scottish Governance 1950–80* (Edinburgh: Edinburgh University Press, 2012); Lynn Jamieson, 'Changing Intimacy in the Twentieth Century: Seeking and Forming Couple Relationships', in *A History of Everyday Life in the Twentieth Century Scotland*, ed. Lynn Abrams and Callum G. Brown (Edinburgh: Edinburgh University Press, 2010). On Wales see Martin Johnes, *Wales since 1939* (Manchester: Manchester

University Press, 2012). On Northern Ireland see Leanne McCormick, *Regulating Sexuality: Women in Twentieth-Century Northern Ireland* (Manchester: Manchester University Press, 2013).

93 On the importance of regional studies of sexuality see Helen Smith, 'Working-Class Ideas and Experiences of Sexuality in Twentieth-Century Britain: Regionalism as a Category of Analysis', *Twentieth Century British History* 29, no. 1 (2018). On sexual cultures of London see Mort, *Capital Affairs*. On youth cultures in post-war London see Felix Fuhg, *London's Working-Class Youth and the Making of Post-Victorian Britain, 1958–1971* (Basingstoke: Palgrave Macmillan, 2021).

94 Sandra (1949), OH-14-01-02; Linda (1952), OH-15-01-03; Jacqueline (1945), OH-15-04-03. Worth, 'Women, Education and Social Mobility'.

95 Diana (1947), OH-15-01-05.

96 Rosalie Silverstone, 'Office Work for Women: An Historical Review', *Business History* 18, no. 1 (1976): 98–110; Gillian Murray, 'Taking Work Home: The Private Secretary and Domestic Identities in the Long 1950s', *Women's History Review* 26, no. 1 (2017).

97 Sally (1946), OH-15-05-02; Hazel (1947), OH-15-04-05.

98 On the devaluation of women's office work see Guerriero R. Wilson, 'Women's Work in Offices and the Preservation of Men's "Breadwinning" Jobs in Early Twentieth-Century Glasgow', *Women's History Review* 10, no. 3 (2001). On young women's increasing social mobility, Penny Tinkler, 'Going Places or out of Place? Representations of Mobile Girls and Young Women in Late-1950s and 1960s Britain', *Twentieth Century British History* 32, no. 2 (2021).

99 Pauline (1944), OH-14-01-03.

100 On working-class youth cultures in this period see Fuhg, *London's Working-Class Youth*; Laura Tisdall, '"What a Difference It Was to Be a Woman and Not a Teenager": Adolescent Girls' Conceptions of Adulthood in 1960s and 1970s Britain', *Gender & History* 34, no. 2 (2022).

Part I

Growing up

1

Becoming sexual

Across the 1950s, 1960s, and 1970s, a new genre of advice literature came to the fore in British publishing. Joining their marital advice counterparts on the shelves of British bookshops were new texts, written specifically for young people about how to handle the changes associated with puberty and adolescence.[1] Authors with a range of different claims to expertise – religious leaders claiming moral authority,[2] doctors and psychologists citing medical authority,[3] teachers and social workers with experience of working with young people[4] – published a range of texts that informed young people of how their bodies would change over the course of their teenage years, explained the reproductive system, described the emotional upheavals associated with adolescence, and offered their views of sex and sexuality. These 'facts of life' texts varied in their tone and in the specific guidance given (some were more overtly pro-chastity than others) and there were distinct changes in the format of the texts and their advice over time (such as increasing levels of visual content). However, the organising logic behind the texts remained remarkably consistent across this period. These books were premised on the notion that adolescence was a period of transformation and one in which sexuality emerged as a central aspect of individual experience. While texts such as Eustace Chesser's *Grow Up and Live* situated its lessons 'On Becoming a Man or Woman', 'Sex Life in Human Beings', and 'The Dangers of Casual "Affairs"' within much broader discussions of 'How Life Came into Being', the six 'systems' of the human body, and questions such as 'Why do we have to go [to school]', books such as George W. Corner's *Attaining Womanhood: A Doctor Talks to Girls About Sex*, first published in Britain in 1953, made the link between sex and the transition from youth to adulthood very direct.[5]

'Facts of life' literature of the post-war period reflected the view that the emergence of sexuality was one of the key components of 'growing up'. This chapter explores the extent to which young women in post-war England thought of themselves in these terms, arguing that notions of maturity were central to girls' understandings of their sexuality. Perceiving sex to be an exclusively 'adult' pursuit, girls wishing to grow up viewed sex as a necessary step in their self-development. Significantly, however, women suggested that this transition was not passive. Girls were acutely aware that they were undergoing this process and often acted in ways to alter the trajectory and pace of change: some tried to use sex as a means of forcing their transition to adulthood, whereas others saw their developing sexual feelings as indicators of maturity, stressing their past selves' need to wait until they were 'ready' to engage in penetrative intercourse. Considering sex education and the acquisition of sexual knowledge as well as women's early sexual experiences and their accounts of virginity loss, this chapter shows how girls of the post-war generation saw sex differently to their predecessors. Whereas the sexual development of previous generations had been orientated towards girls' marital and reproductive futures, young women growing up between 1950 and 1980 desired sexual maturity as an end in itself.

The facts of life

In mid-twentieth-century England there was an increasing sense that adolescents ought to be made aware of the physical and psychological changes that their bodies were going through. Although debates would rage across this period about precisely which forms of sex education were most appropriate, morally right, and socially useful, there was growing consensus that more damage was done by perpetuating ignorance than was usually done through (some form of) sex instruction. Where ignorance had previously been linked to innocence, in the post-war period ignorance itself was increasingly seen as problematic; campaigners argued that menarche and first intercourse were potentially traumatic if girls were not been adequately prepared for them.[6] Contrary to pre-war sexual cultures in which young women reported feeling 'unprepared for the corporeal changes associated with puberty',[7] by the 1950s it had become 'an accepted axiom in modern education that children should be told the truth about the facts of life'[8] and that they had a 'right to sexual information'.[9] In its landmark 'Little Kinsey' survey of sexual attitudes in 1949, Mass Observation celebrated that 'the battle [had] been won' over sex education, that it was 'now, officially and professionally at least, respectable' and that 'approval of sex education [was] as wholehearted as it [was] widespread'.[10]

Sex education

In addition to prompting the proliferation of commercial and academic guidance literature, this belief that young people (particularly girls) needed to be forewarned about the 'facts of life' was evident in changing attitudes towards school-based sex education.[11] School-based sex education had been (in Jane Pilcher's term) 'an absent presence' throughout the first half of the twentieth century.[12] Although some schools taught their students about puberty and human reproduction, it was ultimately deemed parents' responsibility to educate their children about such matters. The Second World War and attendant concerns about the moral and physical health of the nation prompted greater interest in the issue and, as a result, the Board of Education produced an advisory pamphlet regarding school-based sex education in 1943.[13] Sex education in schools remained non-compulsory but over the next three decades several advisory reports and handbooks were produced to help schools design provision should they wish to offer this. While changes should not be overstated, by the 1970s many schools offered sex education and some programmes had moved away from focusing purely on the biological and reproductive aspects of sex to a more holistic and relationship-oriented curriculum. Moreover, where programmes had initially been designed around parental rights, these were increasingly overridden by a concern for young people's interests and well-being.[14]

The testimonies reflect experiences of a wide variety of educational experiences – state and private, selective and non-selective, secular and religious – and although a significant minority of women claimed to have received no formal sex education, most of the oral history participants and Mass Observers studied here suggested that they had received some form of adult-led sex education during their adolescence.[15] The nature and form of this varied significantly, however. For some women, their parents (usually their mothers) had taken the lead in teaching them about the 'facts of life'. Others described school-based instruction of various types. In some schools reproduction and the 'facts of life' were covered as part of the religious or biology curricula;[16] in others they were offered as a separate form of hygiene or health instruction.[17] Yet while women incorporated descriptions of sex education within their sexual life histories, they often dismissed school-based sex education as having been irrelevant or insignificant.

In interrogating interviewees and Observers' critiques of sex education we should be conscious of the ways in which individuals' accounts were potentially composed in reference to contemporary debates.[18] Within the oral history interviews, discussions of sex education were one of the most common places where the temporal distance between past and present collapsed. Asked about their experiences of sex education during adolescence, Sandra, Tracy, Ruth, and Caroline all offered responses that directly compared their experiences to how they had gone on to handle sex education with their own children and/or what they observed in contemporary society.[19] The refraction of memory through the lens of the present is a ubiquitous feature of oral history interviews but was potentially heightened in this case by ongoing public debates. In 2014/15, when most of these oral history interviews were conducted, a high-profile campaign to have sex and relationship education become a mandatory part of the English school curriculum was gaining momentum.[20] While none of the interviewees referenced this directly, many of the key terms and premises of the campaign (such as the importance of discussing the emotional as well as biological aspects of sex) were invoked in women's accounts.

In these contexts, many critiques of mid-twentieth-century sex education were distinctively retrospective and it is hard to fully tease apart historical judgements from those shaped by the intervening decades. We see this, for example, in Olive's assertion that 'we were provided with the basics at school [but] I don't think there was enough emphasis on the emotional side of sex' and in Tracy's reflection that 'they told us about the mechanics of it, they didn't tell us about the feelings and the thoughts and they didn't tell us about the emotional side of it either'.[21] Echoing contemporary debates over sex and relationship education, Tracy lamented the lack of emotional education but it is not clear whether this was something her teenage self had wanted or expected or if this was a judgement based on her later life experience. Acknowledging these dynamics does not mean, however, that women simply projected twenty-first-century values and expectations back into their accounts of the past or that their accounts of sex education were innately contrived. Of course, much of the impulse underpinning contemporary campaigns and attitudes came from individuals' frustrations and criticisms of their own experiences in earlier periods.

Through a careful reading of this large body of testimonies it is possible to identify a number of key trends and themes within girls' mid-century experiences of sex education. While many critiques were retrospective, others hint at more contemporary frustrations with and perceived limitations of adult-led sex education. Central to many accounts was a sense that in the mid-twentieth-century there were fundamental mismatches between what adults and young people understood the purpose of sex education to be, what it needed to incorporate, and how it could be best delivered.

It was not uncommon for women to initially claim that they had received no sex education only for these assertions to be complicated by later aspects of their testimony. Christina, who was a teenager in the 1960s, asserted that her sex education was 'virtually non-existent' but later suggested that her class had received 'a talk at school when [she] was about 11'.[22] Janice's testimony followed a similar pattern. When asked if she had received any sex education at school she replied:

> No. None whatsoever. At school we had this one bit of education at the end of the first year of senior school, Year 7, which I think ostensibly taught us about periods and I don't remember any other sex education at school … We must've done something when we were doing O Level Biology, must've done, but it doesn't stand out.[23]

Here, interviewees utilised a language of 'non-existence' not as factual statements about the *type* and *quantity* of sex education they were given but as expressions regarding the *quality* of education they received. Claims of non-existence did not necessarily reflect a culture of sexual silence or a lack of sex education but instead highlight a clash of sexual cultures in which educators' sense of what they needed to teach girls did not align with what girls (and their future selves) expected or felt themselves to require.[24]

Jill reflected that 'we all knew the facts of life from a biological angle, if not from a social one' and this feeling that sex education programmes failed because they prioritised biology over other aspects of sexuality was repeatedly articulated by interviewees and Observers of all ages across this demographic.[25] Jane, for example, did biology at school and explained that 'I think we probably had diagrams of the reproductive tract of the rabbit, and maybe even of the human (shock, horror!) but as far as the "how" of sex (the mechanics) went, I'm certain we were kept pretty well in the dark!'[26] While schools may have covered reproduction this did not always translate into educating students about the specifics of human intercourse. At the same time, links between sex, relationships, and emotional feelings were also presented as having been neglected. As Andrea explained: 'All I had learnt at school had led me to believe that sex was only for reproduction. I had heard people talking about enjoying sex, but I didn't know what they meant.'[27] In these instances, women recognised their schools as having offered sex education but that asserted that its coverage left significant gaps in their understanding and often raised more questions than it answered.

These ambiguities were reflected in testimonies that expressed uncertainty as to what 'counted' as sex education. In 1943 a Board of Education pamphlet had dismissed using animal examples as a form of sex education on the grounds that 'it is doubtful whether many children see the human implications from their limited study of small mammals', yet interviewees' testimonies suggest that many teenagers of the 1960s and 1970s were taught about animal reproduction.[28] Asked about whether she'd been given any sex education, Valerie responded, 'Well, we did zoology, right? So I knew vaguely what sex was. I mean in the actual straight physical act of sex, I suppose.'[29] In her interview Daphne recalled animal anatomy sessions but could not quite identify the real role or significance of this:

Oh god, you know I remember one biology lesson, um, and it, it was a sex education lesson I think, well, I think it was meant to be but it was, it was about something to do with rabbits, god knows. God knows what it was![30]

When Julie was asked, 'Did you have any sex education at school?', her response was cautious and speculative: 'Not that I remember. Maybe something about rabbits at senior school but that was a Catholic convent, so they would have been quite limited.' The fact that interviewees jumped from questions about sex education to these accounts of animal reproduction suggests that adolescents were able to see a correlation between animal biology and human reproductive processes and these sessions clearly made enough of an impression on these women that they incorporated them into their narratives of sexual development several decades after the fact. Yet, the status of such education was often fraught.

It was not simply the content that women recalled as having been misjudged; they suggested that the timing and form of adult-led sex education was also a barrier to its usefulness. The question of when was the right time to introduce children to the 'facts of life' preoccupied educators in the post-war period. While some authorities suggested that young people needed to know the basic biological facts by the age of eleven,[31] others stressed that it was the emotional rather than physical age of the child that was important.[32] When it came to girls, however, menarche often forced the issue as many mothers and teachers felt compelled to prepare their daughters (practically as well as intellectually) for menstruation.[33] Several interviewees and Observers suggested that adults timed their educational interventions poorly, however. For some, the problem was that schools and parents pre-empted the issue and attempted to educate their daughters before these young women were capable of comprehending what they were being told.[34] Women suggested that school-based sex education sessions were too sophisticated for girls just entering puberty: Christina was given a talk at school when she was eleven but 'that talk assumed we knew an awful lot more than we actually did'.[35]

More commonly, women suggested that adult interventions came too late; girls had already learnt key information before their parents and teachers intervened. Perceiving adults to have little to offer in addition to what they already knew, girls such as Rosemary and Joyce brushed off attempts to discuss sex. Rosemary's school had brought in an external speaker to talk to the girls 'about more grown up parts of sex. In other words, boys and touching' when she was around fourteen. Her assessment of this was blunt: 'that was crap'. She went on: 'I just remember we thought it was funny and we treated it as a joke. To be honest it was a bit late.'[36] Joyce had initially been given sex education at secondary school and had found it 'quite enlightening'. Her and her friends' attitudes had shifted, however, when they were offered sex education again at fifteen: 'by then we really did think we knew it all' and so they attempted to embarrass the teacher by submitting 'appalling' questions to the question box around which the lesson revolved.[37] Although women recognised adults' attempts to teach them about sex, they stressed that these interventions were mistimed. In these instances, the adequacy of adult interventions was related to girls' levels of maturity: the content could be important but if delivered at the wrong time it might be dismissed by girls with different interests and preoccupations. Adults timed these interventions in the hope of setting the pace for girls' sexual development, yet young women undermined this agenda by acquiring information before their parents expected.

These issues of content and timing were also exacerbated by the way that sex education was delivered. As members of older generations who had not necessarily been socialised to discuss sex openly, many parents and teachers were deeply uncomfortable in their roles as sex educators.[38] It was common for women across this cohort to mention how visibly awkward adults were when the matter of sex was raised.[39] Theresa recalled a teacher 'blushing scarlet' while trying to teach reproduction.[40] Daphne told of how she had inadvertently tortured a teacher by failing to recognise other people's embarrassment:

> I remember to my absolute shame that I really wanted to understand what this poor woman was trying, and she was so embarrassed, everyone else in the class except me obviously was embarrassed and I actually put up my hand and asked a question and I don't remember the a–, I don't remember the question, I don't remember the answer because I suddenly realised I should not have done it. 'Cos I made this poor woman's life even worse.[41]

Although many schools, teachers, and parents felt compelled to educate young women on matters of sex, this did not necessarily come easily to them. We can see here how the discourse of one generation can shape the experiences of the next, even once the discourse itself has been discredited and replaced. As one parent complained in a letter to *The Spectator* in 1966, doctors and sex educators, '[tell] us what to do, as if we do not already know and [make] the ludicrous assumption that we are all equipped to do it'.[42] Although many adults of the post-war period may have agreed on the principle of sex education, it often proved more difficult to translate this into practice.

Adults' severe discomfort with talking about sex resulted in passive approaches to sex education. Teachers often lectured on the subject whilst parents simply gave their daughters educational reading material.[43] Though women were sympathetic to their 'poor' teachers, they critiqued having been denied the opportunity to ask questions about what they were learning, feeling, and experiencing. Iris noted, for example, that her school assumed that they were preparing girls for sex in their biology classes but that the coverage was inadequate and offered little room for interrogation: 'Biology lessons in the first year of grammar school were supposed to be sufficient to answer any questions but only gave the bare facts. We could not possibly have asked for more details from our teacher.'[44] Similarly, Pauline described how the sex education lessons that her and her classmates had been 'terribly excited about' simply involved being presented with pamphlets:

> And, it was very very tame because the teacher we had, Miss Wright, who's a very stern lady, and all that happened was that she came out and slammed down these leaflets, 'Read these!' [Both laughing] Yeah. So, we had a booklet on, y'know, what happens to boys in puberty. Mmmm. What happens to girls in puberty. And how the two ends connect, y'know.[45]

As Pauline's testimony suggests, this culture of one-way instruction was actually exacerbated by the influx of new sex education materials including commercially produced 'facts of life' literature and videos on reproduction and hygiene.[46] These materials could be used to circumvent dialogue between teachers, parents, and children on these subjects. Girls whose parents provided them with reading material emphasised that this was shrouded in a culture of discretion. Ruth's younger self had sensed that being given a book on the topic of sex was her mother's way of introducing the topic without having to discuss the matter verbally:

> My parents wouldn't tell me anything ... at all.
>
> *Did you ask?*
>
> Well. I don't know if I did, because I don't think I dared. Because I had this book thrust at me, which perhaps coincided with periods starting (right) which was never spoken about either (Oh. OK. Right) nothing was spoken about.[47]

In 1958 a piece in the *British Medical Journal* lamented the attitude of parents who were content 'merely to leave pamphlets on the subject [of sex] within easy reach of their children' but these practices evidently persisted.[48] In many schools and households this appears to have been the compromise that facilitated a degree of sex education without miring adults in the more awkward aspects of the subject although it left many young people's desire for knowledge unquenched.

In these ways, post-war sexual culture was characterised by something of a 'generation gap'. This dissonance was not necessarily combative and, on reflection, women did attempt to give their schools and parents some credit for their attempts to provide sex education. Nevertheless, there was a significant feeling of distance and disconnection between the chronologies of adolescence held by young women themselves and those that adults constructed. Although adults constructed a framework of adolescent development in which they perceived themselves to have a crucial role in guiding and assisting young people, their interventions were seen as inadequate, leaving many girls feeling half-informed. Feeling that the truth was being withheld from them, girls pursued sexual knowledge on their own.

Alternative sexual knowledges

Adults in the post-war decades may have attempted to impose order on young women's transition to sexual maturity through carefully timed sex education but many women described their actual acquisition of sexual knowledge as having been rather more piecemeal. While adult-directed sex education formed a part of this, books, films, and conversations with siblings and friends were also key sources of information. Women often portrayed these as 'alternative' forms of knowledge acquisition, a way of making do in the face of a lack of adult-led teaching. As Amanda put it, 'I had no sex education from anyone. All knowledge was gained from friends, reading books and films.'[49] Yet these learning processes were commonly presented as having been more authentic than those offered by adults. Driven by curiosity and self-interest, girls pursued information that directly related to their current (and future) experience. Whereas adults' attempts at sex education relied upon arbitrary judgements about when girls were ready for information, these alternatives allowed girls to mature into sexual knowledge at their own pace.

Especially in childhood and the early stages of adolescence there was a value in simply knowing anything about sex. Understanding sex as something hidden, unknown, and taboo, girls just wanted to know more about this mysterious idea. Even before they hit puberty, for instance, young people's curiosity often led them to encyclopaedias and dictionaries.[50] Having encountered words or ideas that they did not understand, curious girls sought to educate themselves using the research skills they had acquired elsewhere to learn more about sex.[51] Crucially, however, girls did not keep this information to themselves. Although girls often inherited the sense that this knowledge was 'secret', they frequently shared it with one another and young women took it upon themselves to teach each other about sex (with varying degrees of accuracy). Kathleen remembered an older girl telling her what happened when you had sex: 'it sounded so bizarre to me I was quite sure that couldn't possibly be the truth!'[52] As Heather recalled, the discovery of this information could be disconcerting but it was comforting to share and interrogate this with friends who had been similarly ignorant:

> I think I must have been about eleven when someone at school told me what men did to ladies to have a baby. ... I do remember the impact it must have had on me because instead of going straight from school after being dropped off by the bus I stopped off at the house of my best friend ... and [we] chewed the details over thoroughly

expressing disgust, fascination, disbelief which we couldn't shake off and often repeated urgh!!'s.[53]

This knowledge was a prized possession: knowing the 'facts of life' offered insight into the world of adults and was deemed a general marker of intelligence and maturity. However, having discovered this knowledge, young women could not escape the fact that this had been withheld from them. Sensing that this was a secret adults were unwilling to share or discuss, girls confided in each other and tried to work through this confusing new landscape together.

As girls got older, their approach to information about sex shifted from 'knowledge for knowledge's sake' to 'knowledge as a practical tool'. Girls were no longer content to know that sex existed, instead they wanted to know more about how it worked as an interpersonal interaction. As girls entered their mid to late teens and began to contemplate sexual activity for themselves, sex was no longer an abstract concept to be 'known' intellectually. Thinking of embarking on a new form of embodied practice, girls wanted to know what sex looked and felt like (both physically and emotionally). Any education they had received at school was often deemed to have been irrelevant to these new practical concerns.

Books could help a little with these new priorities and many girls turned to fiction as a source of insight. Several women remembered adolescent encounters with *Lady Chatterley's Lover*.[54] Kathleen described this as having been 'very helpful' although she noted that even *Chatterley* in all its infamy was 'tame' in its depiction of sex.[55] This sentiment was echoed by Mass Observer Glynis who similarly found 'sexy' texts disappointing:

> I remember going into a bookshop in guide uniform and keeping a lookout while my friend stole a copy of *Fanny Hill* which we took back to camp. It was most disappointing to find that the language was old fashioned and the sex implied. We had been hoping to find out what it was 'like'.[56]

As Chris Hilliard, Marcus Collins, and others have noted, in the decades after the Second World War formal censorship of 'obscene' material declined and print and visual media of a sexual nature proliferated.[57] By the 1970s, facts-of-life literature, depictions of sex in films, novels, plays, and television, and soft-core pornography in various forms had gone 'mainstream'.[58] Yet even girls who were consuming this culture found it wanting in terms of its ability to inform them about sex. As such, for girls in their mid to late teenage years the most prized forms of sexual knowledge were experience-based knowledges of sexual practice. Feeling that their friends were the only people who could truly understand their feelings and the specific conditions of post-war sexuality, girls saw their peers as important sources of information.

As discussed in more detail in Chapter 4, girls had to carefully navigate this sexual landscape; although sexual experience could be a valuable form of knowledge, young women were keen to maintain their reputations as 'nice girls'. Moreover, as penetrative intercourse was so closely associated with intimacy, those engaging in sexual activity within long-term relationships often attempted to maintain a degree of discretion. When it came to 'low-level' sex acts or penetrative intercourse that were deemed to be 'experimental', however, girls could be keen to share their experience. Sally described how she and her friends 'talked about sex, all of us, quite a lot' and these discussions were central to many young women's school-based socialising.[59]

These discussions did not simply function as a source of shared intimacy, however. Instead, women indicated that they functioned as a form of sex education in their own right. Having suggested that her school-based sex education at a convent school in the mid-1970s was 'horrendous', Tracy recalled learning about sex from older girls:

> I think I can remember in year, I dunno, it must've been the 3rd year so that would've been about 12 or 13, some friends had elder sisters and they um, were discussing about what they'd done with boys and I remember us all thinking, 'Oh my God, that's absolutely disgusting! Did you really let a boy do that to you?!' And, couple of years later we were doing the same thing! [HC laughs] Um, but I remember, yeah, we were sat listening to my friend, ah yeah, I s'pose I would've been about 13, terrible 13, listening to that.[60]

Tracy placed this sex talk at the centre of her narrative of sexual knowledge acquisition; observing and talking to older girls was an important way in which she came to know about sex. Unlike adult-led sex education that revolved around marriage, reproductive biology, and penetrative sex, these shared stories spoke more directly to girls' immediate interests and concerns, such as what it felt like to 'snog' a boy at a dance or to engage in petting on the way home from a date. While the information gleaned in these contexts was potentially less factually accurate than that given by adults (and certainly adults were concerned by the misinformation circulated this way), it was deemed to be more authentic and directly useful to girls' lives. Understanding themselves as undergoing a process of becoming sexual, girls gained a sense of what was to come by listening to those that were perceived to be a few steps ahead.

These reflective testimonies largely confirm Christine Farrell's contemporaneous assertion that peer discourse was 'often the only source of "uninhibited" exchange of sexual information and experiences'.[61] Yet although girls may not have been shy about communicating their experiences, several women suggested that there was something fundamentally different about knowing about sex in theory and experiencing it first-hand. In Doris' words, 'I knew, if you like, the human anatomy side of things but I certainly didn't know, you know, what it was about until I did it.'[62] This was echoed by Ellen, who 'had a bit of Sex Education at school' but who described herself as having 'learnt most of it through practical experience, "on the job", as they say!'[63] Although many girls told stories about their sexual exploits to their friends, there was a limit to what could be conveyed verbally. Girls could tell each other everything and still their knowledge of sex remained incomplete as talking failed to adequately communicate the physical and emotional sensations associated with sex. Just as girls growing up in the interwar decades held 'the evidence of one's own body' to be the most reliable form of sexual knowledge, so many girls of the post-war generation believed that, as an embodied experience, sex had to be experienced to be fully 'known'.[64]

Sexual experience

For many young people sexual experience was deemed to be the most profound form of sexual knowledge but, in the same way that girls' bodies did not become adult instantaneously, girls' sexual activity was also incremental and conceptualised in terms of discrete, sequential stages. Imagined as a learning process in which girls were moving from ignorance to enlightenment, girls' experiences of sexual activity were often organised around ideas of development.

Stages of sexual activity

Most girls did not jump straight in to having penetrative intercourse; instead, adolescent romantic and sexual lives were characterised by a gradual progression through a range of increasingly 'sexual' physical interactions. Taking the testimonies as a whole, similarities in narrative and chronological structure suggest that there was a 'standard' order in which sexual activity was practised. Participants described moving from holding hands and kissing through various forms of 'petting' to penetrative intercourse. Women framed this progression as a learning process through which they became familiar with their bodies and their feelings. Non-penetrative sex acts were often framed as part of a continuum that was building towards the pinnacle of 'full' sex:

> *Had you had physical relationships with other people?*
>
> Heavy petting? Oh well, well, yes, inevitably we all tried to push things as far as we could without actually doing the dastardly deed! So yes you gradually build up to, a bit of groping and things.[65]
>
> Then I met the guy that I was, who I subsequently married, eventually, a long time later, when I was about, coming up to 17. And that's when it, y'know, then, that's when we really started to get into heavy stuff, leading up to having sex.[66]

Women's testimonies articulated an understanding of sexuality that viewed sex acts such as kissing and petting as experiences that girls needed to have in order to become ready for 'full' sex.

This continuum conceptualised sexuality as something that had to be learned. As Hazel expressed: 'You would gradually explore each other more and more without going the whole hog. That's how you learn, isn't it?'[67] Women framed their early sexual experiences as a time of familiarisation and learning. Characterising their childhoods as a period of total ignorance about their sexual potential, women suggested that they only gradually came to learn about what their bodies could do and the sensations they could experience. Although this transition was understood to be 'natural', its newness could be unsettling. While activities such as kissing and petting were deemed to be considerably less sexual than penetrative intercourse and 'heavy petting', to girls who perceived heterosexual interaction as a radically new part of their social lives, the expectations to engage in these activities could be stressful and anxiety-inducing.

Cheryl, Gloria, and Christine each recalled the prevalence of kissing and petting at social events in their youth and candidly noted their teenage selves' nervousness and discomfort. Each of the girls responded to expectations of interaction differently. Gloria described the expectation 'to give a kiss' to boys at the dance halls in Manchester as 'very daunting' and therefore set about 'avoiding it where [she] could'.[68] Christine similarly recalled some 'fairly scary parties, when everybody was, sort of necking in various corners'.[69] Gloria and Christine emphasised their sense that they were not yet 'ready' for sex. Cheryl remembered a party she went to when she was sixteen where there were lots of couples petting and her feeling of being 'totally out of my depth'.[70] She went on to describe the boys at the party as being 'too advanced' for her. Understanding sexuality as something developmental, Cheryl characterised her youth as a time of gradual 'growth' that she went through at her own pace.

Elsewhere, adolescence was presented as an exciting time of cautious exploration and discovery through hands-on experience. Sarah, for example, framed her early sexual activity as a process of initiation in which her boyfriend gradually introduced her to new experiences and activities: 'A [her boyfriend] was quite passionate. I learned French kissing and was quite shocked when he asked me to handle his penis. It seemed such a naughty thing to do but I got used to it!'[71] Going on to stress that 'fumbling and groping was as far as it went', Sarah understood this activity as part of a longer process of sexual development. Similarly, Theresa suggested she 'experimented quite a lot' with her teenage boyfriend so that when it came to having penetrative intercourse itself 'it wasn't a sort of completely unfamiliar process'.[72] Having engaged in 'dry fucking' and 'feeling about', Theresa and her partner had come to 'know' as much about their bodies as they could do without actually having penetrative intercourse itself. For Theresa and Sarah penetrative sex was a significant threshold and one that they built towards rather than something experienced spontaneously.

Guidance literature of this period often presented non-penetrative intimacies (in particular 'petting') as a risky precursor to sex, directly linking intimate contact such as breast fondling and mutual masturbation with penetrative intercourse.[73] The connection between these activities had been cemented in the early twentieth century by sexological and marriage guidance literature that positioned manual stimulation of the genitals as an important part of the 'foreplay' essential for preparing wives for imminent intercourse.[74] As such, magazine columnists and the writers of health guidance for teenagers often stressed the dangers of engaging in non-penetrative sex acts as it was easy for young couples to get 'carried away' and accidentally have sex which they would subsequently regret.[75] Girls were repeatedly told of the dangers of 'tempting boys' and commentators insisted that sexual intercourse was the 'normal end' of 'stimulating of the sexual parts'; girls 'should know what happens to a boy's body when he gets excited and accept their own responsibility in the matter'.[76] Within these frameworks, engaging in petting and other non-penetrative sex acts was to tempt fate as penetrative sex was all but inevitable.

Teenagers themselves did not necessarily see sex in this way, and women's reflective testimonies suggest that far from falling prey to hormonal abandon, their adolescent lives were governed by carefully managed regimes of control.[77] Interviewees and Observers repeatedly stressed how, as teenagers, they engaged in physical intimacies with their boyfriends but stopped short of actually having sex. Gail told of doing 'all sorts of petting and stimulation but not "go[ing] the whole way"'.[78] As Daphne put it: 'The lines were fairly, fairly strictly drawn, sort of, fairly heavy petting but not much more.'[79] Reflecting on their teenage sexual lives, women did not recall feelings of overwhelming passion but emphasised their careful management of their sexual activity. Eileen stressed that even going to bed with boys did not translate into inevitable intercourse: 'Ending up in bed at parties was the norm, but not necessarily to have proper sex. The most damage that was done was an aching wrist!'[80]

This control was embedded within the categorisation of sex acts. In contrast to the 'slippery slope' of some guidance literature, women explained that their experiences of sex were framed and defined by specific taxonomies of sexual activity. Physical interactions with members of the opposite sex were organised and categorised into hierarchies with specific sex acts having a distinct status and place within the scheme.[81] Sexual activity was conceptualised as a set of ascending stages, each of which was more 'sexual' than the last. Although the specific categorisations varied, the use of numbers to classify different physical interactions into stages and levels remained remarkably consistent across this period and was described by women growing up across the 1950s, 1960s, and 1970s.[82]

> The popular term for ['experimentation'] was petting and was graded on a scale of one to ten at our school. I can't remember all the stages but it was probably from holding hands to kissing and touching breasts and so on to what was called heavy petting although I am not sure exactly what the criteria for that was but would probably be touching private parts and arousing and satisfying each other, number ten being full sex.[83]
>
> It was number 1 to 5. ... I s'pose thinking in reverse 5 obviously was 'all the way', 4 was letting him feel down below, 3 was letting him feel the top, I think 2 was kissing and I guess number 1 was holding hands![84]
>
> What was the ranking that we used? 1 snog, 2 ... I think it was like 4 or 5. [pause] It was, yeah it was snog, top, we used to call it like top, [whispering] 1 snogging, 2 top, 3 bottom ... yeah, like poking, 4 would be like blowjobs and ... things [stops whispering] and then 5 was sex I think.[85]

The 'direction' of progression was also consistent: it generally proceeded towards increasing levels of genital contact, although different groups used slightly different scales and definitions of activity. Certain peer groups differentiated between active/passive engagement: in some schema stimulating a partner's genitals was deemed to be something different and more 'advanced' than having your own genitals stimulated.[86] To Kathleen the difference between 'petting' and 'heavy petting' lay in an 'over'/'under' clothes distinction, whereas for Mandy and her friends it was the body parts being touched that defined 'heaviness'.[87] Both Kathleen and Mandy's frameworks moved through ascending levels of sexual contact though their peer groups had different criteria for judging sexual intimacy.[88] As discussed in more depth in Chapters 3 and 4, this elasticity in definitions and varying interpretations of what 'sex' meant created useful grey areas which young women exploited for their own ends (be they the desire for sexual activity or a desire not to engage).

Pleasure narratives

Understandings of sexual activity as a central component of the transition from childhood to adulthood also informed expectations of pleasure within young women's sexual experiences. While each individual's experience was unique, two distinct narratives of sexual pleasure (or its absence) emerged in women's testimonies and both suggested that girl's pleasure was often subservient to a more pragmatic desire to transition to maturity.

The first of these pleasure narratives described pre-penetrative experiences as unenjoyable, but endured; girls engaged in sex acts not because they felt sexual desire or anticipated pleasure but because they believed that this was just what girls of their age did. Responding to the Mass Observation Directive on 'Sex', Evelyn described her first relationship with a boy called C. Although she included this relationship in her sexual life story, she specified that this relationship had little to do with sexuality: 'I must be honest too and admit that although I liked C, I didn't fancy him in a sexual sense; kissing was fine, he was good at that, a bit of touching here and there, but no more.'[89] This sense of sexual activity being divorced from pleasure or self-interest was similarly evident the narratives of women like Julie and Gail who 'knew' what pleasure was through masturbation but saw this as 'a very separate thing' to what they did with boyfriends.[90] Gail described having spent 'hours' in her mid-teenage years masturbating but claimed that this erotic interest did not translate into her physical interactions with boys: 'Once I'd started having boyfriends, I think I was probably too nervous to allow any of those sexual feelings into the kissing and petting.'[91] Remembering these interactions as having been orientated around the boys' pleasure, Gail saw her past self as having engaged in such activity as 'an experiment'. For girls of this generation, engaging in these activities did not necessarily revolve around pleasure seeking; they did not always anticipate pleasure or expect to orgasm as a result of kissing or petting with boys.

This did not necessarily mean, however, that girls were unwilling to engage in these activities; rather, girls simply had different motivations for engaging in sexual activity than sexual pleasure alone. Particularly in their mid-teens, girls engaged in these interactions out of a sense that that was simply what was expected of them and that these were essential waypoints to reaching maturity. Marjorie described her experiences of 'heavy petting' ('This meant allowing a boy to touch your breasts and put his hand into your pants') and stressed that although she didn't find this particularly pleasurable, she willingly engaged in such activities: 'I didn't like it very much, yet wanted it to happen. I wanted to know what it was that everyone talked about in such glowing terms.'[92] Women such as Gail and Marjorie suggested that their adolescent sexual activity was driven less by a desire for pleasure than by curiosity and a social imperative to keep up with the expectations of their friends and partners. Within British culture sex has long been associated with notions of pressure and obligation and, as explored further in Chapter 3, girls of this generation were often pressured and coerced into sexual activity by their partners.[93] In these testimonies, however, we can see dynamics of expectation in a different form. These accounts indicate that many girls were driven by a more selfish sense of expectation and obligation. When choosing to engage in sexual activity, they were not simply responding to the expectations of their male partners but were pursuing their own imperatives of maturity, sexual enlightenment, and experience.

The second pleasure narrative was very different in how it characterised pre-penetrative sexual activity, foregrounding the pleasure of non-penetrative sex acts but suggesting that this was often thwarted by the imperative to 'move on' to penetrative intercourse. Women presented their early erotic experiences as being more pleasurable than their post-penetrative sex lives. The language used in their testimonies positioned the early stages of relationships and sexual development as having been particularly erotically charged. Deborah spoke of the heightened sexual tension of her adolescent sex life:

> We did lots of walks in the country which of course progressed to heavy petting, usually lying in the heather. My boyfriend used to groan with desire and tell me how painful his erection was in the hopes that I would let him relieve it!! We also spent hours in his sports car writhing around the gear lever and steaming up the windows.[94]

Other women were keen to stress their partners' sexual prowess and described their boyfriends as having been skilled and attentive lovers.

> My first love affair was the first with sex, and this took years to arrive at. We were busy with the 'fingers' stage, but it was when I was on holiday in Cornwall ... that I had my first orgasm, and that was just so mind blowingly amazingly wonderful. My boyfriend said 'I've been waiting ages for that to happen for you.' And it was wonderful ever after til we broke up 5 years later.[95]

> I was 17 when I got my first real boyfriend. Kissing him set off all sorts of sparks and feelings. We would meet up in the park and he would do amazing things with his fingers.[96]

Within these narratives it was these early sexual experiences that women most explicitly recalled through vocabularies of pleasure and eroticism. In contrast to the sex that they would go on to have as adults (within marriage or otherwise), which was often associated with penetrative intercourse, women suggested that these early expressions of sexuality were notably more pleasurable. Mandy even went so far as to express regret that this stage did not persist longer into her marriage: 'When I got engaged I was still technically a virgin. Lots of foreplay of each other but no penetration ... I do remember that the fingers etc were very pleasurable and I remember feeling sad that we got to "bonking" too quickly once we were married.'[97] Echoing the sentiments of second-wave feminists who would critique heterosexuality for its phallocentrism, Mandy's use of the term 'bonking' suggests a degree of dissatisfaction with her married sex life and its move away from 'foreplay' to penetrative intercourse.[98]

These testimonies reveal the liminal status of adolescent heterosexuality and the sexual activity associated with this. These accounts highlight the almost-gravitational pull of penetrative intercourse and its characterisation as the defining sexual act around which all heterosexuality revolved. At the same time, however, they emphasise how sex acts that would in later life simply become incorporated into 'foreplay' were, in adolescence, distinct expressions of sexuality and ones that women found particularly enjoyable. Although women repeatedly constructed their adolescent sexual activity in relation to a larger process that built towards 'full' sex, they suggested that activities such as petting and cuddling had appeal of their own.

Understanding sexual activity as a series of ascending 'stages' helped girls orientate themselves within their sexual landscape and within their own personal development. Each of these phases was conceptualised as being more 'sexual' than the last, meaning that girls felt themselves to be becoming increasingly sexual as they 'progressed' along this journey. Geraldine described several phases of her sexual development: she first 'got off' with a boy when she was fourteen; she had a more serious boyfriend at fifteen; she did 'everything but' penetrative sex with J, the boyfriend she had at sixteen; and she lost her virginity with her older boyfriend P at seventeen. Linking her increasingly 'sexual' feelings to her increasing age, she explicitly framed her adolescence as a period of becoming sexual. She stressed that she had not always felt 'sexual' even though she engaged in heterosexual intimacies; her sexuality was something that she grew into. 'Getting off' with a boy at a disco when she was fourteen and having him feel her breasts was 'exciting' but 'in a forbidden way rather than sexual'. At fifteen, however, she was going 'a little further' and 'felt sexual now though and quite a lot of sexual tension'.[99] Geraldine linked losing her virginity to being 'grown up'. In her testimony, as in so many other women's, however, the precise nature of the link between maturity and penetrative sex was somewhat undefined.

Virginity

Women of the post-war generation were more likely to have sex outside of marriage or engagement than their predecessors. The 1991 National Survey of Sexual Attitudes and Lifestyles found that only 13.8 per cent of women born between 1946 and 1955 were married at first intercourse, compared to 38.5 per cent of women born between 1931 and 1945.[100] In the 1950s and early 1960s, demographers, epidemiologists, and medical professionals drew attention to rising levels of extra-marital pregnancy, the falling age of marriage, and increasing rates of venereal disease among young people.[101] These were soon joined by a series of sociological and journalistic studies, surveys, and polls investigating shifting sexual values and behaviours.[102] While the press was drawn to the more sensational stories of moral decay and the corruption of contemporary youth,[103] sociologists suggested that many of the changes in behaviour could be explained by 'permissiveness with affection', a term which described young couples who were pre-empting marriage by having intercourse in the context of engagement or long-term romantic relationships.[104] As the period went on, however, this explanation became less compelling, prompting *19* magazine to ask in 1968, 'Where have all the virgins gone?'[105] In their view, '[v]irginity for an unmarried girl is, as everyone knows, a disappearing ideal' and as their reporter Lucy Abelson found when tasked with finding out 'what makes a girl give up her virginity', the reasons were 'many and varied' and 'love was no longer the only reason'.

The testimonies of interviewees and Observers corroborate Abelson's findings. A substantial proportion of interviewees and Observers had penetrative intercourse for the first time outside of the context of marriage and/or engagement, with a partner who they did not subsequently marry.[106] While sex *could* play an important role in romantic intimacy (see Chapter 3), in post-war England having sex did not *necessarily* signify the longevity of a couple relationship. Although many of these women were in long-term relationships at the time of virginity loss, others had one-night stands or more fleeting interactions that transcended traditional models of sexual relationships. Although women such as Eileen, Beatrice, and Jean justified their first times by claiming that they were in love,[107] other interviewees and Observers suggested that their decision to have penetrative intercourse for the first time had little to do with emotional commitment or romantic intimacy. It was possible for sex to be what Glenys called 'a purely physical fling'.[108] Catherine did not mention romantic love anywhere in her descriptions of her early sexual experiences, she '[didn't] remember feeling anything much during sex – I just did it I suppose because that's what you did'.[109] In a rare reference to embodied desire, Cheryl asserted that her two sexual relationships prior to marriage were 'pure lust', she 'didn't love them at all'.[110]

Women of the post-war generation suggested that, as they grew up between 1950 and 1980, it was increasingly possible for first intercourse to be experienced outside the framework of romantic love. The accounts of first intercourse examined here suggest that the prerogative of achieving personal fulfilment through sexual initiation could take priority over the socially mandated ideal of being in a stable, loving relationship. This is not to say that girls explicitly rejected the possibility of going on to have monogamous, emotionally invested relationships but rather that they perceived first intercourse to have meaning beyond an embodied expression of romantic love. Reflecting on their adolescent experiences, many women conceptualised first intercourse primarily in terms of what it meant as a milestone in their own personal journey to adulthood rather than as a moment of profound interpersonal bonding.

Being a virgin

For many young women, adolescent sexuality was framed by the concept of virginity. Virginity not only described a fact of girls' sexual experience but gave girls an identity based upon their level of sexual experience. Girls were raised to believe that their virginity was a status to be valued. As oral history interviewee Diana recalled: 'I was taught that men were only out for one thing and girls had to protect this amazing thing they had which was their virginity.'[111] Within this framework, girls were taught that sex had consequences for who they were and how they were seen by others. Amanda indicated that it was not only adults communicating discourses of chastity but that her peers bought in to this attitude as well:

> I belonged to a generation that thought virginity was a prized possession, which was another reason why it took so long for me to go 'all the way'. Boys seemed to be quite impressed if one was still a virgin, and I thought since it's gone, that's it, I'll have lost that special thing.[112]

Amanda's highly gendered construction of virginity echoed that identified by Michael Schofield in his study of teenage sexuality in the early 1960s. Fifty-one per cent of boys interviewed for the study indicated that they 'would like' to have sex experience prior to marriage while 64 per cent wanted to marry virgins; 57 per cent of girls agreed with the statement that 'If a girl has sex before marriage she gets a bad reputation'.[113] As Schofield articulated, girls 'wish[ed] to protect their own virginity but expect[ed] boys to gain sexual experience, and [found] it acceptable that the boys should be able to do what they rule out for themselves'.[114] In this context, virginity was bound up with a girl's social value and worth.

Across the long 1960s, teenagers were repeatedly urged by parents, teachers, and social commentators to 'save themselves' until marriage. Within some households and communities, the insistence on chastity was rooted in religious faith and culture. Asked if virginity was an important concept to her adolescent self, Vivienne replied: 'It was, obviously, I just accepted it as part of Catholic teaching.'[115] In other contexts, the need to refrain from sexual activity was framed in less moral and more practical terms, stressing that pre-marital sex might make it difficult for young women to adjust to marital sex life later on. A pamphlet produced by the Girl Guides Association warned young women that 'Few things are so likely to lead to frigidity in marriage as promiscuity.'[116] Elsewhere, the exact reason why girls should remain chaste was less clearly defined, it was simply what was right. When she was asked about her youthful understandings of sex and virginity, Julie replied: 'My mum was definitely that you married the person and then you had sex and then you had a family. That was, sort of, the stereotypical thing that we were born into, that we were, that was what she wanted for us and that was important.'[117]

Yet while testimonies showcase the continued presence of these chastity discourses, they also reveal how these were resisted, adapted, and challenged by young women growing up at this time. In particular, the testimonies suggest that girls of the post-war generation absorbed some of the existing discourses on sexuality while dismissing or deprioritising others. Where virginity had previously been a possession or status of value, this was not necessarily the case for the post-war generation. As later chapters explore, young women of this era were increasingly willing to trade in their virginity for enhanced intimacy with a partner and/or for social status among their peers. At the same time, having bought in to adult discourses which indicated that having sex for the first time was potentially transformative and which framed adolescent sexuality as a 'natural' development on the way to adulthood, many girls felt that they needed to have intercourse in order to become sexually mature. Losing their virginity was framed less as giving away a prized possession and instead functioned as a way of cutting ties with their youth and childhood. As Kathleen explained, upon having sex at seventeen, 'I was very relieved to no longer be a virgin, to have entered the grown-up world and know what it was about'.[118]

The notion that girls needed to experience sex in order to become adults goes some way to explaining the increasing pressure that girls felt to have sex as they got older. Numerous interviewees and Observers, for example, used a language of 'lateness' to describe their experiences of sex.[119] These women, born decades apart, suggested that as they approached their twenties, they increasingly felt that they were missing out on an important part of life by not having had penetrative sex. Jane described her first experience of sex as 'an act of desperation' reflecting her nineteen-year-old self's sense that she had 'left it rather late'.[120] Elsewhere, Glenys specifically noted that she had sex for the first time with her married manager after an office Christmas party because 'by this time I really felt I was missing out'.[121]

Having been born in 1952, Audrey reached her mid-teens in the late 1960s. In her interview she spoke of her and her friends' heightened awareness of virginity as a status and the complicated feelings they had about how it defined them:

> *Was your virginity something that was particularly important to you?*
>
> Yes and no. In that ... from, I s'pose from about 15, it would probably've been around then, when we actually knew that somebody else had lost theirs at school ... it became something that was talked about. Who has and who hasn't, that sort of thing. So it was a thing that we were very conscious of. It was also something I really remember, I can actually remember the conversation with somebody about, actually, on reflection it's horrendous, talking to my friend G we were going to play ten-, actually I did play tennis a bit sometimes, um, and I remember saying, 'I wish somebody would rape me so I could lose my virginity'. Which now, I spent 5 years working on a rape crisis line, so now just the thought, but, it was unknowing, it was, 'I want to get rid of this thing'. So it was a big thing and I wanted to get rid of it. Yeah. Awful![122]

As early as her mid-teens Audrey had a growing sense that her virginity was something to 'get rid' of. It was not the case that she saw first intercourse as insignificant or meaningless – she and her friends considered it a 'big thing' that they were 'very conscious' of – but it was a status she wished to shed. To her, having sex for the first time was not about conferring meaning or intimacy onto an existing relationship but was about her own sense of status and identity.

This sentiment was echoed by other women who remembered their teenage selves very consciously considering their status as virgins. Eileen suggested that her younger self had anticipated sex to be a moment of transformation and that she specifically linked this to a broader process of growing up. She and a friend discussed their desire to have shed their virginity before heading to university:

> Every Sunday evening, my best friend and I used to go to church. We would then pop into our favourite pub in town, and get a bus home around nine o'clock. One evening, around the time of our A levels, she just came out with, 'We're off to university in September. What are we going to do about our virginities?' 'I think we should lose them,' I replied. 'Right,' she said, 'the next opportunity, we should do it'.[123]

Linking sexual initiation with the beginning of university, Eileen's narrative tied together two significant rites of passage, presenting them as part of one overarching maturity project. If leaving home was one marker of becoming an adult, girls such as Eileen did not wish to be lumbered with the remnants of their youth in the form of sexual inexperience.[124]

The sense that first intercourse marked an important moment of transition for young women and one which they wanted to carefully manage was conveyed consistently within testimonies through the presentation of first intercourse as a choice. In contrast to some of the other transitions of adolescence over which they had no control (not least their bodies' physical developments through puberty), many girls were keen to exert control over the speed at which they reached maturity through sexual activity. Women often framed their narratives in such ways as to emphasise the elements of deliberation and active decision-making that underpinned their sexual activity.[125] The choice to have sex was presented as a wholly rational process with such accounts of first intercourse being almost entirely devoid of sexual language or desire.[126] Christine discussed losing her virginity in a very flippant manner:

> *So can you tell me a bit about the first time you had sex?*
>
> Erm ... I think it was boring and painful, quite honestly [HC laughs] ... I couldn't understand what all the fuss was about. [...]
>
> *Do you remember ... erm ... why you wanted to have ... I assume you wanted to have sex? Do you know why that changed?*
>
> I just wanted to get it over with ... to get that initial hump ... over the hump, as it were.[127]

Asked whether or not she enjoyed her progression towards sex, Alison confirmed that she did but specified that this was not the primary reason she went on to have sex:

> *Was [sexual activity] something that you were enthusiastic about and that you enjoyed and that you wanted to experience?*
>
> I think so but I think it was more to get it out of the way. I don't think it was because I had any expectation other than to know that I'd had sex and not be a virgin and know what it was like; it wasn't so much I thought, 'Oh this is gonna be wonderful and I'm really ready for it and I'm so in love,' in fact he was a bit of a arsehole. [...]
>
> *Was virginity an important thing to you?*
>
> It wasn't a big deal but I think I thought I'd gone so far with him that was the next stage and I, I think I was keen just to find out what it was like.[128]

In retrospect at least, the desirous and embodied aspects of sex were presented in both of these testimonies as being less worthy of comment than the identity work performed through the act of first intercourse.

As discussed further in Chapter 3, some women of this generation presented the sexual culture of this time as highly pressured and felt that they had been coerced into engaging in sexual practice when they were younger. However, many interviewees and Observers strongly emphasised that having penetrative intercourse for the first time was a conscious choice. Women such as Barbara and Anne portrayed themselves as having had equal agency for engaging in, if not having initiated, first intercourse. When Barbara turned seventeen in 1969, for example, she 'decide[d] that it was about time [she] knew what was going on'. She described how her and her (older) boyfriend 'engineered a situation where it would happen' and then reflected on her feelings after the event:

> I wouldn't say I enjoyed it, it was an interesting experience. I wanted to know what it was like, I didn't have an orgasm, I don't think he would've known what to do, to be frank, but I thought, 'Right, I've done it, that's one hurdle over with, I can get on with my life', you know.[129]

Anne described a similar dynamic. Not only was she an active participant because she wanted to have sex, she coordinated the event to suit her needs. In her words, she 'took the lead':

> *Was it something that you had planned? Had you spoken to him and said, 'I would like to have sex with you,' and then it? Or ...*
>
> I don't remember that. It didn't happen because he insisted on it. So there must've been some degree of collaborative conversation taking place. Ahhh ... [gnashes teeth] I think I took the lead actually. Y'know, so I said to you about to some extent manipulating the situation so that you felt in control, so that you could control the c-, any communications about it.[130]

Anne wanted to have sex but was acutely aware that her mother would not approve and so she felt compelled to manage the situation in order to maintain a sense of control. Within her narrative sex had very little to do with pleasure but it was by no means a passive experience. Despite the fact that there was roughly twelve years between their experiences of first intercourse at sixteen and seventeen, both Anne and Audrey emphasised a process of sexual decision-making in which they were motivated less by sexual desire than by curiosity and a 'need' to rid themselves of their virginities.[131] Having sex for the first time was positioned as a key symbol of maturity and a form of self-discovery.

While the testimonies often intimated that multiple factors contributed to the decision to have sex, women often identified curiosity as their driving motivation, portraying their adolescent selves as having been inquisitive about sex. Although Tracy found the experience of first intercourse 'awful' and 'horrible' at the time, she presented the story of her first time as an amusing anecdote:

> *Can you tell me a bit about [having sex for the first time]?*
>
> [Laughing] Okay, yes I can tell you. It was on our dining room floor. Um, and I think he already had a condom on. And I remember it was absolutely awful because my dog, we had a dog at the time and he was very interested in what was going off so he kept trying to sniff around us and I pretended like I'd done it loads of times. So, y'see and I think I even made him go home with it on! It was awful, I said, 'You can't put it down my toilet.' It's awful![132]

The awkwardness of the experience had subsequently become a source of humour for Tracy. She was one of the few oral history interviewees who described the act itself in any detail when asked to recall first intercourse but she had to be prompted to discuss her motivations for having sex:

> *So had you ... um, had you decided that you wanted to have sex?*
>
> Yeah, <u>I think I wanted to give it a go by then yeah</u>. Yeah, definitely, definitely.
>
> *So, had you done very much before then?*
>
> Yes, yes, yeah. But um, only with him really. I, I liked him, he was a chef at the time and I trusted him and he was nice and he hadn't been with a lot of girls. [...]
>
> I think I was just, <u>it was just kind of an experiment</u> and I thought, y'know, if you told me a bit more about it I wouldn't've had to have f-found out for myself really.
>
> *So part of it was just curiosity?*
>
> Yeah I think so. <u>I just wanted to know what it felt like I think</u>. Even though they'd gone, 'Oh, you should save yourself [inaud] you should save yourself,' that's what they used to drum into you at school.[133]

Tracy's account reads as an incomplete rendition of various virginity tropes. She briefly alluded to notions of romance and relationship-based rationales for having sex ('I trusted him and he was nice and he hadn't been with a lot of girls'), tapped in to ideas of rebellion ('if you told me a bit more about it'), and suggested that a desire for self-discovery contributed to her decision to have sex ('I wouldn't've had to have f-found out for myself really'). By far the most consistent and coherent impetus for having sex however was that of curiosity (see underlined). She repeatedly stressed her desire to experience something new and her feeling that having sex would shed her of her ignorance and offer her a degree of enlightenment.

Virginity and transformation

Many testimonies presented first intercourse as a rite of passage but they also suggest that the exact nature of the relationship between sex and maturity was not always clear-cut. Although individuals continued to link sex with ideas of maturity and framed sexual initiation as a process of 'becoming', the causal link between sex and adult status was unstable. While interviewees and Observers associated first intercourse with a sense of transition, there were tensions both across and within the testimonies regarding the exact nature of this transformation.

Many women framed their experiences of having penetrative sex for the first time as a moment of consolidation; the act of first intercourse signified the maturity that they already perceived themselves to have acquired. Joyce, for example, described having sex for the first time as 'an initiation'. To her younger self it represented 'getting something done that needed to be done, really'.[134] In so far as women described having sex as a choice, they often emphasised that this revolved around judgements of whether or not they were 'ready' to engage in 'full intercourse'. Quite what made girls 'ready' varied; Gail emphasised her age and relationship status ('I didn't have full sex until I felt ready for it, in a long-term relationship at the age of 20'[135]), whereas Michele suggested that this was more a question of 'knowing her own mind'.[136] For some, the issue was a general sense of maturity while for others their numerical age mattered as evident in their discussions of the age of consent. Across this period the legal age of consent was sixteen but women offered different assessments of how this influenced their sexual decision-making. Linda, who was born in 1952, indicated that this legal consideration was hugely influential and directly structured her sexual experience. She suggested that she and her peers would 'never have dreamt of' having penetrative sex prior to being 'legal' and that being 'of age' was central to her justification of sexual activity.[137] Diana, by contrast, was more sceptical of this deliberation. Asked why she had waited to have sex until she did at sixteen,

Diana raised the issue of consent law: 'Well somebody said, "You waited until you were 16" but I'm not sure ... I don't think I ever made that calculation.'[138] Describing her virginity-loss experience as spontaneous, Diana characterised her adolescent sexuality as less carefully managed than those who were wary of sticking to the code of the law, her decision to have sex was instead portrayed as just a natural progression within her relationship and in her sexual development.

This sense of consolidation or capping off was similarly evident in women's characterisations of first intercourse as a type of experiment. Janice and Anne both framed their experiences of first intercourse as an experiment that tested the boundaries of their already-earned status as adults.

> When I got to 16, I s'pose I was, for the age, quite promiscuous and I was curious, I wanted to know. So the first boy I did have sex with he wasn't a boyfriend, it was a one-night stand and it was a total failure, because I wanted to know what it was like, that was it, I wanted to know what it was like.[139]
>
> *And how long had you been together before you slept together?*
>
> Oh, not long. Not long. I was quite keen on that idea. Um ... I like experimenting with any, kind of, it-it's just, 'Hmm? Really?'[140]

To 'experiment' implies that one has enough knowledge to be curious and by framing their first experiences of intercourse with this language women such as Janice and Anne implied that they felt themselves to have already achieved a degree of sexual maturity prior to having sex itself. Understanding sexual activity through a hierarchical lens in which behaviours built towards penetrative sex, girls were accustomed to feeling 'sexual' prior to engaging in penetrative intercourse. As such, it was possible for girls to understand sex as simply the next step in their sexual development. Whilst penetrative sex did possess heightened status and retained a potential for transformation, in these models it was seen as a natural progression.

Elsewhere, however, the transformative power of penetrative sex was more radical. Several women suggested that, after having had sex, they felt different. Julie surprised herself by having sex whilst away on a year abroad, she described the experience as 'quite momentous': 'I remember the next day thinking "Oh, this is what it feels like to be a woman who's had sex"!'[141] For girls like Julie, having penetrative intercourse did not simply equate to having added something new to their sexual repertoire. Rather, they felt themselves to have been profoundly changed by the experience. Kathleen had sex for the first time with a neighbour after she had moved away from home into a shared flat in London:

> I remember it as a Saturday night and uh, next day I was due to go home for Sunday lunch with my parents and I wondered if they would be able to tell that I was a different person. It's so silly isn't it.
>
> *Did you feel like a different person?*
>
> Yes I did. I did. I felt much more grown up. [...]
>
> *And was virginity, the idea of virginity something that was important to you?*
>
> No.
>
> *Had you ever expected that you would be a virgin when you got married?*
>
> No. I was very, quite relieved to no longer be a virgin, to have entered the grown up world and know what it was about.[142]

In Kathleen's narrative the transformation penetrative sex entailed was directly linked to the notion of growing up. Experiencing sex not only allowed her to 'know' what sex was but marked her entrance into adult sexuality.

This sense of transformation was not merely retrospective, however. Many girls anticipated that sex would be transformative and indeed used sex as a means of hastening their progression to adulthood. In her testimony, Hilda explicitly presented having sex for the first time as a component part of growing up, listing it alongside other transformations of adolescence: 'I think I saw it as a part of growing up a bit like having periods, shaving under my arms and learning to use make-up.'[143] This notion of sex as one of many changes was echoed and expanded upon in Alison's oral history testimony. Alison suggested that during her adolescence in the late 1970s, she believed that by enacting adult behaviour, you became an adult – the performance of adult behaviour was constitutive of adult status. In this way first intercourse served the same purpose as other adolescent firsts such as consuming alcohol and smoking. She described how these behaviours had little appeal in and of themselves but were pursued by teenagers such as herself who saw them as milestones on the way to adulthood.

> I don't, don't think I had any particular expectation about whether I'd enjoy it or anything I just, um, thought it was great that I was doing it so it's, I guess it's a little bit like starting to smoke, what, I mean why would you smoke? Let's be honest. But you kind of feel you're a bit grown up. That first drink, that first cigarette, that first sex, same sort of thing, it's not so much, 'Will I enjoy this?', it's something that you want to do because that's what grown-ups do. I think I was very much in that, yeah.[144]

Reflecting upon her teenage self decades later, however, Alison was highly sceptical of this viewpoint. She noted how this youthful logic represented a fundamental misunderstanding of what it was to be grown-up: she now believed that engaging in a dialogue about sex would have been more 'adult' than actually having sex.

> By the time I was actually having sex, um, I think I just felt sophisticated that I was having sex, but now looking back I realise how young and naïve I was 'cos obviously if you're talking about it that's far more grown up and sophisticated but I, I was just doing it.
>
> *And how did you feel, I mean, I know you say you kind of felt sophisticated, is that how you felt afterwards? Was-?*
>
> Yeah. Yeah, yeah. Whereas now I realise that was quite childish 'cos actually I wasn't thinking what do I want from it and what, what would actually be nice, I was just thinking, 'I'm having sex!' [Both laugh] 'So grown up!'

In her youth, Alison thought that she could make herself 'grown up' through sex. With hindsight she felt that the progression to adulthood actually took much longer and involved far more than a single moment of transition.

Conclusion

Women framed their narratives of adolescent sexuality as a process of 'becoming sexual'. Inheriting a developmental framework from their parents and teachers, girls thought of their teenage years as a time when they transitioned from being children to being adults and sexuality played a key role in this process. Characterising childhood as a time of sexual ignorance and adulthood as a time of sexual activity and wisdom, coming to learn about sex through formal teaching and experience itself was a process of sexual 'becoming'. An engagement with sexual knowledge and activity was crucial to girls' 'growing up'.

'Knowing' about sex was important for young women in the 1960s and 1970s as they began to navigate a new sexual landscape in which sex was no longer primarily confined to marriage. For women of previous generations who believed that they would only have sex with one person in their lifetime, having sex for the first time (be it within the context of marriage itself or engagement) was framed as the beginning of a mutual endeavour and shared experience with their spouse and penetrative sex was incorporated into their sexual repertoire.[145] For women of the post-war generations, sexual knowledge and experience were framed differently. While sex required a partner and had tangible social presences and consequences, the significance of sex was increasingly internalised and girls of this era were less likely to imagine their first sexual partner as being their only sexual partner. Girls were coming to perceive sexual feelings and practice as being indicative of some internal truth. Significantly, in so far as sex was conceptualised as a form of identity project, it was understood as an individual pursuit that was not necessarily bound to romantic relationships. Girls did not necessarily think of themselves as possessing a specific sexual 'identity', but their sexuality shaped and reflected how they thought about themselves and their relationships.

The testimonies considered here encourage us to understand sexuality as having its own life cycle and inherent logics of age. They push back against analyses which assume that sexual subjects are 'adult'. Moving away from a binary of childhood sexual ignorance versus adult sexual subjectivity, both adults and young people in the post-war period understood adolescents to be sexual and saw adolescent sexuality as distinctive. The logic underlying constructions of youthful sexuality was one of development and transition but this did not mean that adolescent sexuality was trivial or insignificant. Instead, it was loaded with meaning, shaping how young people thought of themselves as well as how they imagined their place in the world. In this chapter, we have seen how youth sexuality was often forward-facing in orientation as young women viewed their sexuality as an integral part of their progress to maturity, and at times used sex as a means of accelerating their acquisition of adult status. As we will see in the following chapter, however, not all aspects of adult sexuality were appealing to young women and considerations of the future played an important role in framing young people's sexual choices.

Notes

1 Hannah Charnock, '"How Far Should We Go?": Adolescent Sexual Activity and Understandings of the Sexual Life Cycle in Postwar Britain', *Journal of the History of Sexuality* 32, no. 3 (2023).
2 Quentin and Irene de la Bedoyere, *Choices in Sex* (London: Burns & Oates, 1964); Malcolm Brennan, *Sex Education: Training in Chastity* (London: Catholic Truth Society, 1974). On Catholic guidance to young people, see Geiringer, *The Pope and the Pill*.
3 Kenneth Barnes, *15+ Facts of Life* (London: British Medical Association, 1961); Wardell B. Pomeroy, *Girls and Sex* (Harmondsworth: Pelican Books, 1970); Benjamin Spock, *A Young Person's Guide to Life and Love* (London: Bodley Head, 1971).
4 Len Barnett, *Sex and Teenagers in Love* (Redhill: Denholm House Press, 1967); Alan H. B. Ingleby, *Learning to Love* (London: Transworld Publishers, 1962).
5 Eustace Chesser, *Grow Up and Live* (Harmondsworth: Pelican Books, 1949); George W. Corner, *Attaining Womanhood: A Doctor Talks to Girls About Sex* (London: George Allen & Unwin, 1953).
6 Julie-Marie Strange, 'The Assault on Ignorance: Teaching Menstrual Etiquette in England, c. 1920s to 1960s', *Social History of Medicine* 14, no. 2 (2001).
7 Roy Porter and Lesley A. Hall, *The Facts of Life: The Creation of Sexual Knowledge in Britain, 1650–1950* (New Haven: Yale University Press, 1995).
8 *The Transmission of Life*, 6th ed. (London: The Girl Guides Association, 1954), p. 5.
9 Maurice Hill and Michael Lloyd-Jones, *Sex Education: The Erroneous Zone* (London: National Secular Society, 1970), p. i.
10 Mass Observation, '"Little Kinsey": Mass Observation's Sex Survey of 1949', unpublished report, printed in Liz Stanley, *Sex Surveyed 1949–1994: From Mass-Observation's 'Little Kinsey' to the National*

Becoming sexual 77

Survey and the Hite Report (London: Taylor & Francis, 1995), pp. 86–87.
11 James Hampshire, 'The Politics of School Sex Education Policy in England and Wales from the 1940s to the 1960s', Social History of Medicine 18, no. 1 (2005); James Hampshire and Jane Lewis, '"The Ravages of Permissiveness": Sex Education and the Permissive Society', Twentieth Century British History 15, no. 3 (2004).
12 Jane Pilcher, 'School Sex Education: Policy and Practice in England 1870 to 2000', Sex Education 5, no. 2 (2005).
13 Board of Education, Sex Education in Schools and Youth Organisations (London: His Majesty's Stationery Office, 1943).
14 David Limond, 'Frequently but Naturally: William Michael Duane, Kenneth Charles Barnes and Teachers as Innovators in Sex(uality) Education in English Adolescent Schooling: c. 1945–1965', Sex Education 5, no. 2 (2005).
15 Sandra (1949), OH-14-01-02.
16 Tracy (1962), OH-14-02-01; Audrey (1952), OH-15-01-02; Linda (1952), OH-15-01-03; Janice (1952), OH-15-03-01; Christine (1947), OH-15-03-03; Doris (1945), OH-15-04-02; Stephanie (1960), OH-15-05-01; Vivienne (1944), OH-15-05-05. In MOP, 'Close Relationships' (1990) see Andrea (1957), A2212; Enid (1950), D1226; Laura (1962), L2499. In MOP, 'Courting and Dating' (2001) see Glenda (1950), G2883 and Veronica (1951), W1813. In MOP, 'Sex' (2005): Joan (1961), J3473; Cheryl (1944), C2078; Geraldine (1959), G3395; Heather (1948), H1703; Iris (1940), H2637; Jennifer (1965), H3341; Mandy (1939), M1979; Maria (1956), M2986; Muriel (1940), P1009; Norma (1943), P3392; Sylvia (1948), T1961.
17 Pauline (1944), OH-14-01-03; Audrey (1952), OH-15-01-02; Joyce (1950), OH-15-03-02; Christine (1947), OH-15-03-03; Rosemary (1958), 15-04-04; Stephanie (1960), OH-15-05-01. From MOP, 'Sex': Betty (1963), B3154; Carolyn (1947), C1832; Eileen (1951), E743; Jennifer (1965), H3341; Mandy (1939), M1979; Marilyn (1955), M3476.
18 Graham Dawson, Soldier Heroes: British Adventure, Empire and the Imagining of Masculinities (London: Routledge, 1994), p. 25; Summerfield, 'Culture and Composure'.
19 Sandra (1949), OH-14-01-02; Tracy (1962), OH-14-02-01; Caroline (1944), OH-15-0205; Ruth (1960), OH-15-02-01.
20 An Education Select Committee inquiry into SRE held in 2014 led to the publication of a report which called from SRE to be statutory. The government response indicated a commitment to the broad principles of the report but no legislative changes were suggested. Further

campaigning eventually led to the introduction of statutory relationships and sex education through the Children and Social Work Act 2017. For a useful overview of the various campaigns leading up to and following on from this see https://www.sexeducationforum.org.uk/about/our-history-30-years-campaigning [accessed: 25 September 2024]. Similarly, anxiety and condemnation of England's teenage pregnancy rate had been a prominent feature of press discourse in the early 2000s when the Mass Observation Directives on 'Sex' and 'Courting and Dating' were circulated.

21 Olive (1954), MOP, 'Close Relationships', G2510.
22 Christina (1950), MOP, 'Close Relationships', C1786.
23 Janice (1952), OH-15-03-01. See also MOP 'Sex': Lesley (1958), L3298; Rebecca (1943), R1025.
24 Linda (1952), OH-15-01-03; Janice (1952), OH-15-03-01; Helen (1950), OH-15-03-07; Maureen (1945), OH-15-05-04.
25 Jill (1959), MOP, 'Sex', H3459.
26 Jane (1951), MOP, 'Sex', H1745. See also Joyce (1950), OH-15-03-02; Valerie (1947), OH-15-05-06.
27 Andrea (1957), MOP, 'Close Relationships', A2212.
28 Board of Education, *Sex Education in Schools and Youth Organisations*, p. 9. Linda (1952), OH-15-01-03; Julie (1960), OH-15-02-09; Hazel (1947), OH-15-04-05; Kathleen (1948), OH-15-04-06; Vivienne (1944), OH-15-05-05; Cynthia (1944), OH-15-05-07.
29 Valerie (1947), OH-15-05-06.
30 Daphne (1941) OH-15-03-05.
31 Cirrel Greet, *Facts of Life* (London: Tom Stacey, 1972), p. vi; Denys John, 'In a Comprehensive School', in National Marriage Guidance Council, *Sex Education in Perspective* (Rugby: National Marriage Guidance Council, 1972), p. 23.
32 Eric W. Johnson, *Love and Sex in Plain Language*, revised edn (London: Andre Deutsch, 1975), p. 9; *The Transmission of Life*, pp. 5–6.
33 Strange, 'Assault on Ignorance'.
34 Sharon (1951), MOP, 'Sex', S2581.
35 Christina (1950), MOP, 'Close Relationships', C1786.
36 Rosemary (1958), OH-15-04-04.
37 Joyce (1950), OH-15-03-02. See also Heather (1948), MOP, 'Sex', H1703; Enid (1950), MOP, 'Close Relationships', D1226; Cheryl (1944), MOP, 'Sex', C2078.
38 On changing cultures of sexual ignorance and discourse in the early twentieth century see Szreter and Fisher, *Sex before the Sexual Revolution*; Lucinda McCray Beier, *For Their Own Good: The*

Transformation of English Working-Class Health Culture, 1880–1970 (Columbus: Ohio State University Press, 2008).
39 Hilary (1956), OH-15-01-01; Linda (1952), OH-15-01-03; Sally (1946), OH-15-05-02. See also MOP, 'Sex': Frances (1961), F3178; Joan (1961), J3473; Muriel (1940), P1009; Rebecca (1943), R1025; Sheila (1958), S3372.
40 Theresa (1954), OH-14-01-05.
41 Daphne (1941), OH-15-03-05.
42 W. B. Hepburn, 'Letters to the Editor', *The Spectator*, 3 June 1966, p. 11.
43 Linda (1952), OH-15-01-03; Angela (1961), MOP, 'Growing Up', A1783; Enid (1950), MOP, 'Close Relationships', D1226; Jill (1959), MOP, 'Sex', H3459; Lisa (1957), MOP, 'Sex', L3037; Lorraine (1951), MOP, 'Sex', L3253.
44 Iris (1940), MOP, 'Sex', H2637.
45 Pauline (1944), OH-14-01-03.
46 Participants who recalled learning about sex through 'facts of life' literature included: Barbara (1952), OH-15-02-03; Enid (1950), MOP, 'Close Relationships', D1226; Angela (1961), MOP, 'Growing Up', A1783; as well as the following in MOP, 'Sex': Bridget (1966), B3185; Eileen (1951), E743; Gloria (1950), G3417; Lisa (1957), L3037; Lorraine (1951), L3253. On the use of videos as sex education see Theresa (1954), 14-01-05; Hilary (1956), OH-15-01-01; Mary (1959), OH-15-05-08; Andrea (1957), MOP, 'Close Relationships', A2212; Hilda (1954), MOP, 'Close Relationships', H1651; Marie (1955), MOP, 'Sex', N3396; Sheila (1958), MOP, 'Sex', S3372.
47 Ruth (1954), OH-15-02-01. See also Lisa (1957), MOP, 'Sex', L3037.
48 A. Leslie Banks, 'Puberty', *British Medical Journal* 1, no. 5064 (1958): 193–96.
49 Amanda (1947), MOP, 'Sex', A1706.
50 Sally (1946), OH-15-05-02; Gail (1958), MOP, 'Sex', G3042.
51 Lynda Mugglestone, '"The Indefinable Something": Representing Rudeness in the English Dictionary', in *Rude Britannia*, ed. Mina Gorji (Abingdon: Routledge, 2013).
52 Kathleen (1948), OH-15-04-06.
53 Heather (1948), MOP, 'Sex', H1703. See also Geraldine (1959), MOP, 'Sex', G3395.
54 Joy (1954), OH-15-04-01; Kathleen (1948), OH-15-04-06; Debbie (1964), MOP, 'Close Relationships', D3289; Vicki (1957), MOP, 'Close Relationships', T2345; Georgina (1959), MOP, 'Sex', G3423; Heather (1948), MOP, 'Sex', H1703.
55 Kathleen (1948), OH-15-04-06.

56 Glynis (1952), MOP, 'Growing Up', G2089.
57 Chris Hilliard, *A Matter of Obscenity: The Politics of Censorship in Modern England* (Princeton: Princeton University Press, 2021).
58 Harry Cocks, '"The Social Picture of Our Own Times": Reading Obscene Magazines in Mid-Twentieth-Century Britain', *Twentieth Century British History* 27, no. 2 (2016); Collins, *Modern Love*; Ben Mechen, '"Instamatic Living Rooms of Sin": Pornography, Participation and the Erotics of Ordinariness in the 1970s', *Contemporary British History* 36, no. 2 (2022).
59 Sally (1946), OH-15-05-02. See also Audrey (1952), OH-15-01-02. See also Linda (1952), OH-15-02-03.
60 Tracy (1962), OH-14-02-01.
61 Christine Farrell, *My Mother Said...: The Way Young People Learn About Sex and Birth Control* (London: Routledge and Kegan Paul, 1978), p. 61.
62 Doris (1945), OH-15-04-02.
63 Ellen (1961), MOP, 'Close Relationships', D2239. See also Sally (1946), OH-15-05-02; Olive (1954), MOP, 'Close Relationships', G2510.
64 Sally Alexander, 'The Mysteries and Secrets of Women's Bodies: Sexual Knowledge in the First Half of the Twentieth Century', in *Modern Times: Reflections of a Century of English Modernity*, ed. Mic Nava and Alan O'Shea (London and New York: Routledge, 1996), p. 166.
65 Hazel (1947), OH-15-04-05.
66 Theresa (1954), OH-14-01-05.
67 Hazel (1947), OH-15-04-05.
68 Gloria (1950), MOP, 'Sex', G3417.
69 Christine (1947), OH-15-03-03.
70 Cheryl (1944), MOP, 'Sex', C2078.
71 Sarah (1952), MOP, 'Sex', S2207.
72 Theresa (1954), OH-14-01-05.
73 Greet, *Facts of Life*; Nancy le P. Warner, *L for Learner: Towards an Understanding of Sex* (London: The Girl Guides Association, 1962), p. 16; *The Transmission of Life*, p. 13.
74 Ellen M. Holtzman, 'The Pursuit of Married Love: Women's Attitudes toward Sexuality and Marriage in Great Britain, 1918–1939', *Journal of Social History* 16, no. 2 (1982).
75 'Letters to Jane', *Honey*, January and February 1961; 'Danger Boy Too Hot to Handle', *Jackie*, 28 March 1964; 'Dodie Wells Answers', *Petticoat*, 22 February 1969; Eric W. Johnson, *Love and Sex in Plain Language*, revised edn (London: Andre Deutsch, 1975), p. 123; Barnett, *Sex and Teenagers in Love*, p. 59.

76 Rose Hacker, *The Opposite Sex* (London: Pan Books, 1960), pp. 98–99.
77 Charnock, '"How Far Should We Go?"'.
78 Gail (1958), MOP, 'Sex', G3042. See also Muriel (1940), MOP, 'Sex', P1009; Hilary (1956), OH-15-01-01; Vivienne (1944), OH-15-05-05.
79 Daphne (1941), OH-15-03-05.
80 Eileen (1951), MOP, 'Sex', E743.
81 The organisation of sexual acts into hierarchies has been noted by contemporary sociologists: Ruth Lewis, Cicely Marston, and Kaye Wellings, 'Bases, Stages and "Working Your Way Up": Young People's Talk About Non-Coital Practices and "Normal" Sexual Trajectories', *Sociological Research Online* 18, no. 1 (2013).
82 The use of numbers also works as a form of euphemism allowing girls to avoid graphically describing their sexual activity. On metaphors in sexual language see Deborah M. Roffman, 'The Power of Language: Baseball as a Sexual Metaphor in American Culture', *SIECUS Report* 19, no. 5 (1991); David Voigt, 'Sex in Baseball: Reflections of Changing Taboos', *Journal of Popular Culture* 12, no. 3 (1978).
83 Mabel (1946), MOP, 'Sex' Directive (2005), M3408.
84 Linda (1952), OH-15-01-03.
85 Tracy (1962), OH-14-02-01.
86 Barbara (1952), OH-15-02-03; Joyce (1950), OH-15-03-02; Valerie (1947), OH-15-05-06.
87 Kathleen (1948), OH-15-04-06; Mandy (1939), MOP, 'Sex', M1979.
88 Amanda described a framework that merged these two approaches, see Amanda (1947), MOP, 'Sex', A1706.
89 Evelyn (1947), MOP, 'Sex', F3409.
90 Julie (1960), OH-15-02-09.
91 Gail (1958), MOP, 'Sex', G3042.
92 Marjorie (1952), MOP, 'Courting and Dating', N1552.
93 Szreter and Fisher, *Sex before the Sexual Revolution*.
94 Deborah (1950), MOP, 'Sex', D826. See also Veronica (1951), MOP, 'Courting and Dating', W1813.
95 Amanda (1947), MOP, 'Sex', A1706.
96 Rachel (1959), MOP, 'Sex', R2826.
97 Mandy (1939), MOP, 'Sex', M1979.
98 Anne Koedt, 'The Myth of the Vaginal Orgasm', in *Notes from the Second Year*, ed. New York Radical Women (New York, 1970).
99 Geraldine (1959), MOP, 'Sex', G3395.
100 Wellings et al., *Sexual Behaviour in Britain*, pp. 71–76.

101 For example, Cyril Greenland, 'Unmarried Parenthood: Ecological Aspects', *The Lancet*, 19 January 1957, pp. 148–51; 'Venereal Disease and Young People', *British Medical Journal*, 7 March 1964, pp. 575–77.

102 Major investigations included Eustace Chesser, *The Sexual, Marital and Family Relationships of the English Women* (London: Hutchinson's Medical Publications, 1956); Virginia Wimperis, *The Unmarried Mother and Her Child* (London: Sir Halley Stewart Trust, George Allen & Unwin, 1960); Schofield, *The Sexual Behaviour of Young People*. *Picture Post* ran a series on 'Sex and the Citizen' across the autumn and winter of 1951. Across the period in question, the *Daily Mirror* ran a series of features on contemporary sexual values including: 'Sex and Youth', *Daily Mirror*, 1 December 1955; 'The Great Love Quiz', *Daily Mirror*, 13 April 1970; 'The Girl of Today', *Daily Mirror*, 10 June 1975, pp. 1, 4–5; 'The Way We Love Now', *Daily Mirror*, 1–3 March 1976.

103 See, for example, the 1958 *Sunday Pictorial* series, 'While Parents Sleep', *Sunday Pictorial*, 23 November – 28 December 1958.

104 Christie Davies, *Permissive Britain: Social Change in the Sixties and Seventies* (London: Pitman Publishing, 1975), pp. 69–70; Geoffrey Gorer, *Sex and Marriage in England Today: A Study of the Views and Experience of the Under-45s* (London: Nelson, 1971), pp. 34–38. The term 'permissiveness with affection' was coined by the American sociologist Ira Reiss, in 'The Scaling of Premarital Sexual Permissiveness', *Journal of Marriage and Family* 26, no. 2 (1964): 188–98, at 197.

105 'Where Have All the Virgins Gone?', *19*, March 1968, pp. 64–67.

106 Of the Mass Observers and interviewees whose marital status at first intercourse is known, only 13 per cent had penetrative sex for the first time within marriage. Seventeen per cent had sex with a fiancé/future spouse outside of marriage and 69 per cent had sex prior to marriage with a different partner.

107 Eileen (1951), MOP, 'Sex', E743. In MOP, 'Close Relationships' see Beatrice (1953), B1215; Darlene (1941s), B1887; Freda (1948), F1849.

108 Glenys (1941), MOP, 'Sex', G226.

109 Catherine (1959), MOP, 'Sex', C3513.

110 Cheryl (1944), MOP, 'Sex', C2078.

111 Diana (1947), OH-15-01-05. See also Helen (1950), OH-15-03-07; Amanda (1947), MOP, 'Sex', A1706.

112 Amanda (1947), MOP, 'Sex', A1706.

113 Schofield, *The Sexual Behaviour of Young People*, pp. 110–11.

114 Schofield, *The Sexual Behaviour of Young People*, p. 112.

115 Vivienne (1944), OH-15-05-05.
116 Le P. Warner, *L for Learner*, p. 16.
117 Julie (1960), OH-15-02-09.
118 Kathleen (1948), OH-15-04-06.
119 Maureen (1949), OH-15-05-04. In MOP, 'Close Relationships': Darlene (1941), B1887; Freda (1948), F1849; Eleanor (1960), H1131; Sherry (1942), S1229. In MOP, 'Sex': Jane (1951), H1745; Rachel (1959), R2862; Pamela (1948), R860.
120 Jane (1951), MOP, 'Sex', H1745.
121 Glenys (1941), MOP, 'Sex', G226.
122 Audrey (1952), OH-15-01-02.
123 Eileen (1951), MOP, 'Sex' Directive (2005), E743.
124 See also Sarah (1952), MOP, 'Sex', S2207.
125 The emphasis on deliberation and premeditation in the accounts of historic virginity loss stand in contrast to studies from the 1990s in which the 'conventional social construction of sex' emphasised spontaneity. Fiona J. Stewart, 'Femininities in Flux? Young Women, Heterosexuality and (Safe) Sex', *Sexualities* 2, no. 3 (1999); Mara B. Adelman, 'Sustaining Passion: Eroticism and Safe-Sex Talk', *Archives of Sexual Behavior* 21, no. 5 (1992).
126 These findings mirror those of late twentieth-century sociology. See, for example, Janet Holland, Caroline Ramazanoglu, Sue Sharpe, and Rachel Thomson, 'Deconstructing Virginity: Young People's Accounts of First Sex', *Sexual and Relationship Therapy* 15, no. 3 (2000); Susan Sprecher, Anita Barbee, and Pepper Schwartz, '"Was It Good for You, Too?": Gender Differences in First Sexual Intercourse Experiences', *The Journal of Sex Research* 32, no. 1 (1995); Sharon Thompson, 'Putting a Big Thing into a Little Hole: Teenage Girls' Accounts of Sexual Initiation', *The Journal of Sex Research* 27, no. 3 (1990).
127 Christine (1947), OH-15-03-03.
128 Alison (1960), OH-14-02-02.
129 Barbara (1952), OH-15-02-03.
130 Anne (1964), OH-14-01-06.
131 Audrey (1952), OH-15-01-02.
132 Tracy (1962), OH-14-02-01.
133 Tracy (1962), OH-14-02-01.
134 Joyce (1950), OH-15-03-02.
135 Gail (1958), MOP, 'Sex', G3042.
136 Michele (1956), MOP, 'Courting and Dating', N2912.
137 Linda (1952), OH-15-01-03.
138 Diana (1947), OH-15-01-05.

139 Janice (1952), OH-15-03-01.
140 Anne (1964), OH-14-01-06.
141 Julie (1960), OH-15-02-09.
142 Kathleen (1948), OH-15-04-06.
143 Hilda (1954), MOP, 'Close Relationships', H1651.
144 Alison (1960), OH-14-02-02.
145 This is not to say that penetrative sex became guaranteed or assumed. See Szreter and Fisher, *Sex before the Sexual Revolution*; Fisher, *Birth Control, Sex and Marriage in Britain 1918–1960*.

2

Sexual presents and imagined futures

Asked if her younger self had marital aspirations, oral history interviewee Barbara replied:

> No. None at all. At that time, I didn't, didn't think I'd ever get married. I had seen the marriages of my mother's generation and I didn't really see anything that I felt I aspired to. Because they were so unliberated if you like.[1]

This sentiment that young women needed to 'get some living done' was echoed by Julie, eight years Barbara's junior:

> *So, did you want to get married?*
>
> Certainly not immediately. I ... wanted boyfriends, I wanted to travel, definitely wanted to travel ... very into travelling and going places and doing things ... erm have a really good job and earn loads of money.[2]

Both Barbara and Julie understood their youth as a time of opportunity and hope as they imagined grand futures for themselves. They did not wholly reject the domestic femininity of their mothers but they yearned to 'be something' before they settled down to marriage and motherhood.

These dynamics of the push and pull between desires in the present and hopes for the future were central to women's experiences of youth in post-war England. Although there had always been a period of transition between childhood and adulthood, this phase of 'youth' or 'young adulthood' took on new significance in this period.[3] As pop culture increasingly targeted and spoke to the distinct experiences and feelings of teenagers, young people were encouraged to embrace this stage of the life course in which they were not constrained by the parent- and teacher-set rules of childhood nor tied down by the adult commitments of having a family.[4] Young adulthood was understood as a time when individuals got to make their own decisions and choose the future that they wanted for themselves.[5]

This chapter traces how matters of sexuality fit into these negotiations between present and future and in so doing it speaks to recent interest in the history of temporalities.[6] The stories that women told about their adolescent sex lives suggest that the hopes girls had for higher education and employment, to go on to have happy marriages and to raise families, were important in framing how they thought about sex and managed their sexual practice in their adolescent and young adult present. Where the previous chapter explored how desires to grow up and become mature could motivate girls into sexual activity, the future could also serve as a brake on their sex lives. Considering girls' attitudes to pregnancy and birth control makes clear that girls were not necessarily ready to embrace adulthood entirely.

While the future was an important structuring influence, however, it was not a fixed mark and the temporalities of youth were elastic and unstable. For adolescent girls self-consciously transitioning from youth to maturity, the perceived nearness of adulthood wavered; it could be both tantalisingly or terrifyingly close and reassuringly or frustratingly far, and these chaotic temporalities translated into variations in sexual and contraceptive behaviour. For some, the fear of pregnancy manifested in the proactive control of their fertility through abstinence, birth control, and abortion. For others, anxieties about the disruptive potential of sex did not guarantee that they would take action to avoid pregnancy. Although the introduction of reliable contraception and the decriminalisation of abortion certainly did change the potential consequences of sex, at no point did these innovations 'divorce sex from reproduction' and young women's sexuality was profoundly shaped by their status as 'not-yet-adults' who had their lives in front of them.[7]

Pregnancy as a threat

The stigma of extra-marital pregnancy

Getting pregnant and having a child outside of marriage was highly stigmatised across the twentieth century.[8] Although the number of extra-marital pregnancies increased substantially between the Second World War and the 1980s, throughout the post-war period this experience remained deeply embedded in cultures of shame and condemnation.[9] Across this period legislation such as the 1959 Legitimacy Act and the 1969 Family Law Reform Act altered the legal status of 'illegitimate' children but the press and popular culture continued to present extra-marital pregnancy as a social nightmare and personal tragedy.[10] *Daily Mail* headlines such as, 'These Girl Mothers Are "Shameless"', 'How Can We Halt Our Terrifying Moral Slump?', and 'Britain's Loneliest Mothers' left little doubt that illegitimacy was undesirable and some elements of the tabloid press used the rise of illegitimacy to bolster claims that post-war Britain was experiencing a decline in moral standards and decaying traditional values.[11] At the same time, in features such as 'We Could Say She's With Relatives', 'Pity the Poor Bastard', and 'Unto Us A Child Is Born ... But Is He Really Wanted?', girls' magazines such as *Honey* and *Petticoat* stressed the agonising dilemmas that resulted from teenagers' unplanned pregnancies.[12]

Teenagers were acutely aware of the stigma associated with extra-marital pregnancy. Daphne, who was a teenager in the 1950s, indicated that warnings on this matter had been explicit: 'it'd been drummed into you ... that having an illegitimate child was next door to the absolute last uh, um, you know, death was better'.[13] This was echoed by Barbara who was a teenager in the late 1960s: 'You were a social pariah if you were illegitimate or you had an illegitimate child. There was a stigma on you. Village gossip was rife, right, and you were also sanctioned.'[14] Describing the situation in the mid-1970s, Ruth stated that 'it was a disgrace, an utter disgrace to get pregnant and it was a utter embarrassment'.[15] Given the pervasiveness of this discourse it is unsurprising that oral history interviewees and Mass Observers suggested that their adolescent sexual lives were shrouded in the fear of getting pregnant. Although the experience of extra-marital pregnancies was a minority one, the threat of pregnancy loomed large within women's narratives.[16] Many women spoke of their adolescent selves' fear of getting pregnant. Within her Mass Observation testimony, Glenys (born in 1941) asserted that 'The fear of getting pregnant and "having" to get married cannot be over-emphasised', whilst Joy (born fourteen years later) stressed that even amongst teenagers in the late 1960s and early 1970s 'there was always a fear you might become pregnant'.[17] Born in 1949 and a university student in the late 1960s, Maureen described having engaged in 'heavy petting' but never penetrative sex. She explained:

> I was scared, so scared that I might get accidentally pregnant and for some reason ... I think I was worried about taking the pill, that I couldn't rely on it, that it wouldn't work, my biggest fear was a teenage pregnancy, that would've been a scandal.[18]

Maureen's fear of becoming pregnant was so deep-seated that even the promise of the oral contraceptive pill was brought into question. For her there was too much at stake and she was not prepared to take the risk by having sex.

Women who abstained from sex until their wedding day often suggested that the fear of pregnancy underpinned this choice.[19] Rebecca recalled that although she and her future husband 'experimented a little' prior to marriage, 'the fear of pregnancy and the stigma attached to that' was enough to stop them engaging in penetrative intercourse.[20] Explaining why she had remained a virgin until her wedding night Muriel stated that '[t]he biggest factor was the fear of becoming pregnant, the second biggest was the idea of telling my mother if the worst happened. Having an illegitimate child was the worst disgrace in those days.'[21] Geraldine and her friends decided that there would only be one option if they became pregnant: 'We would have to drown ourselves in the river.'[22] As teenagers in the 1950s, 1960s, and 1970s, pregnancy was understood by girls as being a disaster that threatened all aspects of their lives.

Far from being an abstract danger, the threat of pregnancy was present and tangible. By the time many girls were 16 they were aware of others within their communities who had 'got themselves in trouble'.[23] Having attended college in an industrial town in the Midlands, Alison indicated that it was 'really common at school [to] hear "Oh, so-and-so has got her pregnant, she's 14, she's 15"'.[24] In other communities this was less common, only intensifying the distress. Christine recalled how her and her friends were shaken when a classmate disappeared:

> One of my schoolfriends did get into trouble, big time, and she had to leave school and we ... that really scared us, I suppose we were about 15 ... It was a long wait to find out about that one, but it did frighten us. Because up to then we didn't believe that something like that could happen to any of us and it did.[25]

Observing how unmarried pregnant girls were treated, pregnancy was a looming danger that threatened girls' immediate existence; pregnancy had consequences in the here and now.

For girls such as Pamela, the imperative to avoid pregnancy was rooted within her family life. She believed that getting pregnant would cause an irrevocable breakdown in her relationships with her parents and she would be made homeless: 'My parents were very strict and frightening – I hadn't to bring trouble home. (One of my father's friend's daughter was expelled from my school for being pregnant at 15 yrs of age). I would be thrown out of home.'[26] Similarly, when Mabel left home to begin nurses training aged 17 her mother threatened her 'with total excommunication' if she became pregnant and she stressed that it was this rather than any sense of 'morals' that prevented her from having pre-marital sex. Although Mabel jumped into 'everything but' with the man she met upon leaving home, '[t]he spectre of my mother still hung in the air around us' and prevented her from having penetrative intercourse.[27]

Besides this potential for extra-marital pregnancy to precipitate family breakdown, girls were also concerned about what pregnancy could mean for their social standing and reputation. As Barbara put it: 'You were a social pariah if you were illegitimate or you had an illegitimate child. There was a stigma on you.'[28] Aged eleven in 1975, Marian was aware of the shame and taboo directed at her neighbour's teenage pregnancy: 'She was 15, only four years older than me and by God, was she frozen out! ... There was this silence about it, none of the grown ups would talk about her and either went silent or gave each other looks whenever she was mentioned.' Watching how this girls was treated had a profound effect on Marian: 'Even though I was fairly young I remember being sure that if I got pregnant then I would stop it, rather than let it ruin my life.'[29] The danger that pregnancy posed was thus immediate and real and it was so potent precisely because it was something that girls witnessed for themselves. Listening to the explicit warnings of their parents and observing the experiences of their peers, girls associated pregnancy with imprisonment, bereavement, and excommunication and, in this way, pregnancy threatened to rapidly unravel their social and personal lives.

Risking imagined futures

The unravelling potential of pregnancy did not just relate to girls' present lives, however. Much of the threat of pregnancy lay in its consequences for the futures that girls and their parents were imagining for them. In particular, girls were concerned that unplanned pregnancy would thwart their aspirations for meaningful relationships and fulfilling careers and would prevent them from making a successful and satisfying transition to adulthood. It was certainly not new for young women to fear pregnancy but the texture of this anxiety took on distinct forms in the post-war period.[30] Put simply, the new opportunities and identities available to young people through mass affluence, the expansion of the education system, and the welfare state raised the stakes of young adulthood for middle-class girls, meaning that they had much to lose by becoming pregnant. Joyce's explanation for not having penetrative sex until she went to university summarised this future-oriented thinking in blunt terms: 'I wouldn't have dreamed of doing anything until I knew I was 100%, well 99%, safe. It was just the idea of ruining, the inverted commas, "ruining" the rest of my life. Because to me, that's what it would have been.'[31]

Women who grew up in the 1950s and 1960s have been characterised as a 'breakthrough' generation.[32] As Helena Mills, Eve Worth, and Lynn Abrams have found, women of this generation perceive themselves to have been gifted with opportunities for freedom, self-expression, and individual fulfilment that were not available to previous generations.[33] Within their testimonies, many women similarly expressed the sentiment that they had been part of an exciting moment of profound social change in which young adulthood took on particular significance as a distinct life phase. As Kathleen explained:

> 1963 I moved from my home in Bromley, which was very suburban and kind of middle-class and repressed as it were, I was very young I was only 16. ... In the 50s young women grew up in their parents' house, got married and moved to a house with their husband and it was quite a new thing, very new thing that young women were actually living independently between living at home and getting married. Um, so there was this sort of sense of independence and you could, you could explore things that you wouldn't've had the opportunity to explore when you were living at home.[34]

The exact dynamics of this young adulthood varied but it was increasingly anticipated that girls would experience life independent of their parents before getting married. Young adulthood was not simply a holding space in which young women searched for a husband and prepared for marriage but was understood as an important period for self-realisation.[35] In Jacqueline's words: 'I was young, I was free, I was young and you know, the world was mine ... I could grow with what was happening around me and change with it.'[36] Modern middle-class femininity was premised on girls making the most of their fortune to live in a world so alive with possibility and opportunity.

Education was seen by many to be the key to girls fulfilling their potential as well as being an opportunity for independence in its own right. The introduction of compulsory secondary schooling for girls through the 1944 Education Act, the raising of the compulsory school leaving age to fifteen in 1944 and then to sixteen in 1973, and the development of new externally examined qualifications ('O' and 'A' levels from 1951, 'Certificates of Secondary Education' from 1965) all functioned to formalise girls' school education and encouraged many middle-class girls into higher education and vocational training.[37] The creation of the 'plate-glass' universities in the 1960s, as well as the expansion of existing 'redbrick' institutions, combined with new grants to support students, made attending university more viable for middle-class girls.[38] Although debates over the value of educating and training women who would 'inevitably' leave the labour market upon marriage and motherhood certainly persisted into the late twentieth century, the post-war period saw heightened educational expectations became normalised within middle-class culture.[39] Women who attended grammar and private schools recalled how their schools and parents expected them to go into higher education or professional training. Asked about how 'academic' her school was, Vivienne replied: '[P]eople who stayed on to sixth form were expected to apply for university or teacher training college. That was what you were supposed to do.'[40]

Parents were often hugely influential in encouraging their daughters' pursuit of further education. Daphne described herself as 'blazing a trail' in her family by going to university in the late 1950s. Her parents had left school in their mid-teens but encouraged her to go to university.[41] Reflecting the expansion of higher education from the 1960s, younger women among this sample recalled not just encouragement from their families but a degree of expectation that they would attend university. Julie, who was born in 1960, indicated that:

> [I]t was totally implied you did your A-Levels and you go to university ... it was assumed that's what you would do. I don't remember having a discussion about whether I wanted to or not, pros and cons, 'is this a good idea?' ... you got certain A-Levels and you went to university.[42]

Anne, who was also a teenager in the late 1970s, indicated that her parents instilled in her a sense that she needed to make the most of her educational opportunities: 'My mum would see me as being somebody who had that opportunity ... and father's kind of constant thing is, "But what are you going to do with your brain?" ... Y'know, it's that, it's the whole thing, "It's all there, take it".'[43]

While higher education and professional training was seen as one route to successful young adulthood, other young women sought independence through work. No longer understood as a mere stopgap between school and marriage, women's work came to be seen as an important way through which young women found and expressed a sense of self.[44] Although some girls had a particular sense of vocation, many young women (especially those leaving school at fifteen and sixteen) were less enthusiastic for careers than they were for the opportunities offered by employment and financial independence. Stories of entering employment often focused upon the perceived freedoms associated with living away from home and earning their own keep.

This narrative was particularly prominent amongst those who worked as secretaries within offices. Although there were opportunities for office work in most towns, for many girls the appeal of such work lay in the chance to live and work away from home; with basic secretarial training girls were able to pursue work in almost any city in the country. Sally grew up in Exeter in the late 1950s and had been educated at a very academic, all-girls school. Against the wishes of her school she decided to leave at sixteen: 'I did well at school, I did my O Levels, I did well, everybody was pleased that I'd do my A Levels, go to university like everybody else at the school did, and I left at 16 'cos I'd had enough, I didn't want to do A Levels.' Sally stressed that she did not have any particular career ambitions, she just 'wanted to get out into the world and enjoy [herself]'. Not knowing what else to do after she had left school, she took a secretarial course and trained in Business French specifically because '[she] thought it would give [her] an extra reason to leave Exeter and go to London and get a job'.[45] Sally was motivated by a desire to be independent and start a new exciting life away from home. Work for her was not a career but a means of achieving the lifestyle that she wanted.

Hazel's situation echoed Sally's. She had also grown up in Exeter in the 1950s and had also taken French as part of her secretarial training. She knew that in order to put her French to work she had to leave her hometown to go to 'a fairly major city, p'raps somewhere like Portsmouth or Southampton with export and travel connections'. But she was also drawn towards London: 'I used to read quite a lot about London and things were just starting to happen in London and I wanted to go and be part of it!' Hazel not only had a clear sense of what work she wanted to do, she chose to go to London where the music and fashion scenes and youth culture 'were just starting to bubble up'.[46] Emphasising the sociability of their living and working situations and the flexibility afforded to them by the near-constant availability of work, women such as Sally and Hazel framed their youthful employment in terms of freedom, exploration, and self-fulfilment.[47]

Looking back on their lives, women associated their young adulthood with feelings of liberation and empowerment yet these heightened expectations made the spectre of pregnancy seem all the more chaotic and troublesome. Across this thirty-year period, middle-class girls such as Wendy and Brenda understood pregnancy as inevitably disruptive and dangerous to the futures they imagined for themselves:

> Being pregnant and unmarried, or even rumoured of being sexually active, was not to be countenanced among nice, grammar school girls who were expected, at the very least, to get enough O levels to get into the lower echelons of the civil service.[48]

> I don't remember any of my friends getting pregnant – we were all destined for university or at least a levels and keen to avoid getting sucked into early domesticity.[49]

As these testimonies indicate, girls' educational and employment aspirations were often set against and existed in tension with expectations of marriage. Although girls were increasingly encouraged to enter the labour force and make the most of their education by embarking on careers, this did not displace the notion that most women would find their ultimate happiness and satisfaction through marriage and motherhood. Some girls therefore perceived remaining in education and delaying marriage as a risk to their destiny as wives and mothers.[50] While many teachers and educationalists viewed girls' interests in boys 'as a distraction from intellectual pursuits', elsewhere girls were repeatedly bombarded with the message that they were destined for marriage and that men 'didn't like women to be too clever'.[51] Girls' futures as wives and mothers were both revered and resented.

Echoing the words of Lorna Sage, who remembered the postwar decades as a time when girls had 'to choose between boys and books', Glenys suggested that during her adolescence the immediate future was determined by the choice between either education or marriage.[52] Those who wanted to get married left school, while those who wanted to get an education put off having boyfriends.[53] Although it was increasingly common for married women to work, in Glenys' mind, her career ambitions were not compatible with forming romantic relationships.[54] Daphne echoed this feeling of incompatibility in even starker terms: 'At that time, I was not going to get married and I had no interest in getting married at all. ... No, I wanted to do something and be something. I wanted to make a mark.'[55]

However, life had a way of complicating these binary distinctions of work versus marriage and the plans that girls made for themselves did not always come to pass. In her testimony, Tracy described her year at school as having been split between 'the goody two shoes class and the naughty class'. Locating herself in the latter (although with the caveat that she did well in school), she went on to explain a key difference between the two groups: 'the swotty ones had that sort of, like it was all planned out, like 25 you're gonna get married and yeah ... We just wanted to find out about sex'.[56] Tracy had looked down on her classmates' domestic ambitions yet she herself got married at nineteen and, at least initially, 'really liked being the little housewife ... I thought it was very grown up!'. Even Daphne, who had so starkly rejected the idea of marriage, met and began her relationship with her future husband while at university. Looking back from middle age, she could recall her younger self's desire to 'make a mark' while knowing the different path that her life had taken: 'The fact that I didn't [make a mark], neither here nor there, I was happy so there you go.'[57]

In so far as they celebrated serendipitous 'meet-cutes', instantaneous romantic connections and the fantasy of being swept off their feet, mid-century romance cultures idealised the experience of deviating from imagined life trajectories.[58] Films and novels encouraged girls to be open to the disruptive potential of romantic love; love was seen to have transformative power that could bring untold joy and happiness into young women's lives. The life-altering potential of love, however, was understood very differently to the life-altering potential of pregnancy and the latter was often positioned as a risk to the former. The relationship between love, marriage, and pregnancy was fraught.

At the same time that shifting expectations of education and work increased the anxiety around unplanned pregnancy, changing understandings of the nature and function of marriage were also reframing the consequences of becoming pregnant. Though women's lives had long been organised around the assumption that they would find purpose and stability in marriage and motherhood, the twentieth century witnessed the rise of 'companionate' marriage,[59] with the post-war decades experiencing what Claire Langhamer has referred to as an 'emotional revolution', which saw romantic love become the idealised foundation of marriages.[60] Marriage was reimagined as a site of self-realisation and fulfilment and the success of marriages lay in the their foundation upon romantic intimacy, emotional connection, and sexual compatibility. For middle-class girls growing up in the post-war decades, the simple fact of marriage was not enough; it was crucial that they found the 'right' partner to share their lives with.

In their testimonies women spoke not only of their desire to get married but of the need to choose their partners wisely. Prompted by the Mass Observation Directive on 'Courting and Dating' in 2001, women described the specific criteria that their teenage selves had looked for in a partner. Glenys, for example, 'wanted someone who would look after [her]'.[61] Similarly, Heather 'expected [her partners] to be gentle with a sense of humour who [she] thought [she] should be able to talk to as if [she] had known him all [her] life'.[62] As explored further in Chapter 3, great emphasis was placed upon compatibility and finding a good fit in a future husband. Placing romance, emotional connection, and temperamental compatibility as the foundations of marriage had consequences, however, especially as modern expectations of marriage and those of sex pulled in slightly different directions. As explored in the following chapters, young women were increasingly likely to engage in sexual activity with young men that they had no (immediate) intention of marrying. The criteria by which young men qualified as sexual partners did not necessarily map on to those expected of future husbands. By having penetrative sex with partners in whom they had little long-term interest, young women risked not only their educational and professional futures, but their hopes of marrying for love.

This risk was heightened as the association of marriage with pregnancy remained extremely strong throughout this period. The notion of pregnant brides was so ubiquitous that it was often assumed that those marrying young were expecting a child; Gwen was a virgin when she got engaged and was indignant when her mother accused her of being pregnant.[63] Similarly, Muriel recalled her mother advising her not to get pregnant immediately upon marriage in case anyone thought that she had been pregnant prior to her wedding.[64] There remained an expectation that girls who became pregnant outside of marriage would go on to get married (ideally before the child was born).[65] In cases of unplanned pregnancy it was believed that getting married was the only way to ensure the livelihood of the girl in question and her child.

Many women described their younger self's intense fear of 'getting pregnant and "having" to get married'.[66] Helen's testimony highlighted the fraught atmosphere surrounding unplanned pregnancy. She described how raising a child outside of marriage was 'utterly unacceptable to our generation's parents' and how although men 'doing the right thing' and marrying their pregnant partners went some way to avoiding 'scorn, shame [and] retribution', these unions were still disapproved of.[67] Families could attempt to gloss over such scenarios and the pretence of respectability could be maintained but social stigma and silent judgement remained. As Wendy noted:

> 'She's got to get married' was still a shameful thing to be said & I remember our next door neighbour assuring everyone her new grandchild was a premature baby & everyone knowing it was not yet retaining the polite fiction.[68]

Many pregnant girls were made to feel that marriage was their only option; especially prior to the legalisation of abortion in 1967, girls living at home often lacked access and resources, not to mention the criminal intent required, to terminate their pregnancy.[69]

Not only were such marriages deemed distasteful at the time but with hindsight their problematic foundations had been 'proved'. This generation of women were the first to benefit from the divorce law reform of the late 1960s and some individuals were keen to stress that 'shotgun weddings' were particularly prone to breakdown.[70] Describing how one of her childhood friends got married in 1968 ('and yes she was pregnant'), Carolyn followed this up by stating that: 'She later divorced in the early 80s which was a shame but happened to a lot of girls who had to get married.'[71] Likewise, Muriel offered little comment on her cousin's shotgun wedding other than specifying that 'the marriage ended in divorce'.[72] Although there were plenty of success stories, marriages founded upon a 'need' to get married were perceived as being especially susceptible to breakdown. These marriages were not portrayed as happy but rather imagined to be somehow superficial or not quite complete. At a time when marriage was supposed to be rooted in love and mutual fulfilment, the idea of being compelled to get married sullied the institution.

Building on Claire Langhamer's model of a post-war 'emotional revolution', we can see how the 'romanticisation' of marriage raised the stakes of extra-marital pregnancy. Girls of this generation wished to marry for love and to share a deep emotional bond with their spouse; they believed that happiness within marriage was dependent upon choosing their own partner and entering into their commitment freely. Pregnancy-prompted marriages and shotgun weddings undermined this model by introducing an element of obligation that weakened the foundation of the marriage. If young couples already intended to marry then unplanned pregnancy could be framed as a catalyst, bringing forward the timeframe for this commitment.[73] For those girls whose dating and sexual lives were focused around leisure, fun, and company rather than love and romance, however, pregnancy was a threat as it potentially doomed them to a life-long union with a man they barely knew or cared for. By getting pregnant unexpectedly, girls stood to lose their opportunity to marry for love. With heightened expectations of what marriage should mean, the fear of being forced into it also increased.

Contrary to the claims that the mass availability of contraception 'relieved the penalties of pregnancy'[74] and 'broke the link between sexual activity and reproduction', these testimonies illustrate how teenage girls were acutely aware of their child-bearing potential.[75] Fear of pregnancy was an important influence informing young women's attitudes towards sex and their sexual conduct. In this way, Lisa Smith's observation that 'as subjects situated on the border of childhood and adulthood, young women have to work even harder to maintain non-reproduction because the consequences of an unexpected pregnancy threaten their own future, their family, and society more generally' was as true of the 1950s, 1960s, and 1970s as it is in the twenty-first century.[76]

Avoiding pregnancy

This 'not-never-but-not-now' approach to having children was, for many young women, underpinned by clear logics of self-fulfilment and realisation. Exploring the actual sexual practices of women of this generation, however, highlights the ephemeral quality of aspirations and future-based logic in the present. In theory, increasing access to contraception should have limited the risks associated with engaging in sexual activity and these testimonies suggest that contraceptive innovation, particularly the invention of the oral contraceptive pill, did enable adolescent sexual activity to function differently to that of the older generation. However, there was not an overnight revolution; many old fears remained and new anxieties came to the fore. The Pill may have increased women's potential to avoid pregnancy but it did not eradicate women's fertility. Even girls coming of age in the post-Pill era of the 1970s were acutely aware of their own reproductive potential and were deeply wary of it. Their use of contraception represented not a denial of their fertility but an active attempt to temporarily resist it in service of their other desires and aspirations. As we shall see, although many girls had rational reasons to use contraception, this did not always translate into their sexual practice. Sexual interactions and encounters forced young women to confront the often clashing demands of their present and imagined future selves. While this provided some girls with opportunities to claim control over their life journeys, other girls embraced spontaneity and prioritised their more immediate desires.

A 'post-Pill paradise'?

In the six decades since its introduction in 1961, the oral contraceptive pill has gained a reputation as one of the most transformative inventions of the modern world. Historians and social commentators have suggested that the Pill 'divorced sex from reproduction', in effect removing considerations of fertility from the sex act itself.[77] Value judgements regarding the cost–benefit of this have varied – while the Pill is considered by some as a feminist triumph that freed women from the tyranny of endless child-rearing, both feminists and conservatives have critiqued the emergence of 'promiscuous' sexual cultures facilitated by reliable contraceptives.[78] In spite of these different evaluations, however, Mass Observer Rita captured the prevailing sentiment in her assessment that 'the Pill changed everything'.[79]

Reflecting on their own lives and experiences, women expressed the view that the Pill has liberated their sexuality. Given that it offered no prompts on this topic, it is striking, for example, how many women responding to the 1990 Mass Observation Directive on 'Close Relationships' used the words 'free' and 'freedom' in association with the oral contraceptive pill.[80] Interviewed in 1991 as part of an oral history project celebrating the thirtieth anniversary of the oral contraceptive pill, Kate described the Pill as the 'cult contraception' of the 1960s and directly positioned changing contraceptive practice as the central cause of altered sexual mores:

> [Laughing] I was very sexually active at university, this was the 'Swinging Sixties', and it was very liberating ... I think in the 60s it was sexy to use the Pill so I think that's what I was, that's what I was offered, if I remember. 'Cos I think they were, not exactly dishing them out like Smarties, but that was, it was considered very safe.[81]

Similarly, Sandra recalled how after arriving in London in 1968, 'it wasn't long before I went on the Pill because it seemed silly not to really'. From that point onwards: 'we were pretty promiscuous really, because, it was just whoopydoo really and it was very ... sort of free and easy, y'know I had lots of, lots of boyfriends floating in and out'.[82] Being on the Pill was crucial to Sandra's sexual activity. One-night stands were 'absolutely fine' because '[y]ou were on the Pill so you were safe'. Central to these accounts of sexual 'liberation' was the sense that the Pill made contraceptive sex 'easy'; once girls were on the Pill they did not have to worry about getting pregnant and it was this detachment from deliberation that allowed women like Kate and Sandra to be 'very sexually active'.

Crucially, however, most women did not see themselves as having existed in a hedonistic 'post-Pill paradise' in which pregnancy was immaterial and promiscuity rife. Rather than portraying contraceptive use as a universal and inevitable practice that facilitated a wild and chaotic culture of casual sex, testimonies stressed instead the deliberations that girls made before deciding to go on the Pill and emphasised the lengths they had to go to acquire birth control. Within their testimonies women suggested that the use of contraception was a conscious choice and a product of psychological, emotional, and physical labour. Women's emphasis on their past selves' proactive pursuit of contraception worked to position them as modern sexual agents; through birth control, women were able to regulate their fertility and subsume it in service of their desires and ambitions.

Women proudly recalled that they had 'put themselves' on the Pill.[83] Having done so in their teens was framed as a marker of their precocious sexual maturity and their embracing of modern sexual culture. Audrey had a tumultuous adolescence – she moved away from home as a teenager in order to escape a difficult home situation and attend grammar school. Even though her living situation was turbulent, when she became sexually active she was 'really, really, really clear' about the need for contraception. She recalled her determination to procure the Pill aged seventeen in 1969:

> Even though my life by that point was completely chaotic I was very organised about going and getting the Pill. And the doctor said, 'You realise if you sleep with someone at this age you're doomed for life, get all these diseases', 'I still want the Pill please'.[84]

Theresa offered a similar account of challenging medical authority to access the Pill:

> I waited 'til I was 18 and went to my GP to, to go on the Pill. I didn't go before because I thought he'd tell my parents 'cos he was a friend of ... the family. And he didn't want to put me on the Pill but ... he said, 'I s'pose you're already doing it.' I said, 'Yes, I am.' '[Tuts] Well then I don't have any alternative,' he said, 'but I don't want to, you better tell your mother.' And I didn't.[85]

Although these stories function on one level to present Theresa and Daphne as defiant and rebellious, they simultaneously worked to stress their former selves' responsible approach to sex.

Within other testimonies, the model of responsible sexuality being performed through birth control practice was less to do with defiant autonomy and more to do with partnership. For couples who understood sex as a means of furthering emotional intimacy and who had mutual hopes for sexual activity, pursuing birth control was seen as a shared endeavour. Women who were in meaningful relationships often used the 'we' pronoun to discuss their contraceptive decision-making.[86] Daphne gleefully explained that her and her fiancé, 'we managed to fool a, um, a, a family planning cli-clinic ... and I did get the Pill before I got married'.[87] While the testimonies described contraceptive practice as an active process that had to be proactively managed, this labour had been shared. Clare and her partner discussed their desire for sex and the need for contraception. Having decided that she should go on the Pill, they went to the family planning clinic together:

> We tried to be responsible and were aware of the dangers of pregnancy etc. I remember we talked about sex and decided I should go on the 'pill' however I was frightened to go to my doctor in case my mum and dad found out. We found a family planning clinic in nearby High Wycombe and we bused [sic] over there together.[88]

As in the self-regulation narratives, Clare stressed that accessing the Pill was not straightforward; to Clare the cost of her parents finding out was not worth paying for the benefits of convenience. Yet, the challenges served to validate this process both as an act of responsible sexuality and as a testament to the emotional bond at the heart of her relationship.

Accounts of Pill use very neatly map onto the accounts of modern middle-class femininity described earlier in the chapter. Though sometimes implicit, there is a logical connection between girls' heightened expectations of work, careers, marriage, and motherhood and their proactive pursuit of reliable contraception in the form of the Pill. Yet, although this experience was central to many of the post-war generation's experiences of sexuality, it was far from universal. Part of this was simply demographic as women born in the 1940s were born too soon to have encountered the Pill in their youth. The Pill was introduced in Britain in 1961 and was not widely available to unmarried women until the late 1960s.[89] Although many older women in this cohort had gone on to use the Pill in adulthood (often as a form of family planning within marriage), information and access to the Pill was limited in their youth. Moreover, just because the Pill was technically available to younger women in the cohort does not mean that they used it. Women who were born in the mid to late 1950s and who grew up in the 1970s reported cultural and material logics for not having used the Pill. Although it was a reference point in their testimonies, women were clear that Pill use was not assumed, self-evident, or necessarily expected in their youth.

Some women explained that access to the Pill was difficult for teenagers and young people, particularly for those living outside urban centres where most of the sexual health clinics were located.[90] Fear of disclosing sexual activity to family doctors who would pass this on to girls' parents was not uncommon.[91] Other women recalled having very deliberately chosen not to go on the Pill. Anne, one of the youngest women interviewed for this project, was born in the mid-1960s and recalled how as a teenager she chose not to go on the Pill due to her desire for secrecy and concerns about its safety: 'Going on the pill was really bad news for 2 reasons: 1, someone might find out 'cos they could see, find the tablets; and 2 because th-, chemically problematic for all sorts of reasons.'[92]

Most commonly, however, oral history interviewees suggested that among their social circles and in their minds, there had been a sense that the Pill was not really for them. Hilary, for example, indicated that, growing up in the south west of England, the Pill was a distant entity removed from her and her friends' sexual reality:

> Yeah, you knew it was available, but you probably thought it was more for family planning for people that were already married and it was a bit risky and a bit dangerous if, if you approach someone to say, 'Well, actually I am having sex' or 'I want sex', and 'Please can I have the pill'. Yeah, you know, we were too naive for that. You know, we weren't worldly wise. Maybe that was being in Devon, I don't know.[93]

Elsewhere, Barbara and Helen suggested that they had associated the Pill with family planning.

> I took enormous risks because we weren't able to get the pill at that time. It was available, but you had to go with your boyfriend and say you were getting married. I didn't have boyfriends like that, so I couldn't get it.[94]

> I think the thing is that generally you tended to go on it if you were in a, a permanent relationship or at least an in involvement. Sad to say that things weren't working out too great and it was far more, you know, occasional this and that. And you didn't necessarily go to your family doctor to start with.[95]

Hilary, Barbara, and Helen were all born in the 1950s and embarked on sexual relationships in the late 1960s and 1970s, at a time of greater awareness and access to the Pill. As young women having sex outside of marriage, however, the relevance of the oral contraceptive pill to their lives was not clear.

Alternative methods of birth control

Of course, myriad forms of contraception existed beyond the Pill and not being on the Pill did not mean that women were not using birth control or managing their sexuality in ways to avoid pregnancy. Though much is often made of women's apparent aversion to using forms of birth control that involved touching themselves or delaying intercourse to apply/insert contraceptives, sexually active young women in the 1960s were open to using 'over the counter' contraceptive technologies that were more accessible to unmarried couples than the GP-controlled methods of the cap, diaphragm, or the Pill.[96] Testimonies confirm that young people used a range of birth control methods, including condoms, withdrawal, the rhythm method, spermicidal foams, and suppositories.[97] To a certain extent, women had internalised late twentieth-century rhetoric that, other than sterilisation and abstinence, hormonal contraceptives were the only truly reliable form of birth control but they nonetheless remembered their younger selves having taken active precautions to avoid pregnancy.

Condoms were a common form of birth control among young couples in the mid-twentieth century.[98] As Jessica Borge, Ben Mechen, and Paul Jobling have explored, shifting sexual mores of the post-war period expanded the consumer market for condoms and 'sheaths' (as they were called) were increasingly available in chemists, barbershops, and in vending machines.[99] What is striking in the personal accounts explored here, however, is the ambiguous characterisation of condom use as a means of controlling fertility and managing sexual practice. In contrast to accounts which framed use of the oral contraceptive pill as a form of proactive intervention that girls took on their own behalf, narratives of condom use could follow this trope or else they were presented as a compromise in which girls left their safety in the hands of their male partners. Writing about contraceptive use within marriage in the first half of the twentieth century, Kate Fisher revealed 'patterns of contraceptive activity which privileged male action and prized female passivity'.[100] This gender divide was blurred in the mid-century, however. Although narratives of Pill use indicate heightened female agency, testimonies also highlight that traditions of male-controlled contraceptive practice persisted among younger generations.

Born in 1946, Julia was among the first 'Pill generation'. However, using the Pill simply never occurred to her as a young, unmarried woman. Rather, she and her future husband used condoms up until they got married. That her partner was responsible for providing condoms was assumed by both parties:

And what type of thing were most people of your age using then?

Condoms, as they're called now, in my day they were 'French letters'.

Where did you get them from?

I didn't personally buy any, the boy I was with bought them, I don't know chemists and things I supposed, hairdressers wasn't it, hairdressers in those days, it wasn't in all public places years ago.

So was it generally left up to the-

The male. Oh yes, definitely so, definitely so yes.[101]

As Julia's testimony suggests, contraceptive practice was gendered because the specific technologies and techniques used to control fertility were gendered. In particular, condoms were understood as being men's business.

While numerous women remembered 'boyfriends using condoms', there was little critical reflection as to *why* exactly this was.[102] Having stressed that the Pill was only available to the married or engaged, Christine asserted that for young couples, 'he had to take care of' birth control.[103] Although girls viewed contraception as essential in avoiding pregnancy and the risk that it posed to their imagined futures, they did not necessarily see it as their job to provide condoms or birth control. Women such as Audrey and Doris claimed that they insisted that their partners use contraception but relied upon these men/boys providing condoms.[104] As Doris put it, in the pre-Pill world, 'It was mostly the boys buying condoms quite frankly, if they put their minds to it.'[105] Pauline explained:

In those days it would've been either from the barber's shop, that'd been traditionally the place, y'know, 'Something for the weekend sir?' Or you were just beginning to get the condom machines coming into the pubs, so, in the men's toilets y'know, so, um, probably out of a machine.[106]

Although condoms were increasingly advertised to women and made available over the counter, condom-selling was still primarily associated with male spaces.[107]

Where women who had used the Pill presented their sexual pasts in terms of self-reliance and responsibility, those who had not used the Pill told slightly different stories that emphasised their past selves' naivety and vulnerability and/or spoke of deferred responsibility. Cheryl, for example, described having sex with two men she 'quite fancied', specifically noting that, 'luckily both were very sensible and took precautions'; her phrasing suggests that she had little involvement in this process of ensuring that their sexual activity was 'responsible'.[108] Similarly, when asked what type of 'precautions' she had used upon having sex for the first time, Kathleen replied that they had used a condom, adding that 'he was quite responsible and all that'.[109] This dynamic was particularly prevalent within couples where there was a significant age difference between partners; girls with older (sometimes married) partners often left such arrangements to their partners who they deemed to be more informed about such matters.[110] In these contexts, age dynamics as well as gender contributed to this male-led contraceptive culture.

Many girls clearly knew about contraception and some were prepared to demand that birth control be used during penetrative sex but these accounts of youthful sexuality did not inhabit the same level of defiant self-care and rational sexuality exhibited by those women who discussed having been on the Pill. In a culture in which contraceptives could be difficult for girls to acquire, not all girls were confident enough to explicitly raise the issue with their partners. In her testimony, Geraldine recalled how she had really wanted to have sex with her boyfriend when she was sixteen but ended up not doing so because she 'was scared to talk to him about the practicalities of contraception'.[111] Stating that contraceptives were 'less readily available' to young women at this time and that she could not go to the family planning clinic as one of her friend's mothers worked there, there was no way for Geraldine to have sex with the security she required without asking him to provide contraception. As such, sex could not occur.

Non-use of birth control

For Geraldine there was a direct link between her imagined future and her sexual and contraceptive practice: not wanting to get pregnant she could not have sex without the use of birth control. As these testimonies are beginning to demonstrate, however, the contraceptive culture of this time was not entirely rational. It is easy to trace a line from girls' heightened expectations of their futures to their consistent use of contraceptives.[112] It is more difficult, however, to account for the young women who engaged in penetrative intercourse without the protection of birth control. Even though girls saw themselves as being 'at risk' of pregnancy, this did not necessarily translate into proactive behaviour on their own behalf; many girls still relied upon their partners to take adequate precautions and many more did not use any form of birth control.

Women such as Sandra and Julie attributed their non-use of contraception to ignorance.[113] Others, however, did 'know better'. Theresa's mother was a midwife and she had 'drummed' it into Theresa that she must use birth control.[114] Moreover, Theresa had high hopes for her future as she wanted to be a doctor. In spite of all this, she did not use contraception the first few times she had sex, a fact she clearly found troubling in the present as she tried to diminish the extent of her perceived irresponsibility:

Did you use contraception when you were having sex?

Not the first times, no.

Did you even think about it?

Oh god, yes, 'cos my mother had drummed, drummed it down my throat! Y'know, I mean, I knew that it was really foolish but-, so to begin, I mean, maybe, we didn't have that much unprotected sex 'cos he was quite, um ... responsible, y'know, he certainly did not want to get me pregnant, no way. So, although we, we, we risked it a, a little bit, he used condoms after that and then when I was 18, I waited 'til I was 18 and went to my GP to, to go on the Pill.

The stilted syntax and hesitation here suggest that Theresa was somewhat uncomfortable recalling this element of her previous sexual life. Although Theresa was prepared to 'confess' having unprotected sex, as the daughter of a midwife and a doctor herself, being interviewed by a researcher evidently interested in sexual health, Theresa felt the need to stress that this was a temporary oversight and highlight her later responsibility.

Young women's assessments of risk did not always revolve around long-term considerations. Asked to explain how her younger self had decided what types of sexual activity she was prepared to engage in, Barbara indicated that it was 'gut feeling' rather than logic fuelling her choices:

> I couldn't say that it was because I feared getting pregnant because my first sexual encounter was without protection and subsequent ones were. So I can't use that as an excuse. Yeah, but I just wasn't ready for it. And when I decided I was ready for it, I went for it.[115]

It was possible for more immediate concerns – namely the desire to have sex – to supersede the 'need' for precautions. Women suggested that when caught without contraceptives they often had sex anyway: Tina noted that she trusted her boyfriend and so 'made up [her] mind to just go along with it', while Carolyn described very patchy contraceptive practice, 'I wasn't on the pill so my boyfriend used a sheath but sometimes we took a chance and didn't bother'.[116] Similarly, Doris described herself as having been very promiscuous even prior to going on the Pill in her twenties. She claimed that she had been aware that it was 'all a bit risky' but that, caught in the moment with a 'gorgeous bloke who was bearing down on you', it was difficult to resist sex:

> [Sex] was clouded over with this fear that, 'Oh I might get pregnant', that, you know, and I did take a lot of risks, a lot of risks ... because I did it in cars and all sorts of things, on holidays, and, in all sorts of places and environments, there was this thing in the back of my mind like, 'Well, I'm being a bit silly here really'.[117]

Doris was aware of the 'risk' of pregnancy but this did not stop her from engaging in 'silly' behaviour.

The feeling of not wanting to become pregnant was not a reliable indicator of whether or not women used contraception as sexually active teenagers. Even girls with great ambitions for their futures engaged in unprotected sex.[118] For some girls the fear of pregnancy was a powerful motivator and their use of contraception became a means of embodying and projecting a sense of their sexual maturity.

Sexual presents and imagined futures 109

For others, however, wariness of pregnancy did not translate into contraceptive use or abstinence. In the heat of the moment, girls' imagined futures could become blurry projections, visible but not necessarily tangible and their relevance to girls' sexual decision-making is less clear. In these instances girls' concerns for their future selves could be temporarily suspended or overruled as they pursued their present selves' desires for social capital, a sense of maturity, and/or intimacy or sexual pleasure. As such, not using contraception should not be considered mere non-decisions or lapses in judgement. For many young women these choices were conscious and represented an alternative assessment of risk and reward. Girls' desire for sex *now* and with *this* partner was enough to transcend their sense of fear. Navigating the contraceptive landscape not only involved considerations regarding the desirability of pregnancy but incorporated decisions about whether or not individuals wanted to have sex at all, about who they wanted to have sex with, and what type of sex they desired.

Responding to pregnancy

In spite of growing awareness and the greater availability of contraception, young women did get pregnant. As described previously, rates of extra-marital pregnancy among young women rose consistently between 1950 and 1980, a state of affairs that was widely decried and lamented by politicians and social commentators.[119] However, individual responses to pregnancy were complex. For some girls the threat that pregnancy posed to their lives (in the present and the future) served as the justification for terminating unplanned pregnancies.[120] At the same time, however, many women kept their babies and have subsequently led very happy lives. Contrary to the dangerous and damaging unplanned pregnancies that they imagined in their youth, unplanned pregnancy could be perceived as a blessing from the other end of the life course.

Abortion

For young women who feared what pregnancy and having a child would mean to their lives, abortion was understood to be an 'escape route', although the nature, status, and meaning of this shifted across the period. Until the 1967 Abortion Act, terminating pregnancies was a criminal offence in Britain. Although in some communities it was an open secret that individuals could end their own pregnancies or find abortionists to assist them, such behaviour was criminal, dangerous, and relegated to the 'backstreet' (both literal and metaphorical).[121] The 1967 Act decriminalised abortion in very particular circumstances. Women were able to acquire an abortion within the first twenty-eight weeks of pregnancy, provided that two doctors agreed that continuing with the pregnancy posed a health risk to the mother.[122] As such, women in England did not have access to abortion 'on demand' and acquiring abortions was not without its complications; there were regional variations in services, doctors could withhold access, and the details of the law were debated repeatedly across the 1970s.[123] Nevertheless, decriminalisation did meaningfully expand access to abortion, providing an important option for women facing unplanned pregnancy.

Given the illegality of abortion prior to 1968, it is impossible to know exactly how many abortions were carried out each year prior to the Abortion Act. Statistics in the years following the Act, however, indicate that increasing numbers of women sought to terminate pregnancies. The number of abortions obtained by under-sixteens increased 45 per cent (to just under 1,700) between 1969 and 1970 and, in 1970, 14,716 girls aged between sixteen and nineteen acquired abortions.[124] Testimonies collected for this project do reflect increasing access and experience of abortion. Helen reflected that, 'in our day [the mid-1970s] everybody had an abortion'.[125] Barbara echoed this in her suggestion that her younger self's willingness to engage in 'risky' sex was facilitated by her understanding that 'it would have been possible to get an abortion'.[126] However, most of the post-decriminalisation abortions discussed by women in oral histories and Mass Observation testimonies related to experiences in their early to mid-twenties. In this context, in which most women were living away from home, abortions were presented as a logical and practical response to a problem that threatened the independence of young adulthood and their future prospects. All of the first-hand accounts of teenage abortion within these testimonies related to the period prior to the Abortion Act. Certainly, these experiences were not 'typical' but accounts of criminal terminations are important indicators of how far some young women and their families were prepared to go to safeguard their futures.

Sandra's parents were aware of her pregnancy and arranged her abortion. As she suggested, however, this experience was immensely detrimental to their relationship. Having become pregnant 'the year before abortion was legal', Sandra told a harrowing story of how her parents helped her to acquire an illegal abortion:

> They didn't exactly call me a harlot or a whore but that was the inference that y'know, that after, and also, the phrase that that generation of parents used was, 'After all we've done for you, this is how you repay us.' ... And I had to go sit in the bedroom upstairs while they were talking about it. And, um ... and then my aunt came up ... So she was the one who- who was, I s'pose she must've been sent up, by the others to talk to me. And she said, 'Y'know, you've got your whole life in front of you, y'know. Um, you have to have an abortion.' So it was all very upsetting. ... Anyway, [the abortion] was very painful and very distressing and I was hysterical and they, they bundled me into the car and took me home. ... And then nobody talked about it afterwards. My dad didn't talk to me, he sort of ... y'know looked at me like I was, they made me feel like I was the worst person in the universe. So I couldn't wait to leave home.[127]

Sandra's parents justified the abortion on the grounds that a child would stifle her future prospects. They saw the abortion as a means of protecting her, yet this protection was not without its cost. In addition to the physical pain of the procedure, Sandra remembered the emotional anguish that came to define her relationship with her parents.[128]

The process of acquiring abortions was slightly different for girls who had already moved away from home. In these instances, girls were often living out the futures that their schoolgirl selves had imagined and were keen to protect their new-found independence and status. While girls continued to fear for their futures, there was also acute concern for their present. Cheryl described, for example, how the 'real world did impinge' on her and her friends when they went to live in London and two of her four flatmates ended up having abortions.[129] Interviewees and Mass Observers who found themselves pregnant in these contexts stressed that the financial independence of young adulthood would not have been sufficient to raise a child. Moreover, as they had not necessarily been in formal relationships with their sexual partners, they could not guarantee receiving financial assistance (or marriage proposals) from the father of the child.

Jacqueline became pregnant through casual sex while working in London in the early 1960s (prior to the Abortion Act) and felt that there was no way she could go through with having a child. As such, she paid a private doctor for an abortion:

> In the end I found, through a friend I found somebody in Harley Street, he had been struck off and um, I went to him, he was a proper doctor, a proper gynaecologist, examined me, 'Yes, you're pregnant' and uh, late, quite late pregnancy, examined me on the couch and played with me, 'Yes, he'll do the operation, downstairs' and he did it with suction, some form of suction. I was put out by, anaesthetised and then sent home in a taxi and that was that.[130]

Jacqueline went on to suggest that many of her friends in London had abortions ('I think 2 or 3 abortions was quite normal'), a situation that she suggested 'sounds horrific today'. She laid the blame for this upon men who wanted sex but who refused to use contraception. Jacqueline suggested that girls in London in the 1960s were encouraged to participate in sexual activity but that they continued to carry the burden of risk.

Pregnant girls such as Jacqueline were, to a certain extent, free to decide the outcome of their pregnancy for themselves; their financial and physical independence from their parents gave them a degree of choice as to how to respond to this dilemma. As Sally noted, however, the sheer weight of this experience could be overwhelming. She had become pregnant in the early 1960s through a long-term relationship she had in her hometown and did not realise that she was pregnant until she had arrived in London for her 'new start'.

> What happened was as soon as I got to London I discovered I was pregnant. At 18 and no way was I going to have this baby. And I can remember the misery of it, I couldn't tell my parents, I didn't have many friends in London ... I went to Harley Street and saw a doctor, God, you know, I have no memory of how I did it, I went to see a doctor and told him I wanted an abortion and he wouldn't have anything to do with me. I can remember coming out and walking down Harley Street and, I don't know why it's so vivid, and going into the Tube station and thinking 'This is terrible, I'm going to throw myself in front of the Tube'. It's the only time I've ever thought of any such

thing in my life and no way was I going to do it, but I was desperate 'cos by now I was about 4 months pregnant.[131]

For Sally, who had waited her whole adolescence to leave home and travel to London, to arrive at her 'new' life pregnant threw all of her plans into disarray. Moreover, as she noted, although girls' friends could try to help and support them, their assistance was limited by their own youth, inexperience, and lack of material resources. To become pregnant in this context was presented as a unique form of desperation. In the end, Sally found a backstreet abortionist through an acquaintance, 'aborted down the lavatory' and ended up in hospital requiring an emergency dilation and curettage, an experience she remembered as both 'awful' and 'terrible'.

Women who had abortions suggested that the realities of their unplanned pregnancies directly mapped on to the fears outlined earlier. For Sally, Jacqueline, and Sandra, to be pregnant outside of marriage was to be alone and without prospects. Like the imagined pregnancies discussed previously, these girls felt strongly that their pregnancies threatened the lives that they had established for themselves in the present and the futures that they still hoped to have. The only way to recover was to terminate the pregnancy. The futures of work and marriage that these girls imagined for themselves made pregnancy threatening and dangerous. Having a child was understood as a burden that they were not prepared to take on. In this context, girls had to make a judgement about their trajectories in the present and the future. While some opted to stay on the same path and thus terminated their pregnancies (or gave their babies away), others embraced change and opted to keep their child. Unplanned pregnancy could be extremely unsettling for young unmarried women, yet recalling the event from the other side of the life course women displayed a remarkable capacity to reconcile themselves with their past selves' choices.

Keeping the baby

At the same time that abortion rates were increasing, the number of babies born to unmarried mothers and/or conceived outside of wedlock also increased.[132] In 1968, 21,809 babies were born to unmarried women under 20 years old and in 1971 a third of brides under twenty were pregnant on their wedding day.[133] Undoubtedly, young women who found themselves pregnant out of wedlock could face immense material hardship and social isolation; many of the fears raised by interviewees earlier in this chapter were not unfounded. However, taking a reflective approach to experiences of unplanned pregnancy forces us to consider more carefully the fact that unplanned pregnancies and 'shotgun' weddings were not only a common social reality but could be the source of much future happiness and contentment. What may have seemed like a crisis at the moment of revelation could, in later life, be subsumed unproblematically into a broader life history.

Across the post-war period, it was common for unplanned pregnancies to result in marriage. Helen, Tracy, Carole, Carolyn, Heather, and Mandy all described close friends or relatives 'having' to get married because of pregnancy.[134] The legal status of children conceived out of wedlock changed several times in the second half of the century but at a community level marriage was often deemed to retroactively legitimise babies.[135] For some girls, getting married as a result of pregnancy simply marked an acceleration of the trajectory that their relationships were already on. As Iris suggested, amongst her group of friends sexual experimentation was 'largely confined to an intended partner' and, as such, the need to 'marry hastily' when they became pregnant was not deeply concerning.[136] This experience was shared by Phyllis who glibly noted that 'being pregnant probably brought [her marriage] forward a bit'.[137] This culture of sexual activity within long-term relationships and the continued expectation that marriage was a viable response to pregnancy can be viewed as one of the key factors determining the decreasing average age of marriage between the Second World War and 1972.[138]

In the working-class communities that Pauline, Alison, and Diana grew up in, motherhood continued to be revered as the primary destination for girls and young women could use sexual activity as a means of achieving adult status through pregnancy.[139] In areas dominated by heavy industry, expectations for girls to have careers and education were often less potent as older cultures of domestic femininity persisted. Explaining her lack of female friends when she was doing her A levels, Alison explained: 'Most of the people at college were men ... Most of the girls in Corby were pregnant 16, 17 and stayed at home with babies so I d-, I don't think I had many girlfriends until I went to university.'[140] In these communities domestic femininity remained revered and the practice of girls 'delaying' marriage through education and employment was less common, changing perceptions of the disruptive potential of unplanned pregnancy.

Mass Observers and interviewees who grew up in middle-class communities often stressed that pregnancy-induced weddings were out of the ordinary and considered with a degree of disquiet. Yet, within their testimonies, some women pushed back against assumptions that such unions could not be successful. Glenys illustrated the fraught reaction to unplanned pregnancies in the mid-1950s but demonstrated that these could have happy endings:

> There was also a girl from the same avenue – 3 years older than me – who was recognizably pregnant when she married her boyfriend. Her mother made her wear cream instead of white, not quite as bad as my aunt who made my poor cousin, 2 ½ years younger than me, wear pink for her wedding, when heavily pregnant with twins! (She went on to produce a second set of twins and is still happily married to the same guy today.)[141]

When describing her teenage life and how she'd learned about sex, Hilary recalled that she had spent a lot of time with friends who 'were having appalling times with boyfriends'. Asked to expand on what she meant by that she went on:

> I think they were having sex unprotected sex and then worrying desperately whether I'm pregnant. ... Yeah, you know, and and this one girl, she did have the baby, you know. And my goodness, it turned out well ... when, when you think you may have spoiled your life, it didn't for her.[142]

The status of such marriages was thus contested. They were simultaneously commonplace and notably 'different'. Reflecting back upon the sexual culture of their youth, women could be unsure how to best characterise such relationships that seemed to contradict both traditional values of sexual restraint and late twentieth-century mores of romantic marriage. Their observations suggested that although unplanned pregnancy undoubtedly changed the trajectory of these young women's lives, their pre-marital pregnancies had not been destructive or life-ruining.

Reflecting on their experiences several decades after the fact, the Mass Observers who had themselves become pregnant outside of marriage contextualised this experience within the frame of their whole lives and characterised their pregnancies (however accidental) as a blessing. Lilian was extremely critical of teenage pregnancy in contemporary society but had herself raised a family following an unplanned pregnancy in her late teens. She discovered that she was pregnant at nineteen and conceded that she had initially been very afraid of having to face her parents' wrath. However, 'the upset soon turned to positivity as we all decided, I would marry J and we would look for a house'.[143] Although she did not get them in the order she may have intended, Lilian's pregnancy crisis resolved itself with an outcome of marriage, motherhood and home ownership, the future she had always wanted for herself. Similarly, Phyllis presented her pregnancy as having given her the opportunity to leave home. She recognised that she was 'probably too young to get married' when she became pregnant in her late teens but stressed that she and her husband were still together forty years later and suggested that 'maybe by [getting married] I actually grew up'.[144] Looking back on their lives with their families, these women presented their pregnancies as a positive experience that enriched their lives. Though these women's lives may not have gone exactly the way their teenage selves had planned, this deviation was far from devastating and could be the source of new identities and feelings of selfhood.

Women's accounts of what they did when they found themselves unexpectedly pregnant in their youth thus demonstrate the unstable nature of girls' imagined futures. Many of those who terminated their pregnancies explained this response by referring to their continuing aspirations for education, careers, and relationships in the futures, suggesting that their imagined futures were a fixed mark which they pursued. The accounts of those who kept their unplanned babies, however, suggest that it was possible for girls' earlier aspirations and imagined futures to be set aside in the face of new circumstances. Ambitions and goals that girls had set their hearts upon in early adolescence were subject to change and could be recalibrated. Crucially, while girls imagined unplanned pregnancy to be a disaster that threatened their future happiness, this was not necessarily the case in reality. Although the process of discovering and reacting to unplanned pregnancy could be distressing, reflecting on their lives four or five decades after the fact, many women (both those who kept their babies and those who terminated their pregnancies) understood their former selves' decisions and were often content with the ways in which their lives had played out.

Conclusion

Exploring the sexual lives of young women born in the decades after the Second World War does much to support Lynn Abrams' assertion that women of this generation 'made the journey from "home-makers" to "self-makers"'.[145] While most young middle-class women were undoubtedly committed to getting married and having families eventually, in the more immediate future they were deeply invested in pursuing education and employment. Many girls were desperate to leave home and earn money for themselves, aspirations that were facilitated by post-war affluence and the expansion of the welfare state.[146] It was now increasingly possible for girls from modest middle-class (and indeed, working-class) backgrounds to leave home for work in major cities or for higher education or vocational training. Becoming financially independent in this way was seen as a crucial step that young women needed to take towards growing up and becoming their adult selves. Although girls continued to dream of falling in love, getting married, and having families of their own, many did not want this to come at the expense of their working lives, nor did they see this in their immediate futures. As such, unplanned pregnancy was deemed to be particularly dangerous, not only because it threatened girls' social status but because it threatened to derail the education and employment that girls believed to be so important to their self-development and fulfilment.

As we have seen, however, girls' imagined futures were inconsistent determinants of sexual behaviour. Looking at sexual practice in detail, considering not just what individuals thought and felt about sex but how they managed their sexuality in reality, reveals that adolescent sexual logic was not always driven by long-term considerations. The interests of girls' future selves could be overridden by their needs and desires in the present. Finding themselves with the opportunity to have sex, some girls suspended their anxieties regarding pregnancy and its threat to their future; in the heat of the moment the risk of pregnancy and the 'need' for contraception or restraint could be disregarded. Although women retrospectively deemed this behaviour to have been reckless, their testimonies suggest that the non-use of contraception represented a spontaneous risk/reward calculation in which they prioritised sex in the present over the threat of pregnancy.

These testimonies thus call into question accounts of 'growing up' that present a neat and linear progression from childhood to adulthood. Undoubtedly, young people were aware of their impending adulthood and, as explored in Chapter 1, many were keen to accelerate this process through sex. However, girls of the post-war generations did not see maturity and adulthood as rooted solely within marriage or motherhood and in many cases they were desperate to avoid these in their immediate futures.[147] Middle-class girls were invested in ideas of young adulthood which offered them a period of freedom between the parental and school-based control of childhood and the responsibilities of adult femininity. At the same time that girls desired sex because they believed it to be a major milestone on the path to adulthood, the details of their sexual practice suggest that they simultaneously resisted the additional markers of maturity (namely motherhood and marriage) that could result from penetrative intercourse.

In these ways it is apparent that adolescent sexuality was directly framed by considerations of the life cycle.[148] Young women's sexual lives were defined by their status as 'not-yet' adults. The consequences of sex, the function of contraception, and the meanings of abortion and pregnancy within their lives were all informed by girls' youth. Their youth effected not only the decision to have sex in the first place, but also meant that the stakes of intercourse and how it was managed in practice had significantly different consequences to those faced by sexually active adults.

Notes

1 Barbara (1952), OH-15-02-03.
2 Julie (1960), OH-15-02-09.

3 Todd, *Young Women, Work, and Family*.
4 Penny Tinkler, '"Are You Really Living?" If Not, "Get with It!": The Teenage Self and Lifestyle in Young Women's Magazines, Britain 1957–70', *Cultural and Social History* 11, no. 4 (2014): 263–337; Keith Gildart, *Images of England through Popular Music: Class, Youth and Rock 'n' Roll, 1955–1976* (Basingstoke: Palgrave Macmillan, 2013); Nick Bentley, Beth Johnson, and Andrzej Zieleniec, eds, *Youth Subcultures in Fiction, Film and Other Media* (Basingstoke: Palgrave Macmillan, 2018).
5 Tisdall, 'What a Difference It Was to Be a Woman and Not a Teenager'.
6 See, for example, the series of Viewpoints on Temporalities in *Past and Present* 243, no. 1 (2019): 247–327.
7 Haste, *Rules of Desire*, p. 186.
8 Jane Robinson, *In the Family Way: Illegitimacy between the Great War and the Swinging Sixties* (London: Viking, 2015); Deborah Cohen, *Family Secrets: Living with Shame from the Victorians to the Present Day* (London: Viking, 2013); Tanya Evans and Pat Thane, *Sinners? Scroungers? Saints? Unmarried Motherhood in Twentieth-Century England* (Oxford: Oxford University Press, 2012); Jane Lewis and John Welshman, 'The Issue of Never-Married Motherhood in Britain, 1920–70', *Social History of Medicine* 10, no. 3 (1997).
9 Office of National Statistics, 'Live Births by Age of Mother and Registration Type, England and Wales, 1938 to 2021', Worksheet 2, *Information on Births by Parents' Characteristic Statistics* (2021), https://www.ons.gov.uk/peoplepopulationandcommunity/birthsdea thsandmarriages/livebirths/datasets/birthsbyparentscharacteristics [accessed: 12 December 2023].
10 Rebecca Probert, ed., *Cohabitation and Non-Marital Births in England and Wales, 1600–2012* (Basingstoke: Palgrave Macmillan, 2014).
11 'These Girl Mothers Are "Shameless"', *Daily Mail*, 19 May 1950; 'How Can We Halt Our Terrifying Moral Slump?', *Daily Mail*, 21 September 1961; 'Britain's Loneliest Mothers', *Daily Mail*, 31 January 1962.
12 'We Could Say She's With Relatives', *Honey*, September 1968; 'Pity the Poor Bastard', *Honey*, February 1972; 'What's It Like to be a Real Bastard', *Petticoat*, 28 June 1969; 'Unto Us a Child is Born … But Is He Really Wanted?', *19*, December 1972.
13 Daphne (1941), OH-15-03-05.
14 Barbara (1952), OH-15-02-03.
15 Ruth (1960), OH-15-02-01.
16 The following women described having become pregnant outside of marriage. Sandra (1949), OH-14-01-02; Helen (1950), OH-15-03-07;

Doris (1945), OH-15-04-02; Jacqueline (1945), OH-15-04-03; Sally (1946), OH-15-05-02. In MOP, 'Close Relationships' (1990): Marcia (1957), H262; Roberta (1943), I1610; Leslie (1954), M1498; Phyllis (1947), P1796; Stacey (1946), Q1834; Rhonda (1962), R1580. In MOP 'Sex' (2005): Kay (1951), K798; Lilian (1946), L1002.
17 Glenys (1941), MOP, 'Sex', G226; Joy (1954), OH-15-04-01.
18 Maureen (1949), OH-15-05-04.
19 Daisy (1946), MOP, 'Close Relationships', B2304; Glenys (1941), MOP, 'Courting and Dating', G226; Wendy (1943), MOP, 'Courting and Dating', W633; Carolyn (1947), MOP, 'Sex', C1832; Lorraine (1951), MOP, 'Sex', L3253.
20 Rebecca (1943), MOP, 'Courting and Dating', R1025.
21 Muriel (1940), MOP, 'Sex', P1009.
22 Geraldine (1959), MOP, 'Sex', G3395.
23 Hilary (1956), OH-15-01-01; Joyce (1950), OH-15-03-02; Helen (1950), OH-15-03-07; Mary (1959), OH-15-05-08. Respondents to the 2005 Mass Observation Directive on 'Sex' who described friends and relatives getting pregnant include: Carole (1949), C1713; Cheryl (1944), C2078; Eileen (1951), E743; Glenys (1941), G226; Iris (1940), H2637; Mandy (1939), M1979; Mabel (1946), M3408; Norma (1943), P3392. In MOP 'Close Relationships': Agatha (1942), A1473; Sherry (1942), S1229; Michele (1956), N2912; Veronica (1951), W1813.
24 Alison (1960), OH-14-02-02.
25 Christine (1947), OH-15-03-03.
26 Pamela (1948), MOP, 'Courting and Dating', R860.
27 Mabel (1946), MOP, 'Sex', M3408. See also Muriel (1940), MOP, 'Sex', P1009.
28 Barbara (1952), OH-15-02-03.
29 Marian (1964), MOP, 'Sex', M3401. See also Lorraine (1951), MOP, 'Sex', L3253.
30 Roberts, *Women and Families*, pp. 63–72; Szreter and Fisher, *Sex before the Sexual Revolution*, pp. 149–61.
31 Joyce (1950), OH-15-03-02.
32 Ingham, *Now We Are Thirty*.
33 Mills, 'Using the Personal to Critique the Popular'; Abrams, 'Mothers and Daughters'; Spencer, *Gender, Work and Education in Britain in the 1950s*.
34 Kathleen (1948), OH-15-04-06.
35 Tinkler, 'Are You Really Living?'; Tinkler, 'Going Places or out of Place?'.
36 Jacqueline (1945), OH-15-04-03.

37 Peter Mandler, 'Educating the Nation I: Schools', *Transactions of the Royal Historical Society* 24 (2014); Bunkle, 'The 1944 Education Act and Second Wave Feminism'; Val Brooks, 'The Role of External Examinations in the Making of Secondary Modern Schools in England 1945–65', *History of Education* 37, no. 3 (2008).

38 Between 1963 and 1970–71 the student population in Britain more than doubled from 216,000 to 457,000. A. H. Halsey, 'Further and Higher Education', in *British Social Trends since 1900: A Guide to the Changing Social Structure of Britain*, ed. A. H. Halsey (Houndmills: Macmillan, 2000). On the changing nature of higher education see Peter Mandler, 'Educating the Nation II: Universities', *Transactions of the Royal Historical Society* 25 (2015); William Whyte, *Redbrick: A Social and Architectural History of Britain's Civic Universities* (Oxford: Oxford University Press, 2015); Dyhouse, *Students*.

39 Spencer, *Gender, Work and Education in Britain in the 1950s*.

40 Vivienne (1944), OH-15-05-05.

41 Daphne (1941), OH-15-03-05.

42 Julie (1960), OH-15-02-09.

43 Anne (1964), OH-14-01-06

44 Spencer, *Gender, Work and Education in Britain in the 1950s*. On earlier cultures of women's work see Todd, *Young Women, Work, and Family in England, 1918–1950*.

45 Sally (1946), OH-15-05-02.

46 Hazel (1947), OH-15-04-05.

47 Other narratives of London-based liberation narratives include: Sandra (1949), OH-14-01-02; Doris (1945), OH-15-04-02; Jacqueline (1945), OH-15-04-03; Linda (1952), OH-15-01-03; Helen (1950), OH-15-03-07. See also Tinkler, 'Going Places or out of Place?'.

48 Wendy (1943), MOP, 'Courting and Dating', W633. See also Glynis (1952), MOP 'Courting and Dating', G2089; Maria (1956), MOP, 'Sex', M2986.

49 Brenda (1956), MOP, 'Courting and Dating', B2728.

50 Stephanie Spencer, 'Girls at Risk: Early School-Leaving and Early Marriage in the 1950s', *Journal of Educational Administration and History* 41, no. 2 (2009); Carol Dyhouse, *Girl Trouble: Panic and Progress in the History of Young Women* (London: Zed Books, 2013), pp. 125–34.

51 Dyhouse, *Girl Trouble*, pp. 125–34.

52 Lorna Sage, *Bad Blood* (London: Fourth Estate, 2000), p. 234.

53 Glenys (1941), MOP, 'Courting and Dating', G226.

54 On changing patterns of married women's work see Helen McCarthy, 'Women, Marriage and Paid Work in Post-War Britain', *Women's*

History Review 26, no. 1 (2017); Claire Langhamer, 'Feelings, Women and Work in the Long 1950s', *Women's History Review* 26, no. 1 (2017); Worth, *Welfare State Generation*; Dolly Smith Wilson, 'A New Look at the Affluent Worker: The Good Working Mother in Post-War Britain', *Twentieth Century British History* 17, no. 2 (2006).
55 Daphne (1941), OH-15-03-09.
56 Tracy (1962), OH-14-02-01.
57 Daphne (1941), OH-15-03-09.
58 Carol Dyhouse, *Heartthrobs: A History of Women and Desire* (Oxford: Oxford University Press, 2017); Carol Dyhouse, *Love Lives: From 'Cinderella' to 'Frozen'* (Oxford: Oxford University Press, 2021).
59 Kate Fisher, 'Marriage and Companionate Ideals Since 1750', in *Routledge History of Sex and the Body 1500 to the Present*, ed. Sarah Toulalan and Kate Fisher (London and New York: Routledge, 2013); Janet Finch and Penny Summerfield, 'Social Reconstruction and the Emergence of Companionate Marriage, 1945–1959', in *Marriage, Domestic Life and Social Change: Writings for Jacqueline Burgoyne, 1944–88*, ed. David Clark (London and New York: Routledge, 1991); Martin P. M. Richards and B. Jane Elliott, 'Sex and Marriage in the 1960s and 1970s', in *Marriage, Domestic Life and Social Change: Writings for Jacqueline Burgoyne, 1944–88*, ed. David Clark (London and New York: Routledge, 1991).
60 Claire Langhamer, *The English in Love: The Intimate Story of an Emotional Revolution* (Oxford: Oxford University Press, 2013).
61 Glenys (1941), MOP, 'Courting and Dating', G226.
62 Heather (1948), MOP, 'Courting and Dating', H1703.
63 Gwen (1953), MOP, 'Courting and Dating', G2640. See also Norma (1943), MOP, 'Sex', P3392
64 Muriel (1940), MOP, 'Sex', P1009.
65 Of the fourteen Observers and interviewees who mentioned becoming pregnant prior to marriage, six did go on to marry the father. Other Mass Observers and interviewees also discussed family and friends who got married after becoming pregnant: Jayne (1941), MOP, 'Sex', H2639; Marian (1964), MOP, 'Sex', M3401; Helen (1950), OH-15-03-07.
66 Glenys (1941), MOP, 'Sex', G226. Glenys also articulated this sentiment in her response to MOP 'Courting and Dating'. See also Maureen (1949), OH-15-05-04; Daisy (1946), MOP, 'Close Relationships', B2304; Glenys (1941), MOP, 'Courting and Dating', G226; Wendy (1943), MOP, 'Courting and Dating', W633; Carolyn (1947), MOP, 'Sex', C1832; Lorraine (1951), 'Sex', L3253.

67 Helen (1950), OH-15-03-07.
68 Wendy (1943), MOP, 'Courting and Dating', W633. See also Jayne (1941), MOP, 'Sex', H2639.
69 On acquiring abortions prior to the 1967 Abortion Act see Tania McIntosh, '"An Abortionist City": Maternal Mortality, Abortion, and Birth Control in Sheffield, 1920–1940', *Medical History* 44, no. 1 (2000); Kate Fisher, 'Women's Experiences of Abortion before the 1967 Act', in *Abortion Law and Politics Today*, ed. Ellie Lee (Manchester: Manchester University Press, 1998).
70 Joanna Miles, Daniel Monk, and Rebecca Probert, eds, *Fifty Years of the Divorce Reform Act* (Oxford: Bloomsbury, 2022).
71 Carolyn (1947), MOP, 'Sex', C1713.
72 Muriel (1940), MOP, 'Sex', P1009. See also Heather (1948), MOP, 'Sex', H1703.
73 Marcia (1957), MOP, 'Close Relationships', H262 and Lilian (1946), MOP, 'Sex', L1002.
74 Haste, *Rules of Desire*, pp. 6, 227.
75 Weeks, *The World We Have Won*, p. 70; Lesley A. Hall, *Sex, Gender and Social Change in Britain since 1880*, 2nd ed. (Basingstoke: Palgrave Macmillan, 2013), p. 163.
76 Lisa Smith, '"You're 16…You Should Probably Be on the Pill": Girls, the Non-Reproductive Body, and the Rhetoric of Self-Control', *Studies in the Maternal* 6, no. 1 (2014), www.mamsie.bbk.ac.uk [accessed: 25 September 2024].
77 Eva-Maria Silies, 'Taking the Pill after the "Sexual Revolution": Female Contraceptive Decisions in England and West Germany in the 1970s', *European Review of History: Revue européenne d'histoire* 22, no. 1 (2015); Elizabeth Wilson, *Only Halfway to Paradise: Women in Postwar Britain 1945–1968* (London: Tavistock, 1979), pp. 97–98.
78 Testimonies reflecting on this dichotomy include: Jane (1951), MOP, 'Sex', H1745; in MOP, 'Close Relationships', Irene (1952), H2418; Janice (1953), J1549; Beatrice (1953), B1215; May (1952), H2420; Ruby (1964), H2505.
79 Rita (1944), MOP, 'Courting and Dating', R1227.
80 In MOP, 'Close Relationships': Ellen (1961), D2239; Josephine (1957), H2173; Ruby (1964), H2505; Jackie (1954), J2235; Leslie (1954), M1498.
81 Kate (1947), 'QWMC: Changes in Birth Control', British Library Sound Archive (hereafter BLSA), British Library, London, C644/06/01.
82 Sandra (1949), OH-14-01-02.
83 Catherine (1959), MOP, 'Sex', C3513.
84 Audrey (1952), OH-15-01-02.

85 Theresa (1954), OH-14-01-05.
86 Heather (1948), MOP, 'Courting and Dating', H1703.
87 Daphne (1941), OH-15-03-05.
88 Clare (1956), MOP, 'Courting and Dating', C2888. See also Hilary (1956), OH-15-01-01; Lisa (1957), MOP, 'Sex', L3037.
89 Cook, *The Long Sexual Revolution*, pp. 263–337; Caroline Rusterholz, 'Youth Sexuality, Responsibility, and the Opening of the Brook Advisory Centres in London and Birmingham in the 1960s', *Journal of British Studies* 61, no. 2 (2022).
90 Wilma (1943), 'Courtship and Dating', W633; Beverley (1944), 'QWMC: Changes in Birth Control', BLSA, C644/01/01.
91 Theresa (1954), OH-14-01-05. Helen (1950), OH-15-03-07; Clare (1956), MOP, 'Close Relationships', C2888.
92 Anne (1964), OH-14-01-06.
93 Hilary (1956), OH-15-01-01.
94 Barbara (1952), OH-15-02-03.
95 Helen (1950), OH-15-03-07.
96 Jones, *Business of Birth Control*; Stuart Anderson, '"The Most Important Place in the History of British Birth Control": Community Pharmacy and Sexual Health in Twentieth Century Britain', *Pharmaceutical Journal* 266, no. 7129 (2001).
97 Participants who recalled using chemical contraceptives included: Jacqueline (1945), OH-15-04-03; Hazel (1947), OH-15-04-05; Kathleen (1948), OH-15-04-06.
98 This conforms to the findings of the NATSAL which suggested that 37 per cent of women born between 1946 and 1965 used condoms at first intercourse. Wellings et al., *Sexual Behaviour in Britain*, p. 63.
99 Borge, *Protective Practices*; Ben Mechen, '"Closer Together": Durex Condoms and Contraceptive Consumerism in 1970s Britain', in *Perceptions of Pregnancy from the Seventeenth to the Twentieth Century*, ed. Jennifer Evans and Ciara Meehan (Basingstoke: Palgrave Macmillan, 2017); Paul Jobling, 'Playing Safe: The Politics of Pleasure and Gender in the Promotion of Condoms in Britain, 1970–1982', *Journal of Design History* 10, no. 1 (1997).
100 Fisher, *Birth Control, Sex, and Marriage*, p. 189.
101 Julia (1946), 'QWMC: Changes in Birth Control', BLSA, C644/19/01.
102 Hazel (1947), OH-15-04-05; Doris (1945), OH-15-04-02; Eileen (1951), MOP, 'Sex', E743.
103 Christine (1947), OH-15-03-03.
104 Audrey (1952), OH-15-01-02.
105 Doris (1945), OH-15-04-02.
106 Pauline (1944), OH-14-01-03.

Sexual presents and imagined futures 125

107 Borge, *Protective Practices*; Jones, *Business of Birth Control*.
108 Cheryl (1944), MOP, 'Sex', C2078.
109 Kathleen (1948), OH-15-04-06.
110 Eileen (1951), MOP, 'Sex', E743.
111 Geraldine (1959), MOP, 'Sex', G3395.
112 On previous policy-makers' misunderstanding of birth control as a 'wholly rational process' see Wilson, *Only Halfway to Paradise*, p. 98.
113 On ignorance see Sandra (1949), OH-14-01-02; Julie (1960), OH-15-02-09.
114 Theresa (1954), OH-14-01-05.
115 Barbara (1952), OH-15-02-03.
116 Tina (1949), MOP, 'Sex', T1843; Carolyn (1947), MOP, 'Sex', C1832.
117 Doris (1945), OH-15-04-02.
118 Fifty-three per cent of female students at a Scottish university in 1972 had not used contraception on the occasion of first intercourse. C. McCance and D. J. Hall, 'Sexual Behaviour and Contraceptive Practice of Unmarried Female Undergraduates at Aberdeen University', *British Medical Journal* 2, no. 5815 (1972).
119 Calculating the exact rate of extra-marital pregnancy is difficult although its increased prevalence is indicated by the increasing births to unmarried women, rising numbers of babies born to parents who had been married less than a year as well as increasing rates of abortion and adoption between 1950 and 1980. David Coleman, 'Population and Family', in *Twentieth-Century British Social Trends*, ed. A. H. Halsey and Josephine Webb (Basingstoke: Macmillan, 2000), pp. 51–55.
120 Many young women also gave up babies up for adoption but this was not discussed within the personal testimonies explored here. The adoption rate peaked in 1968 when almost 25,000 babies were adopted. Eleanor Grey, in collaboration with Ronald M. Blunden, *A Survey of Adoption in Great Britain*, Home Office Research Studies 10 (London: HMSO, 1971). On the history of adoption in early twentieth-century Britain see Jenny Keating, *A Child for Keeps: The History of Adoption in England, 1918–45* (Basingstoke: Palgrave Macmillan, 2009).
121 Fisher, 'Women's Experiences of Abortion before the 1967 Act'.
122 Sally Sheldon, Gayle Davis, Jane O'Neill, and Clare Porter, *The Abortion Act 1967: A Biography of a UK Law* (Cambridge: Cambridge University Press, 2023); Brooke, *Sexual Politics*; Hoggart, *Feminist Campaigns for Birth Control and Abortion Rights in Britain*.
123 Sheldon et al., *Abortion Act 1967*; Ashley Wivel, 'Abortion Policy and Politics on the Lane Committee of Enquiry, 1971–1974', *Social History of Medicine* 11, no. 1 (1998).

124 'Sex and the Sixth Form', *19*, November 1971, p. 54.
125 Helen (1950), OH-15-03-07.
126 Barbara (1952), OH-15-02-03.
127 Sandra (1949), OH-14-01-02.
128 The experience of pregnancy intensifying problems between parents and children was something articulated by Doris (1945), OH-15-04-02; Jacqueline (1945), OH-15-04-03 and Marcia (1957), MOP, 'Close Relationships', H262.
129 Cheryl (1944), MOP, 'Sex', C2078.
130 Jacqueline (1945), OH-15-04-03.
131 Sally (1946), OH-15-05-02.
132 Coleman, 'Population and Family', pp. 51–55.
133 Office of National Statistics, 'Birth by Parents' Characteristics, England and Wales:2015' (2016), www.gov.uk/government/statistics/births-by-parents-characteristics-in-england-and-wales-2015 [accessed: 26 November 2024]; 'Sex and the Sixth Form', 19, November 1971, p. 54.
134 Helen (1950), OH-15-03-07; Tracy (1962), OH-14-02-01; Carole (1949), MOP, 'Sex', C1713; Carolyn (1947), MOP, 'Sex', C1832; Heather (1948), MOP, 'Sex', H1703; Mandy (1939), MOP, 'Sex', M1979.
135 Helen (1950), OH-15-03-07. The 1926 Legitimacy Act legitimated children born out of wedlock provided that their parents subsequently married and that neither of them had been married to a third party at the time of birth. This was amended in 1959 when legitimation was extended to children conceived through adultery. The 1976 Legitimacy Act reformed law further to allow children of void marriages to be considered legitimate providing that the parents reasonably believed themselves to be married at the time of conception and that the father was domiciled in England or Wales at the time of the birth.
136 Iris (1940), MOP, 'Sex', H2637.
137 Phyllis (1947), MOP, 'Courting and Dating', P1796.
138 Coleman, 'Population and Family', p. 56.
139 Pauline (1944), OH-14-01-03; Alison (1960), OH-14-02-02; Diana (1947), OH-15-01-05. See also Yvette (1959), MOP, 'Courting and Dating', Y2926 on the tendency for girls to get married and start families very soon after leaving school. Tisdall, 'What a Difference It Was to Be a Woman and Not a Teenager'.
140 Alison (1960), OH-14-02-02.
141 Glenys (1941), MOP, 'Sex', G226.
142 Hilary (1956), OH-15-01-01.

143 Lilian (1946), MOP, 'Sex', L1002.
144 Phyllis (1947), MOP, 'Sex', P1796.
145 Lynn Abrams, 'Liberating the Female Self: Epiphanies, Conflict and Coherence in the Life Stories of Post-War British Women', *Social History* 39, no. 1 (2014): 18.
146 Worth, *Welfare State Generation*.
147 On the importance of marriage and motherhood to working-class femininities see Tisdall, 'What a Difference It Was to Be a Woman and Not a Teenager'.
148 Charnock, 'How Far Should We Go?'.

Part II

Relationships

3

Boyfriends and sexual partners

In studying the importance of growing up and becoming mature to young women's sexual lives, the chapters in Part I have presented a highly individualised account of post-war heterosexuality. The narratives we have explored have been populated with a range of characters but largely concentrate on individual sexual subjectivities and how these were informed by young women's imagined futures. Our focus now turns to consider more closely the relationships that young women had with those around them and how these shaped girls' sexual behaviour. While young women remain our protagonists, figures and groups who have been in the background to this point shall now come centre stage in order that we can examine their roles as core characters and sometimes antagonists in the history of post-war sexual change. Where sexuality is often considered at the macro level of culture or the micro level of individual subjectivity, the following discussions focus their attention on the local and social discourses that mediated these. As the following three chapters reveal, girls' social worlds had a profound influence on their sexual lives. Put simply, how girls understood sexuality and the choices they made in managing their sexual activity were directly informed by the relationships (both intimate and otherwise) that they had with the people around them.

This chapter focuses on the dynamics between young women and the men with whom they had romantic relationships and engaged in heterosexual activity. These men played vital roles in women's sexual life histories but they have a somewhat ambiguous status in women's accounts. Some men and relationships loomed large in women's narratives, functioning as key chapters or turning points in their sexual life histories. Elsewhere, however, male partners were peripheral and/or unremarkable in women's testimonies, even as women recounted major life events.

To an extent this reflects the specific nature of personal testimonies. Testimonies gathered through both oral history and the Mass Observation Project have a tendency towards the egocentric – much of their value lies in their capacity to foreground individual feelings and experience in the historical record.[1] Moreover, testimonies were garnered through questions and prompts and respondents did not have infinite time to record their life histories. Their testimonies are inevitably partial and naturally they (de)prioritised some stories, events, and relationships over others.[2] However, the often peripheral status of men within women's accounts is not simply a quirk of testimonial sources. Instead, it reflects the varied and changing nature of heterosexual partnerships. Across the second half of the twentieth century it became increasingly common for individuals to have romantic relationships and sexual interactions with more than one partner.[3] While 48 per cent of women born in the late 1930s and early 1940s had only one opposite-sex sexual partner in their lifetime, this was the case for only 20 per cent of women born in the late 1950s and early 1960s. Where only 19 per cent of that older cohort reported having more than five sexual partners, this figure rose to 47 per cent for those born between 1958 and 1965.[4] Many of these partnerships were important in women's life histories, representing great loves or relationships in which women had invested significant amounts of time and/or emotion. Yet, it was also increasingly the case that women would have more casual encounters. As new imperatives for engaging in sexual activity emerged – to feel grown up, to achieve status, to pursue pleasure – the relationship status of sexual partnerships took on new (at times, diminished) significance.

The testimonies explored here highlight the immense messiness of young people's sexual relationships. Young women's relationships, the emotional worlds within and around these, and the role of sex in defining interpersonal dynamics were complex and often contradictory. Considering women's experiences from their pre-teenage years to their early twenties, the accounts of intimate partnerships and relationships pull in different directions and push against analyses of heterosexuality that concentrate solely on courtship and marriage.[5]

By stepping back from considering heterosexual relationships solely through the lens of courtship or romantic love, not only is it possible to observe the myriad dynamics and formations that made up girls' relationships with young men, but we also create space to see the complex emotional registers that characterised young people's intimate lives. In the post-war period, the relationship between sex and intimacy was recalibrated, becoming increasingly knotted. At the same time that intimacy was understood to be a prerequisite for sexual activity, it was believed that sex had the potential to foster and enhance intimacy. Negotiating these imperatives became a central dynamic in many young women's relationships.

Intimacy beyond courtship

In 2001, social historian Claire Langhamer commissioned a Mass Observation Project Directive on the theme of 'Courting and Dating'. Taken together, the Directive prompts – which ranged from 'What were/are your criteria for the "perfect" partner?' to 'How do you think the behaviour of courting couples has changed over the course of your life?' – encouraged Observers to reflect on intimate relationships beyond marriage. Though the Directive repeatedly drew on the language of 'courtship', its authors recognised that this concept may not have equal purchase to all respondents and it invited Mass Observers to define what they understood by the term. Though the definitions varied, women of the post-war generation consistently described 'courtship' as a specific relationship formation. For many women, 'courtship' represented a particular moment within a young couple's relationship; it was the time between a couple's initial interactions and their engagement. Courting couples were monogamous and their relationships were conducted with a view to get married; although courtship may have involved sexual 'experimentation', this involved testing boundaries within a singular relationship rather than a phase of 'seeing' many different potential partners. This characterisation was common across the cohort and women born in the 1940s articulated this view in much the same way as those born in early 1960s. Although there were sixteen years between them, Doreen's (b. 1959) definition of courtship as '[s]erious dating i.e. with a view to commitment to marriage or living together' was similar to that of Rebecca (b. 1943) who described it as 'that period of time in which a man and a woman get to know each other, to know each other well enough that they want to spend the rest of their lives together'.[6]

Within their definitions many Mass Observers expressed the sense that courtship was firmly rooted in the 'distant past':[7] over 60 per cent of the Mass Observers considered here explicitly described courtship as 'old-fashioned' or otherwise alluded to it being outdated.[8] Some Observers used this as a means of contrasting the present with the past as in Amanda's comparison between the 'gentle tentative' affairs of the post-war decades and the 'instantaneous shagging [of] today'.[9] However, other Observers suggested that courtship was a dated concept even during their youth. Eileen stressed that her and her friends 'didn't call it courting' in the 1960s and 1970s, although 'that word was still something [their] mothers used'.[10] Similarly, Glenys associated the term with her 'elderly father': 'I still, now aged 60, feel it is a slightly cringe-making word!'[11] Women suggested that the terminology, if not the entire concept, of 'courtship' was already redundant by the time of their adolescence in the decades following the Second World War. They did not deny that such a practice had ever existed, simply that it did not apply to them.

Rather than simply displaying shifts in terminology, the responses to this Mass Observation Directive reflect profound changes in the nature of intimate life across the second half of the twentieth century. In contrast to tidy models of marriage-orientated courtship, these responses and the testimonies considered below reveal the messy complexity of young women's intimate lives in post-war Britain.[12] As we saw in the previous chapter, marriage remained an important aspiration for many women and their testimonies placed particular importance on the relationships that did lead to marriage. But girls did not necessarily expect all of their relationships to be heading towards long-term commitment, nor did they expect sex acts (especially 'low-level' ones) to only occur within formal or emotionally committed relationships. Within their testimonies women recounted crushes, sexual interactions, games, dates, and one-night stands that do not fit neatly within 'courtship' frameworks. For women of the post-war generation, sexuality, and intimacy manifested within a wide range of relationship formations.

Before Prince Charming

While personal accounts call into question the utility of 'courtship' as an all-encompassing concept for describing adolescent and young adult relationships, some women's testimonies do confirm the persistence of future-oriented relationships. At school in the early 1970s, Hilary 'wasn't particularly desperate for boyfriends' and she was caught off-guard when she went to art school and began a relationship with the man who would become her husband. Her account of them meeting at a party sits neatly within the romantic tropes of the period.

> We met at a party in a bathroom and spent the evening together, as did my other friends with other boys. And I didn't think much of him at first sight. But as the evening wore on, you know, they were pairing off and deciding to sleep with each other or go somewhere else, you know. And I thought, 'No, I'm not doing that', you know, although he'd been very clingy and lovely. And I, I looked back as I left and, and I thought, 'I'm gonna be with him for life'. And that's, it's the God's honest truth and love at first sight in our case is true.[13]

For women such as Hilary, their youthful intimate lives were defined by a great love, with the majority of their sexual experience taking place within this relationship. Within these accounts, heterosexuality encompassed both sexual feelings and interactions as well as romantic love, intimacy, and deep affection.

Yet, even women whose own accounts revolved around great loves indicated that this was not the only form of heterosexual experience available to women of their generation. Observing the world around them, girls compared their relationships and interactions to those of their friends and peers. Within their testimonies, women often contrasted their experiences to those of other girls. Maureen, for example, compared her choosiness with other girls' desperation: 'Some girls of the time would want a boyfriend at any cost. Well, I've never been like that. I only would want a boyfriend if they were perfect for me and otherwise, I'd rather be on my own.'[14] Similarly, Julie asserted that her teenage self 'wasn't in the group that were trying to get boyfriends'.[15] Beyond simply identifying variety of experience across their generational cohort, in recounting their youthful life histories, interviewees and Mass Observers also revealed the complexity of their own relationships.

Though she experienced love at first sight with her future husband, Maureen's testimony went on to reveal that both her and her husband slept with other people before they got married.[16] While Pauline described falling in love with her future husband as a revelation ('I suddenly realised what it was all about'), this realisation struck her so profoundly because she was already in a relationship, heading towards engagement: 'it wasn't really until I met A that I realised what was missing'.[17] Though relationships that led to marriage were often prominent in women's testimonies, these rarely made up the entirety of women's intimate histories.

Echoing discussions in Chapter 1, testimonies indicate that intimate relationships, interactions, and dynamics were, in their own way, often developmental and aspects of romantic and sexual life featured in women's lives long before they had any serious intentions of forming marriage-facing relationships. Mirroring the escalation of sexual activity women pursued and experienced in their youth, accounts of intimate relationships often suggested that the nature of girls' relationships and interactions with boys changed as they got older. Particularly in their late childhood and early teenage years, young women had 'crushes' or 'fancied' boys and older men. Mass Observer Daisy attended an all-girls' grammar school from the age of ten to eighteen, meaning that boys were 'an unknown quantity': 'Not unnaturally I developed "crushes" on any personable member of the opposite sex with whom I had contact – brothers of friends, boys at Sunday School, the "boy next door". When I spent any period of time with these idols I was tongue-tied.'[18] Maureen's similar gender-segregated schooling did not prevent her from noticing members of the opposite sex, though the objects of her desire were more grown up:

> We went to a dance once at my brother's school. And there was a Spanish teacher there who I did take a huge fancy to because he was much older and very good looking and very sort of interesting and and unattainable, really. ... I was quite fussy. But that's not to say I didn't sort of fantasize about boys, but they were always slightly unattainable ones. And uh, there was another teacher at my school as well who I sort of had did have a crush on. And he was, yeah, he was Spanish as well. I did like, I mean, even as just the smell of Gauloises and that sort of thing was so alien to the convent that it was just seductive. That kind of thing.[19]

Objects of desire could be tantalisingly close (such as Julie's crush on the local butcher boy[20]) or devastatingly remote (though that did not stop Linda and her friend practising their kissing technique in anticipation of The Beatles coming to town).[21] As Maureen explained, these feelings did not necessarily revolve around the expectation or desire to have intimate interactions with these boys and men, the fact that these objects of desire were, in her words, 'unattainable' was part of their appeal.[22] The fact that women mentioned these crushes in their testimonies indicates, however, that they understood such feelings to have been part of their sexual development.[23]

Compared to the relationships that many women experienced in their mid to late teenage years, and in early adulthood, women characterised their first forays into heterosexuality with a sense of lightness and innocence. Asked, 'Do you remember when you first started noticing boys?', Joyce responded with a very specific memory:

> OK, I think I was 12. In fact, I know I was, and he lived next door and his name was [P]. And he was 13. ... We went for a walk and we'd known each other as next door neighbours for about six months. I think they moved in and he was very nice looking, I thought, and we walked off up [the hill] and we held hands after we got out of sight of all the houses and it was hot and we lay down on the grass. And we talked and looked at the sky. And he said, 'Do you mind if I kiss you?' And I said, 'OK, then.' So he went to kiss me and I went 'Ohh! Not on the mouth! On the cheek!' So he spent the next 15 minutes kissing me on the cheek. And then we walked home and I think that's as far as it's ever got, right. But that was the first time I'd ever actually got interested enough to let anybody kiss me anywhere.[24]

In contrast to the emotional weight (both good and bad) that she associated with later relationships, early experiences such as this first kiss were not encumbered with expectation.

This was echoed by Audrey, two years Joyce's junior. In her oral history interview, Audrey suggested that 'boys were theoretical until about [the age of] 15'. Asked to expand on this further, she described a series of fleeting interactions in her early teenage years:

> Well, that 12 year old holiday there was a friend of my cousins who was obviously interested in me and I was interested in him but nothing much really happened but there was that frisson, you know? And

then nothing! [Both laugh] Um, till, I remember when I was 14 I went to a dance at the village hall and it was, the [sighs] The Animals', 'House of the Rising Sun', good track, had my first kiss! Oh! I can remember that, can't remember anything about him! [Both laugh] I think we met once more and went to the cinema and it wasn't anything so, um, yeah. That was the point at which it became, yeah. And then a few more, two or three more similar um, not going anywhere relationships.[25]

Rather than focusing her sexual and romantic life history solely upon the relationships that had a future, Audrey incorporated these 'not going anywhere' relationships into her account. Her testimony placed little emotional weight on these interactions but they nonetheless formed part of her relationship life history and the humorous tone of her testimony belied a sense of nostalgia and fondness for these early forms of heterosexuality.

The emotional lightness of women's accounts of early physical intimacies was, in some cases, a product of context, reflecting the fact that kisses were not always the result of intimate relationships. Games such as 'Postman's Knock' and kiss chase saw kisses wielded in play, for example. Though these interactions could be emotionally charged, this was not necessarily the case.[26] Similarly, for girls interested in theatre, it was not uncommon for their first kisses to be 'in character' rather than the result of romantic intimacy.[27] As explored later, kisses could serve as important thresholds and barometers of romantic interest, but they also existed outside this context. To understand the complex web of dynamics and meanings that underpinned youthful sexuality in this period, it is productive to use sexual acts rather than specific relationships or emotions as our starting point.

Serial monogamy, one-night stands, and sex outside relationships

While most women indicated that their early interactions with boys were not future-facing or necessarily concerned with romantic feelings or intimacy, their accounts of their mid to late teenage years and early adulthood depicted a messier state of affairs. Though the exact details and trajectories varied, most women described having had numerous heterosexual interactions within a variety of relationship formations. Many women portrayed their former selves as having been serial monogamists; they had a number of boyfriends throughout their teenage years. Joyce described having had several relationships with young men. Across her school and university years she had an Ethiopian boyfriend, a boyfriend from a school in her town, a boyfriend who played the harpsichord, a boyfriend who moved to Germany, and she went out with 'about four' rugby players.[28] Similarly, Sandra, 'had a lovely two years' at college in Essex in the 1960s:

> I had some really really sweet boyfriends. Y'know. I think young men were quite gentlemanly then. ... I had a lovely boyfriend who was about six foot and really thin ... And I remember going out with somebody else who had a room in the halls there at the college.[29]

Within oral history and Mass Observation testimonies, such relationships were often only mentioned briefly but the implication was that these were mutually acknowledged and monogamous relationships. The seriousness of these relationships could vary, however. Some girls had individual boyfriends for months or years while other couples' relationships were more temporary. In Janice's experience: 'The lads I went out went out with used to last maybe six weeks. That was a long time. I mean that it was quite quite serious!'[30]

As this chapter will go on to explore, it was common for 'higher level' sex acts to take place within romantic relationships. However, heterosexuality was not confined to such relationships and physical interactions took place outside these formations. For example, in their mid to late teens, some girls engaged in sex acts within the context of much less formal relationships. Girls would kiss and 'fumble' with boys they met at dances and parties or boys that they were 'going out with' or 'dating' but had not yet made any emotional commitment to.[31] Holidays away from home also featured in women's testimonies. Young women did not necessarily have any expectations that they would have long-standing relationships with young men they met on holiday (especially if they were abroad) but this did not stop them from (in fact, in some cases it actively encouraged them into) having holiday romances.[32]

Once they were older, usually living away from home in London or other major urban centres, some young women embraced sexual cultures revolving around single encounters or one-night stands.[33] Using stories about her flatmate to demonstrate the 'sexual atmosphere' in London in the early 1960s, Jacqueline recalled:

> [My flatmate] had loads of boyfriends and, um, I remember we had loads of parties too, because parties were, if you fancied somebody you just invited everyone you knew and then you, and the person you fancied, hoping to get off with them. [Both laugh] So, but she, she used to have, she used to sleep with them all.[34]

This was mirrored by Doris, who contrasted twenty-first-century sexual mores with those she experienced in London and overseas in her late teenage years and early twenties in the 1960s: 'I think what young people do now is they have serial relationships one after another, but I don't think that, um, I mean, then it was just no holds barred quite frankly, and lots of one-night stands and things.'[35] The key features of these urban sexual cultures were sexual excitement based upon immediate attraction, anonymity, and freedom from constraint and much of the appeal lay in the promise of imminent sexual pleasure and the thrill of interacting with strangers. Within these contexts, physical intimacy was not associated with emotional intimacy or expectations that a one-night stand would translate into an ongoing relationship.[36]

Barbara's testimony offers a useful demonstration of the various different relationship formations that made up young women's intimate lives. Her early experiences of heterosexual relationships began around the age of thirteen. At this stage she had boyfriends that she met at her local youth club. She stressed that 'that was the stage of fumbling. Rather, it wasn't sex'. She also suggested that these were not necessarily deeply committed relationships: 'It was romantic because you could, you could talk yourself into thinking you thought this boy was gorgeous, you know, but you could equally talk yourself out of it quite quickly if something else came along.' At seventeen, having decided 'that it was about time [she] knew what was going on', Barbara 'engineered a situation' to have penetrative sex for the first time. Asked if she knew the older man with whom she had intercourse, she replied: 'Oh, hardly at all. And I, I saw very little of him after. He just disappeared into the night, not into the night. But you know it, it was just interesting. And he went his way and I went mine.' Barbara then moved to London with a friend when she was eighteen. Once there she had a string of sexual relationships and encounters:

> I can only tell you about the central London situation where there were loads of young people, loads of hormones. Uh, really, sort of couldn't, they couldn't care less. I fear I had any number of sexual contacts. I, I couldn't tell you how many. If I wanted one, I had one. It might last a few days. It might last a few weeks. It never lasted longer than that. I didn't get a steady boyfriend till I was in Holland in my 20s. But the sex was there.[37]

Barbara's testimony recounts a youthful intimate life very different to the kinds of relationships associated with 'courtship'. The sexual encounters of her youth took place in a range of different relationship contexts and included encounters that may not even be considered 'relationships'.

Estimating that she had had hundreds of sexual partners, Barbara's level of youthful sexual activity was at the higher end of the cohort considered here. However, the ambiguity of relationship formations and dynamics that she described was not uncommon. While some intimate interactions and sex acts took place and were given meaning through the clearly defined (romantic) relationships in which they took place, other young women's experiences were much less neat. When asked to describe the first boy she really remembered, Rosemary talked about her friend's cousin with whom she spent time when she was twelve and thirteen:

> I went to his 17th birthday party so he was about 16. So we weren't boyfriend and girlfriend, obviously, but I knew, he made it clear, you know, I just knew that he liked me ... When I was about 13 he used to work somewhere and he rode, he had a motorbike and he went past the end of our road, so I used to walk the dog when he was coming to that, and he used to stop and talk to me. And we used to stand. And he used to sometimes, he'd usually stop and we'd have a little cuddle.[38]

Rosemary recalled this relationship as having been important to her although such a dynamic does not fit neatly within any standard relationship categories.

Equally ambiguous, though in a different context, Ruth suggested that student life at Oxford Polytechnic in the late 1970s was 'a great big bowl of experimentation': 'I think there was a lot of seeking out of relationships at that time because people hadn't experienced it through their teenage years and probably had been suppressed through culture or by background or by parenting.' Switching between the language of 'boyfriends' and 'friendships with men', Ruth described the fleeting and emotionally uncomplicated relationships of her student years:

> There were loads of chaps ... it was just lovely, you'd sit in the back of a punt and just be snogging away and having a really good time and then you'd eat strawberries [HC & R laugh] it was just completely farcical. Or I'd go out with someone for a couple of weeks ... free-love kind of thing really. So a lot of friendships with men didn't actually lead to sex.[39]

As these testimonies suggest, for women of the post-war generation, heterosexual identities and practices far exceeded the boundaries of courtship, dating, or 'going out'. There was no single, linear connection between emotional intimacy, relationship status, and sexual practice. Instead, young women's sexuality was forged within a complex web of feelings, interpersonal dynamics, and encounters and the role of intimacy in mediating this was malleable.

Physical and emotional intimacies

For young women in post-war England, sexual activity was not confined to marriage, engagement, or 'courtship'. Many young women engaged in sex acts (including penetrative sex) with a range of different men with whom they shared little in the way of emotional intimacy. For girls engaging in sex acts out of curiosity, a desire to grow up, or simply to satisfy sexual desires, there was not necessarily any expectation that they love, like, or even know their partners. Any intimacy forged between couples in these circumstances was momentary and physical. In other contexts, and for other young women, however, sexual activity was very closely associated with emotional intimacy. At the same time that British culture was becoming 'permissive' and sex outside marriage was becoming more commonplace, the romanticisation of heterosexuality across the mid-century had also forged new links between sex and intimacy.[40] As emotional openness and interpersonal intimacy were increasingly understood to be core components of medium- to long-term relationships (even those that were not necessarily destined for marriage), girls' relationships with boyfriends and male partners were central how they thought about sex.

The precise relationship between sex acts and emotional intimacy was not fixed, however, and shifted between contexts. Dynamics of sexual activity and emotional intimacy were similar to those between sexual activity and notions of maturity. At times, shared sexual activity was seen as being *constitutive* of intimacy: the experience of being physically intimate with someone was understood to forge bonds of intimacy. In other instances, however, emotional intimacy was framed as being a *prerequisite* to physical intimacies, with young women being unwilling or unable to engage in sex acts without having some form of emotional connection (most often shared romantic love and trust) with their partner.

Sex in the creation of intimacy

In certain contexts, physical interactions functioned as catalysts for emotional intimacy. Working with a definition of 'sex' that exceeds traditional distinctions of penetrative/non-penetrative sex and instead incorporates all forms of different-sex physical interaction, it is clear that, among teenagers in the 1950s, 1960s, and 1970s, it was not uncommon for sexual encounters to pre-date and/ or prompt the emotional commitment and attachment that accompanied formal relationships. Within the youth leisure cultures of the mid-century, girls would hold hands, dance with, and kiss boys that they had only just met. When Judith was fourteen she and her friends used to go to the cinema and the park in search of boys. These interactions incorporated kissing but Judith stressed that these were not really relationships and the boys were largely interchangeable: 'At first I would just see the same boy each Friday at the cinema, then one week he would not be there and someone else would talk to me and I would see him for a few weeks, just at the cinema and being walked to the bus.'[41] Dancing with and kissing boys upon first meeting was not only socially acceptable but could act as a means of identifying future relationship prospects.[42]

Moreover, there was a belief that relationships were not 'real' until they had been secured by some physical contact such as holding hands or kissing. Magazines such as *Jackie* and *Honey* often tried to warn girls off kissing or petting with boys 'too soon' but through their advice columns, articles, cartoons, and stories they stressed the almost-magical power of a kiss and its potential to transform girls' relationships.[43] Girls were repeatedly told that they would and should not want to kiss a boy until they knew them a little, but readers' complaints when boys failed to kiss them at the end of a date suggest that a relationship was not rendered official or complete until that physical contact had been made.[44] Girls worried that a boy's failure to kiss them was a sign that they did not like the girl or that they were not serious about pursuing a relationship. Implicit within their discussions was the notion that to kiss a boy marked a shift in the relationship. By agreeing to go on a date with a boy girls indicated that there was some potential for a relationship but the real change occurred when this potential was sealed through physical intimacy.

Underpinning this was the foundational belief that these acts of touch were central to the distinctiveness of heterosexual relationships. These physical interactions were what distinguished romantic relationships from friendships; different-sex relationships needed physical interactions in order to transcend being merely platonic. In response to Mass Observation's 'Courting and Dating' Directive, Denise and Amanda both sought to express the ways in which even contact as 'innocent' as hand-holding could be charged with feeling and anticipation:

> At the time I was courting, fortyish years ago, the first 'daring' step would be just holding hands. I say 'just' but even that can give a very pleasant feeling of closeness, next would be a fairly quick goodnight kiss and kiss on meeting.[45]

> A peck on the cheek was very tentatively sort after, sought after? On the first date, which if things continued, progressed on future occasions to hands accidentally knocking together before they were actually held. But oh the thrilling stab of luscious pain when that clasp took place![46]

Their excitement at these 'low-level' physical interactions stemmed from the understanding that these types of interactions were transformative. By holding hands or moving on from pecks on the cheeks to kisses on the lips, young couples were making a statement about their relationship, one that not only cemented the bonds that had already been established but which also acted as a testament of their desire for the relationship to continue.

Physical intimacies could transform partner dynamics, taking friends and acquaintances to lovers and romantic partners but they could also halt developing intimacy in its tracks. At a time when 'compatibility' was seen as essential to functional marital and couple dynamics, physical interactions could act as a litmus test for future relationships.[47] Especially in the very early stages of a relationship, unsatisfactory physical interactions could quash the relationship before it began. If a boy's attempts at physical intimacy were deemed unsatisfactory that could put an end to the pairing. On one of her first dates Penelope's partner took her to the cinema but his attempts at physical intimacy were enough to put her off the relationship entirely: 'He finally took me to see *West Side Story*, sat me in the back row and insisted on snogging me so unbearably I never went out with him again.'[48] Penelope suggested that this was a rather simple decision to make – her partner's 'unbearable' kissing technique was grounds to terminate the relationship.

As girls got older and began to think more seriously about future-facing relationships, penetrative sex itself became a way of testing the viability of a relationship. As Marion wrote:

> I always used to get fairly intimate very early on (if all the 'signals' were right I hasten to add!) When I was younger, I used to think that if sex wasn't great, then the relationship was unlikely to match it – which led to quite a few 'one night stands'. I have no regrets to that – though I'm not sure I'd be too pleased if my daughter did the same!! Usual double standard I suppose ... For example, I slept with my husband within 24hrs ... and never looked back![49]

For women such as Marion who equated good sex with a good relationship, it was quicker and easier to test the sex than it was to wait the weeks, months, or years it would take to ensure that the relationship was emotionally satisfying. Understanding emotional compatibility as something which revealed itself slowly, Marion wanted a quicker test of the relationship's potential. Marion's testimony thus demonstrates the extent to which sexological and marriage guidance rhetoric that established inextricable links between sexual satisfaction and marital happiness had gained credence within lay heterosexuality by the late 1970s.[50] While advice literature continued to suggest that sexual skill could be trained and practised, there was a growing sense that sexual compatibility was actually based upon innate 'sexuality'.[51] This notion that a good relationship was founded upon an essential sexual chemistry meant that women increasingly used sex to test a relationship before becoming too emotionally invested in it. Understanding sex and relationships to function in this way encouraged some women to begin a sexual relationship long before they might have done otherwise in the name of efficiency. Within this discourse, having multiple sexual partners was not antithetical to future marriage but worked in service of it. Viewing both emotional intimacy and sexual compatibility as related, but distinct, components of happiness within relationships, women used the latter to test the potential of the former.

Sex acts as expressions of intimacy

Once girls had entered relationships with young men, questions of intimacy and how this translated into physical interactions often intensified. Heightened feelings of attraction, affection, trust, and care became bound up with the special regimes of touch that distinguished romantic and heterosexual relationships. We saw in Chapter 1 that post-war teenagers understood sexuality to be cumulative and progressive. While, as we saw there, this was associated with notions of growing up and maturity, there was also a sense that girls' sexuality developed within their relationships and that their desire and willingness to engage in sex acts was tied to the nature and longevity of their partnerships and the depth of emotional intimacy shared within them.[52]

When discussing the rules and conventions of adolescent sexuality in the mid-twentieth century, some women suggested that their progression through the taxonomy of sex acts was determined by the nature of specific relationships. Testimonies often outlined the ways in which certain sexual acts were deemed to require levels of intimacy and trust that were only met within long-term relationships. In Geraldine's words: 'There were rules. On a first date you could kiss. After a few weeks he could feel your breasts. After about 6 months he generally got his hand in your knickers but not much further.'[53] How girls felt about their partners and the nature of their relationships determined what types of behaviour they were prepared to engage in with a boyfriend or partner. Carole insisted that 'sex was not on the agenda and wouldn't be until marriage' but suggested that other forms of sexual activity also required careful negotiation: 'Petting wasn't allowed until a couple of months into the relationship i.e. when there was more commitment and the boyfriend was judged to be trustworthy.'[54] The temporal parameters that Carole imposed on her sexual activity reflected her sense that kissing and other sexual acts such as 'petting' required a degree of intimacy that could only be acquired through familiarity and commitment. Understanding sexual activity as a cumulative process, negotiations regarding boundaries and limits defined girls' sexual landscapes long before girls were contemplating penetrative sex.

Nevertheless, these deliberations were undoubtedly heightened around penetrative intercourse. For many women, penetrative sex was only desired and appropriate within the context of long-term relationships and many waited until marriage or at least until they were engaged to have intercourse.[55] Heather described how, having made the commitment to marry her partner, her previous desire to wait until marriage dissipated:

> I had this strong conviction right up to my finally getting engaged to get married that a decent girl wouldn't let a man go all the way until they married. Virginity was all important to me as it was to quite a few of my friends – or so they said. By the time I became engaged opinions were changing and most couples, I suspect, had sex once they intended marrying. Just before I married my friend and I both confessed that we hadn't waited after all and we thought we were very modern indeed![56]

Though they had not made a legal commitment to one another yet, through becoming engaged Heather had made an emotional and personal commitment to her partner which recalibrated her sense of how sex might feature in her relationship. Tradition stressed that the wedding night was the appropriate time for couples to incorporate penetrative intercourse into their intimate lives but couples made their own decisions about what felt right within their own relationships. In Veronica's experience: 'One day it just happened and we both felt it was right and good and not shameful or sinful in any way.'[57]

Many other girls were less concerned to 'save themselves' for marriage, but even they frequently deliberated whether their partner was the right one with whom to have sex. Maria suggested, for example, that she was not opposed to pre-marital sex in principle, but that she was holding out for a special relationship: 'After my first boyfriend, relationships became more serious, but I kept my virginity, perhaps because I never felt that the chap in question was "the one".'[58] Similarly, in their teenage years, Glenys and her friends were waiting for a meaningful relationship: ' "Heavy petting" was what went on as the relationship developed but myself and girlfriends felt that "saving" ourselves for "Mr Right" was what it was all about.'[59] Significantly, however, the 'right' partner did not have to be one that girls associated with love or romance; expectations of intimacy did not necessarily translate into emotional commitment. For girls like Anne it was more a case of finding a boy who would be discrete: 'I decided that he was ideal candidate ... because I could manage his behaviour so that I could be more like the woman I wanted to be without my mum finding out.'[60] Anne's criteria of what was 'right' and her expectations of intimacy were less concerned with emotional connectedness than with making sure her partner respected her enough to keep her sexual activity secret. Similarly, Tracy did not describe the partner she first had sex with as a great love but 'I liked him ... and I trusted him and he was nice and he hadn't been with a lot of girls'.[61] For girls, intimacy incorporated not just considerations of love and sexual desire but also trust and a sense of safety.

Although having penetrative sex for the first time was framed as being a particularly significant milestone (both personally and within girls' relationships), it did not function as a final destination and negotiations of interpersonal intimacy were often repeated across women's lives. Whereas Judith suggested that sexual initiation radically changed her sexual landscape, becoming an assumed aspect of future relationships ('Once you have slept with someone it is just natural to sleep with others after that'), many other women described considerable continuity between the trajectory of their first and future relationships.[62] First intercourse did not mark a point of no return; young people's sexual lives were not simply reduced to inevitable penetrative intercourse once the threshold of the first time had been crossed. Women often repeated this process of moving through the stages with each new relationship. As Jane's testimony suggests, girls developed their own codes for sexual conduct, setting their own pace for experiencing sex acts with new partners: 'When I first started going out with men (1970) sleeping with them on the first date was definitely a no-no. On the first date one might kiss (possibly quite passionately) but only on later dates would I expect to progress beyond that!'[63] The perceived perils of reputation loss and pregnancy that informed individuals' first time experiences did not necessarily disappear once girls had penetrative sex. The expectation that intimacy was a prerequisite for sex did not dissipate either; many girls continued to feel that sexual practice was a form of commitment warranted only within certain relationships.

Continuing negotiations of intimacy are demonstrated through interviewees' and Mass Observers' discussions of oral sex. Though historians have suggested that oral sex may have become 'integrated into everyday sexual practices' during the 1960s and 1970s, references to oral sex were infrequent within testimonies and oral history interviewees often had to be prompted to discuss it.[64] When oral sex was mentioned it was often framed differently to other non-penetrative sex acts. Although Tracy listed 'blowjobs' as being the 'stage' of sexual practice that immediately preceded penetrative sex, other interviewees and Mass Observers suggested that it existed outside of this schema of proto-penetrative sex.[65] In the words of one Mass Observer: 'I don't think many couples in the sixties were aware of oral sex.'[66] Most of those who did discuss oral sex suggested that they engaged in it only after they had experienced penetrative intercourse.[67] Confirming the findings of previous studies, most of the accounts examined here suggest that oral sex was considered to be the most intimate form of sexual activity and was therefore deemed to represent a stage beyond vaginal intercourse.[68] The casualisation of oral sex was viewed as one of the most significant changes in sexual culture over their lifetimes. As Lilian colourfully put it:

> The media on the one hand makes girls more promiscuous, in magazines, giving advice on HOW TO GIVE ORAL SEX!? – What's that all about? As the contributor said on GRUMPY OLD WOMEN, 'I thought a BLOW JOB was something *after* you had gone all the way. And *not* an apperitif in between a quick fondle and a FRENCH KISS!?!?['][69]

While adolescent taxonomies of sexual activity often presented penetrative intercourse as the pinnacle of sexual activity, testimonies such as these suggest that such hierarchies were incomplete; while kissing, heavy petting, and penetrative sex may have been milestones for uninitiated teenagers, 'adult' sexuality had its own dynamics and negotiations regarding intimacy and sexual activity persisted long after first intercourse had occurred. For women like Lilian what was striking about contemporary sexuality, therefore, was not necessarily the repertoire of modern sexual activity but the meanings (or lack thereof) associated with it. Though the long 1960s are often viewed as a time when sexual mores became more liberal, the testimonies considered here demonstrate the extent to which sex continued to be bound up with notions of intimacy, though the links between these were fluid and at times contradictory. Moreover, as the next section demonstrates, this interconnection was not always romantic and its ramifications far from healthy by contemporary standards of sexual well-being.

Persuasion and coercion

Understanding sexual activity as a means of establishing and deepening as well as expressing emotional intimacy created a potentially fraught dilemma for young women. In their testimonies, women repeatedly made reference to cultural norms which insisted that it was 'natural' for young men to encourage their partners to engage in sex acts. Many women interpreted their own youthful experiences through the lens of persuasion, if not coercion. Personal accounts illustrate how girls' desires for emotional intimacy could be, and were, manipulated by young men who used this logic to needle and persuade their partners to have sex with them. While the vulnerability associated with sexual activity was essential to the intimacy-fostering potential of these interactions, it could also be manipulated by girls' partners.

In recent years, the #MeToo movement and campaigns such as Everyone's Invited have drawn attention to the forms of everyday sexual harassment and assault experienced by women. Much of what is discussed in the following pages supports the findings of these campaigns and the arguments of feminist activists and scholars that sexual harassment, assault, and rape were endemic in British sexual cultures across the twentieth century.[70] The testimonies considered here, however, were recorded prior to the #MeToo movement, offering perspectives from the vantage points of the 1990s, 2000s, and 2010s. Being interviewed in 2014 and 2015, for example, the trials of Jimmy Savile and Rolf Harris and the investigations associated with Operation Yewtree were a common point of reference for oral history interviewees either during the interviews themselves or in pre-/post-interview conversation.

Exact responses to these cases varied but it was clear that these criminal trials and the furore they unleashed in the press had prompted women to reconsider the sexual cultures of previous periods. Some testimonies suggest that, in line with broader cultural change, women had re-evaluated experiences of their youth in later life, coming to understand themselves as having been subject to 'assault' or 'rape' rather than some unspecified unpleasantness.[71] In some cases, the treatment of these women would have been criminal at the time but there were also grey areas and points of ambiguity. As we will see, the sexual cultures of the 1950s, 1960s, and 1970s comprised of much that many twenty-first-century commentators would consider unacceptable or troubling. Yet, having grown up in a society in which harassment was ubiquitous and the prioritisation of male desire normalised, many women had an ambivalent or conflicted sense of how their lives fit within this picture. In their youth many had understood certain behaviours as unpleasant but normal. Though women had been hurt by individual partners, many continued to believe that men pressing their partners to have sex was a natural feature of male sexuality. That (young) men were able to use appeals to girls' emotional commitment to them as a tool for this coercion reflected the extent to which notions of intimacy were embedded in post-war cultures of heterosexuality.

Boys try, girls deny

By the 1950s it was widely understood that that sexual drive was a characteristic of biological sex. Over the first half of the century, sexologists such as Havelock Ellis and Theodoor van de Velde, as well as marriage guidance counsellors like Marie Stopes, published works and advice literature that portrayed men as being 'naturally' more sexually aggressive than women.[72] It was understood that young men had both greater desire for sex and a natural instinct to pursue women. Sexual desire was innately gendered, creating specifically gendered sexual practice. Sex advice of the mid century increasingly emphasised the importance of mutuality in sexual relations but within these frameworks men were still expected to be the active party in sexual encounters.[73] While mutual satisfaction was the intended outcome of sexual acts, the process itself was understood to rely upon male desire and initiation.

The trope of the male initiator underpinned much of the adolescent sex guidance of the post-war period. Facts of life literature from across the 1950s, 1960s, and 1970s informed their teenage audiences that 'men's passions are … more easily aroused than women's',[74] that 'the boy's sexual feelings … lie much nearer the surface' than girls',[75] and that it was 'natural for a boy to try to persuade a girl to have sexual intercourse with him' for '[h]e is only responding to the instincts of nature'.[76] Magazine agony aunts echoed the understanding that 'boys are much more easily aroused than girls'[77] and warned girls that they were likely to have to 'fend off' boys 'who seem interested in nothing but sex' throughout their adolescence.[78] As Susan Freeman has argued in an American context, post-war sex education initiatives did not promote predatory male sexuality but in normalising boys' desire and repeatedly suggesting that girls' sexual impulses required coaxing they nonetheless contributed to a culture of male sexual entitlement.[79]

Interviewees and Mass Observers' accounts of their everyday experiences and interactions confirm the ubiquity of male sexual entitlement. As women such as Jacqueline and Norma articulated, to be a teenage girl at this time was to be sexualised and to have to deal with the unwanted attentions of men. It was not unusual for boys to grab at and 'claim' girls' bodies and/or for men to catcall girls and women on the street.[80] For Jacqueline, who grew up in central London, an oppressively lecherous atmosphere was the defining quality of London in the 1960s:

> I lived in London. Beba's [sic] had just started and um, she was just down a side street in Kensington and … the dressing [room], because it was a tiny shop, about the size of this room, there was a curtain at the corner and that was where people changed and the curtain actually didn't fit so the men used to walk past a lot, looking at the

girls changing ... Men were not very grown up in those days, they were not, they were terribly repressed sexually so consequently all these women walking around with hardly any clothes on or very short skirts and showing their suspender belts, their suspenders and you know, it was a nasty atmosphere. There was a lot of, you know, you got touched up on the Tube, people always um, not always, but quite often get people masturbating against you if you were squished together, there was quite a lot of really, wasn't unusual to see a man with his dick hanging out on the Tube.[81]

Jacqueline described this as a very particular moment in time in which the 'new' sexuality of the 1960s had yet to fully overhaul the '1950s ethos' and 'Victorian' mindset of previous generations. Hilary echoed the sentiment that her generation's youth coincided with a particularly unpleasant sexual culture. She asserted that 'the 1970s were rather grubby and sordid and, and nasty'. She went on:

There was an atmosphere of sleaze and that that I think us women had to be even more careful of how we went about things and there were what were called dirty old men. I think they've always have been but, look, you know when all this thing came up about Jimmy Savile and whatnot for my generation, I don't think it's any surprise at all. And there's some guilt that we all knew, but nobody did anything about it.[82]

Elsewhere, however, the feeling that men sought power by verbally and physically harassing women was presented as an almost timeless and universal experience. The testimonies considered for this project are awash with accounts of unsettling, even traumatic, incidences of sexual intimidation. Of the thirty-three women interviewed for this project nine recounted some form of what would now commonly be considered sexual assault, harassment, or rape.[83] As a teenager, Caroline had strangers attempt to hold her hands and grab her body as she walked down the street.[84] Eileen was pushed against a wall while a boy forced his hands into her knickers.[85] Tina was lured to a secluded spot by three brothers who threatened her and grabbed her clothes.[86] Jane and Doris had men follow them as they walked home.[87] These stories were often presented with no details to distinguish the date or broader context, which has the effect of making them seem suspended in time.[88] These interactions were portrayed as menacing and unnerving, and as Eileen explicitly stated, this tainted her feelings about sex for a long time after the fact.[89] Disturbing as they may have been in the moment, however, these types of interactions were not viewed as unusual or surprising; within their testimonies women often made reference to the ubiquity of these occurrences. Gloria prefaced her accounts of being followed by a man in central Manchester and being 'rubbed against' in a football crowd with the chillingly detached statement that 'I had a couple of unpleasant experiences as most girls do'.[90] Rather than being the preserve of a rare subset of men who attacked vulnerable girls, these behaviours represented a commonplace manifestation of male sexual entitlement.

Beyond street harassment and assault, the orientation of sexuality around male desire and interest was evident in young people's intimate relationships. The sense that it was the boy's role to initiate sex and push girls' boundaries was repeatedly expressed within personal testimonies. It was implicit in many of the taxonomies of sexual behaviour described by Mass Observers; their models of sexual progress were primarily organised around the increasing accessibility of the female body with little mention made of an equivalent expectation of male bodily exposure. For example, Amanda's account of adolescent sex was rooted in 'upstairs/downstairs', 'inside/outside' distinctions, but these were all focused on her clothing and body: 'The general progression was "upstairs outside, upstairs inside" (bra). "Downstairs outside, downstairs inside" (nickers [sic]) followed by "fingers" which was when a boy "felt you up".'[91] This distinction was even more explicit in men's testimony where sexual activity was couched in the language of a military manoeuvre:

> The next stage is usually fondling and in my case as, I suspect, in most, it begins with the male hand progressing from knee to thigh and thence to between the legs. Or from shoulder to neck, down the blouse and into the bra.
>
> Once these two targets (the nipple and the vagina) become familiar territory and access readily allowed the next goal is to get the penis manouvred [sic] towards the vagina.[92]

Neither Amanda or George made any reference to a process by which girls touched or undressed their male partners; their testimonies suggest that girls were to be explored rather than explorers themselves.

As alluded to in Chapter 1, among those women who did make reference to touching and stimulating boys' penises, this was often portrayed as something quite transgressive. Sarah described her first boyfriend as having been 'quite passionate' and although she portrayed their relationship as having been exciting she noted that she was 'quite shocked' when he asked her to handle his penis.[93] Girls like Glynis were happy to participate in certain sexual activities but they were more comfortable being passive receivers of contact than having to be proactive themselves. She recalled that, when she was in her early teens, her boyfriend 'rubbed himself against me and fondled my tiny breasts' but she was 'reluctant to touch his penis'.[94] Similarly, Gwen described one of her partners' 'erroneous' belief that she would sleep with him and suggested that his insistence that she 'hold his penis' directly contributed to her decision to end the relationship.[95]

This resistance represented a somewhat counter-intuitive understanding of sexual pleasure and girls' role within it. Within this culture, pleasure was primarily associated with boys' stimulation of girls' bodies and girls were not necessarily prepared to actively masturbate or stimulate their male partners. Yet, this dynamic did not necessarily represent the prioritisation of female pleasure. Although women like Glynis recounted having their breasts and genitals fondled, such descriptions were often devoid of any mention of sexual pleasure – there was not necessarily any expectation that boys were skilled at such performances, that girls would enjoy the sensation, or that such stimulation of girls' bodies would lead to female orgasm.[96] Barbara recalled that the 'progression' of sexual activity was organised around boys 'reaching' certain parts of girls' bodies:

> The boys tried to undo your bra straps and fumble with your breasts and if they really wanted to chance it they tried to get into your knickers and that was it. They might press up against you in a rather, sort of obvious way, um, but it was, well, if you were a strong enough character as I was, it was up to you then how far you let it go.[97]

The stimulation of girls' bodies was thus often framed in terms of male 'achievement' rather than female enjoyment. Women implied that male pleasure and the quenching of the boy's urges was the driving force behind such activity.

Framing male orgasm as the ultimate end point of sexual contact, girls' active participation was not necessarily required; boys were capable of pleasuring themselves with little active stimulation from their partners. Girls came to realise that their boyfriends and partners could be stimulated by the sight and feel of their bodies and that the fricative contact the boys 'needed' to orgasm could be gained by rubbing and 'dry humping' (what Michael Schofield called 'genial apposition').[98] As such, girls who did not feel comfortable playing a more active role in sex could relax in the notion that they simply needed to offer their bodies for their partners to achieve the sexual pleasure they desired. For many young couples this was a mutually satisfactory arrangement that facilitated both boys' and girls' differing rates of sexual interest but elsewhere this prioritisation of male pleasure and desire and the willingness of girls to be passive participants in their own sexual activity could be exploited, fostering power dynamics within relationships that were extremely difficult for girls to navigate.

Before going further it is important to note that many young couples in the long 1960s embarked on sexual relationships that were shared, mutually enjoyable endeavours. For these couples, sex deepened their sense of emotional intimacy and was seen as having strengthened the relationship. Heather gave a lengthy description of her and her husband's early relationship, detailing their early dates building to a lovingly told story about how he proposed.[99] In her testimony, Heather framed their pre-marital sexual activity in the context of their developing relationship and their building a future together; within her narrative the fact of sexual activity cannot be separated from her partner's continuing desire to build a relationship with her family ('He slept on our settee every Saturday night') nor the new home they were setting up for themselves ('Shortly before the wedding we bought a small cottage and spent each weekend getting it ready which gave us a lot more privacy'). Heather gave little detail about the first time they engaged in penetrative sex but she squarely situated this experience within their engagement, a time that she remembered very fondly. Sex was inextricably linked with her and her future husband's developing relationship and commitment to one another.

Even sexual relationships that were short-lived and did not result in marriage could be remembered fondly several decades after the fact. The nostalgic warmth of these memories was reflected in testimonies such as Hazel's, that described her early sexual experiences as a time of shared learning.

> [B]ut yes you would gradually explore each other more and more without going the whole hog. That's how you learn, isn't it?
>
> *And was that, um, reciprocal?*
>
> Yes, yeah. Yes ... generally we were learning together.[100]

Looking back on these relationships (long-term or otherwise), sexual activity was presented as a means by which couples became closer to one another. Here, 'learning' sex together was understood to have been a powerful form of bonding that positively influenced how girls thought about these relationships. The vulnerability and joy that accompanied such experiences contributed to a couple's increasing sense of intimacy. Within other relationships, however, the emotional connotations of sex were more fraught, revealing, and themselves creating, complicated dynamics between partners and their understandings of intimacy.

The Mass Observation Directive on Courting and Dating asked respondents whether they had ever ended a relationship due to differing expectations of the role of sex. Almost 20 per cent of this cohort of women Mass Observers responded positively, describing a range of relationships that broke down due to sex.[101] Women used this prompt as an opportunity to reflect upon the power dynamics of their adolescent relationships, describing times when they ended a relationship, or were themselves dumped, because their male partners wanted to 'go further' or faster than they were prepared to. Here and in the oral history testimonies, teenage relationships were portrayed as a constant negotiation in which boys pursued sex whilst girls sought to wait until it felt 'right'. Describing the sexual culture of her youth, Hazel simply stated that, 'Obviously boys always push don't they'.[102]

In recounting their youthful sexuality, women indicated that they spent much of their time managing their partners' desire. Girls like Joy were constantly having to resist boyfriends' advances: 'if you went out with a boy you'd you know, kiss, that's fine but then it might be they'd touch your top half and that was base, base 2 or something like that, I can't remember and then you'd have to fight them off from anything else'.[103] As Linda put it, 'the boys were just out for any opportunity and that was acceptable. It was the girl's job to keep the boys in check ... That was the unwritten rule that it was the girl's place to stop anything happening'.[104]

Diana recalled the emotional toll that these negotiations took on her:

> *When you were 'heavy petting' did you enjoy that? Did you find that pleasurable?*
>
> I did quite, but I found the management of it quite exhausting as well. 'Cos at that stage I was trying to not do it, um, but it was managing ... Yeah, some of the time I enjoyed it, other times it was like, 'Ugh, leave me alone' 'cos it's just so, yeah, 'cos he was pushing, pushing, pushing all the time.[105]

Though it was frustrating, both in their youth and at the time of recording their testimony, women framed young men's testing of girls' resistance as a normal dynamic of adolescent sexuality.[106]

Testimonies repeatedly emphasised the anxiety that questions of sex provoked among young women. For the most part, girls of this generation had been raised and socialised to believe that they needed to be 'good' and save themselves, if not until marriage then at least until they were engaged. The notion that 'boys try, girls deny' was common.[107] Yet, once girls entered in to relationships the values they held in abstract became more complicated to maintain. As Charlotte wrote, 'I was brought up to think that ideally sex came after marriage, but one soon found that things weren't as simple as that so you have to make it up as you go along'.[108] It was not simply the case that the heightened emotions of new relationships and their attendant feelings of desire were harder to control, however. Many women suggested that from the earliest moments of relationships they were encouraged by their partners to 'go further' and 'do more'.[109] How best to deal with these pressures was unclear. Girls did not always wish to abandon the morality they had been raised with, nor did they want to risk reputation loss and pregnancy. However, they liked and often loved their boyfriends and did not want to lose them either. Teenage girls' sexuality thus became the site of conflict between the clashing values of 'traditional' and 'modern' sexual cultures.

Particularly for girls in their mid-teenage years, the outcome of this dilemma was often a series of increasingly heated exchanges over the question of sex and then the end of the relationship. Either the girls would get tired of boys who could not control themselves, or the boys would get tired of waiting.[110] Either way, however, this process was often fraught and women recalled a great deal of distress as a result of being caught between their hearts, their morals, and their fears about pregnancy. Many young women were immensely hurt by the ways in which boys treated them. Looking back on her experience, Dorothy attempted to contextualise the behaviour of teenage boys but had little tolerance for their actions: 'I realise that rampant hormones have a lot to do with this nasty behaviour but it is really not acceptable to make a girl feel that she is frigid, a tease, unattractive and/or stupid just because she doesn't want some grubby, spotty young men inside her pants.'[111]

The constant pressure girls felt as they moved between relationships could be extremely disheartening. Sarah described her later school years as 'a very tough time' as her refusal to go beyond 'kissing and cuddling' led her adolescent relationships to stall and to her gaining a reputation as being 'frigid'. This situation did not ease when she went to college where expectations of sex continued to plague her relationships:

> [The polytechnic] provided a whole new range of opportunities. The problem was that I was still shy and naive. For instance if boys asked me back for coffee I thought that was all they meant – a kiss and cuddle perhaps but nothing more. At college though – particularly in the 70's when there was no AIDS to worry about, sex was regarded as the normal end to an evening. I was still a virgin with no intention of changing my state. I met lots of boys but sex was always the problem and I got very disillusioned.[112]

Although boyfriends pushing for sex was understood to be a timeless, natural impulse, women like Sarah indicated that these negotiations took on a new character in the 1960s and 1970s. Penelope, for example, described most of her sexual experiences as having been 'pressured' and she directly associated this with the advent of the oral contraceptive pill:

> It might seem strange to say this, but much of my experience with men has been being pressurized into sex. This began when I was 14 & continued. Younger men are quite crude with their pressure ...

> I think the Pill changed everything & led men to take the lead and press for instant sex (whereas before they'd been more prepared to hold back and court a woman) and my generation foolishly gave in to them.[113]

For Penelope, the oral contraceptive pill changed the gendered power dynamics in sexual relationships and created new expectations for women to engage in sex. Crucially, however, while she condemned these 'new' male attitudes, she also lamented the fact that she and her female peers actively participated in this culture.

This idea that the changing sexual mores of the 1960s and 1970s influenced gender dynamics within sexual relationships is well-noted within existing scholarship.[114] Since the 1970s, feminists have drawn attention to the ways in which this era of so-called 'sexual revolution' created new pressures and forms of oppression that have harmed both men and women.[115] Critics have suggested that rather than the liberalisation of sexual constraints leading to more open and fluid sexual cultures in which individuals felt able to pursue a wide range of sexual desires on whatever timeline and in whichever contexts felt right for them, old cultures of sexual repression were simply replaced by new cultures of sexual expectation. Helen recalled the increasing pressure she felt within the more casual sexual relationships and encounters of her late teens and early twenties:

> *Did you feel pressure with any of the men?*
>
> Oh yeah. I mean so much so that you just … just not to be evicted on the street, you know? Because yeah. Definitely there was a lot, yeah.
>
> *And do you feel that that got worse as you got older? Did you feel there was more pressure?*
>
> Yeah, yeah, yeah, definitely yes … The ones who are very fond of me wouldn't have pressed, the ones I had the more stable relationships with and they, you know, it was accepted, you know. But definitely later on they really couldn't give a toss. You just sort of did it.[116]

As the constraints on sexual conduct were relaxed, intercourse became increasingly expected and it was more often assumed to be the normal outcome of even very fleeting heterosexual interactions.[117] Where this shift has often been located in the cultures of 'adult' sexuality and the anonymity of urban nightlife, women's testimonies help to reveal its manifestation in the bedrooms, living rooms, and backseats of suburbia.[118] Women's accounts make clear that new cultures of expectation did not solely gain their power from their foundation in abstract discourses of 'normal' sexuality but instead found such purchase as they were rooted in girls' feelings of emotional obligation. Although some girls were able to extricate themselves from relationships where too much was being asked of them, others were not and were persuaded into sexual activity they did not necessarily want for themselves.

That sex could create intimacy and represented a demonstration of love and commitment made it difficult for girls to say no to their partners' requests for sex. Particularly for vulnerable girls, the promise of intimacy was extremely compelling. However, it could easily transform into a sense of obligation, pressuring girls into activities they did not desire. Having become very attached to an older man when she moved out of home, Kathleen eventually left her life working in London to join a commune run by this man. Once at the commune the man pursued her for sex and although she did not want to sleep with him she found it very difficult to resist in case her rejection disrupted or ruined the other aspects of their relationship that she enjoyed: 'It was a strange situation because in a sense he was like my best friend, he was the person I felt most attached to but I felt obliged to like, service him, in return for what I was getting from him in other ways, you know.'[119]

This sense of obligation and men's manipulation of girls' vulnerability was similarly articulated by Dawn whose Mass Observation testimony recalled her traumatic experiences of sex with her future husband. In the early stages of her account she stressed her immense naivety regarding sex – throughout her teenage years she remained wholly ignorant about what sex entailed, not even knowing where her vagina was. She met her future husband at seventeen. He was eight years older than her and, despite her explaining to him that she was going to be a virgin when she got married, he '[took] advantage' of her:

> I am a soft person, bit of a push over. I can't bear to upset anyone. So when my husband to be got sexually aroused by kissing me he told me that I had to 'help' him or he would be in agony. I didn't

understand, but he said it was my fault he was like it and I had to help him. So I let him penetrate me he said it would be ok and he would withdraw, what ever that meant. He was older and wiser than me so I gave in. I bled all over my mums front room carpet. Well after that he wouldn't take no for an answer, after all I had let him once so I had lost all rights to say no.[120]

Although she had grown up believing that sex was for marriage, Dawn relented to her boyfriend, not wishing to hurt him or ruin their relationship. The power dynamic she articulated here persisted throughout their marriage and it was only decades later that she came to feel that his insistence that she have sex 'weather [sic] [she] wanted it or not' was 'rape'.

Several other Observers indicated that their first sexual experiences with their future spouses were, to a degree at least, coerced. Gwen, Shirley, and Yvette each described their lingering hurt and resentment at their partners having used sex as a bargaining chip within their relationships. Gwen claimed that she had been 'ambivalent about sex' but that her future husband 'insisted we had to sleep together if I was serious about the relationship. I still resent that'.[121] Similarly, Yvette recalled: 'I slept with my husband to be after 6 months of courtship although I didn't feel entirely happy about it and felt "pressured" slightly by him to do it, or lose him.'[122] Within their testimonies, women suggest that their emotional commitment to their partners was wielded as a form of leverage. Arguably, these men may have desired sex because they themselves wished to demonstrate their commitment to the relationship, seeing sex as a means deepening intimacy and expressing their love for their partners. Nevertheless, the way in which these Mass Observers framed their experiences suggests that they perceived these interventions as coercive and that their partners had deliberately drawn upon the association between sex and intimacy in order to persuade them to have sex. Young women were made to feel that their relationships would be in jeopardy if they refused. Far from being an expression of love that girls and women engaged in freely, in the long 1960s many young women found sex to be an obligation and form of emotional exploitation. As mid-century sexual cultures forged new links between sex and intimacy, these links could be used to push against girls' boundaries rather than encouraging young men to respect them.

Conclusion

Between 1950 and 1980, the relationship formations within which girls engaged in sexual activity proliferated. Not only was it increasingly common for girls to engage in pre-marital sex but they were also more likely to engage in sexual activity (penetrative or otherwise) with a range of partners. Taking a broad definition of sex allows us to see, however, that the post-war period represented significant continuities rather than radical change. The sexual cultures explored here mirror those of previous generations; 'petting' and non-penetrative sexual interactions were by no means inventions of the post-war generations.[123] What was changing were girls' perceptions of what kind of relationships were appropriate for incorporating such activities and the relationship stages at which it was acceptable to move from one form of sexual activity to another. Central to these changes and to the messy patterns of sexual behaviour among post-war adolescents were shifting and contradictory understandings of intimacy and its place in sexual relationships.

This chapter has shown that sex was understood to be both formative and constitutive of emotional intimacy. Girls often saw sexual activity as a form of interaction that required a degree of pre-established intimacy – many girls expected to know their partners before engaging in sexual activity and the level of prior intimacy required increased with the level of sexual activity proposed. At the same time, however, it was also believed that engaging in sexual activity was a crucial means of fostering a sense of intimacy within a relationship and that relationships would be incomplete until consummated. Girls could hold both these views simultaneously and, rather than being mutually exclusive, these understandings could be self-perpetuating. Girls therefore had a range of discourses through which to understand and articulate their choice to engage in sex or not.

Where Chapters 1 and 2 drew attention to narratives of proactive choice and deliberate decision-making that underpinned many women's testimonies, the testimonies considered here are a powerful reminder that not all choices are innately empowered. Understanding sexual cultures in the past requires us to attend to the power dynamics and emotional regimes that informed individuals' choices. For many young women, heterosexuality in this period was defined by experiences of coercion and emotional manipulation. These women may have chosen to engage in sex (using today's parlance, these were consensual acts) but these were not positive choices made out of desire, longing, or curiosity but were expressions of love or affection shrouded in fear, sadness, and guilt. Viewing adolescent sexuality through the lens of intimacy rather than romantic love allows us to observe the micropolitics that governed young people's sexual behaviour and the vast array of emotions that informed girls' actions. The emotional components of relationships were not mere backdrops to sexual decision-making but were often pivotal to these deliberations and their outcomes.

Notes

1 Barbara Allen, 'Re-Creating the Past: The Narrator's Perspective in Oral History', *The Oral History Review* 12 (1984); Elizabeth Tonkin, *Narrating Our Pasts: The Social Construction of Oral History* (Cambridge: Cambridge University Press, 1992); Sheridan, 'Mass-Observation as Life History'.
2 Alessandro Portelli, 'What Makes Oral History Different', in *The Oral History Reader*, ed. Robert Perks and Alistair Thomson (London: Routledge, 2016).
3 On cultures of 'dating' after 1970 see Zoe Strimpel, *Seeking Love in Modern Britain: Gender, Dating and the Rise of 'the Single'* (London: Bloomsbury Academic, 2020).
4 Soazig Clifton, Elizabeth Fuller, and Dan Philo on behalf of the Natsal team, *National Survey of Sexual Attitudes and Lifestyles (Natsal-3) Reference Tables*, Table 27, www.natsal.ac.uk/sites/default/files/2020-11/natsal-3-reference-tables.pdf [accessed: 25 September 2024].
5 Histories of courtship include: Claire Langhamer, 'Love and Courtship in Mid-Twentieth-Century England', *The Historical Journal* 50, no. 1 (2007); Stephanie Ward, 'Drifting into Manhood and Womanhood: Courtship, Marriage and Gender among Young Adults in South Wales and the North-East of England in the 1930s', *The Welsh History Review* 26, no. 4 (2013); Laura Harrison, *Dangerous Amusements: Leisure, the Young Working Class and Urban Space*

Boyfriends and sexual partners 165

in Britain, c. 1870–1939 (Manchester: Manchester University Press, 2022), pp. 31–63.

6 Doreen (1959), MOP, 'Courting and Dating' Directive (2001), F2930. Rebecca (1943), MOP, 'Courting and Dating', R1025.
7 Fiona (1946), MOP, 'Courting and Dating', F218.
8 Responses to the MOP, 'Courting and Dating' that expressed this sentiment: Brenda (1956), B2728; Anita (1954), C2053; Anna (1941), C2091; Charlotte (1943), C2654; Annette (1960), C2844; Deborah (1950), D826; Denise (1943), D2585; Donna (1955), D2824; Dorothy (1951), E2836; Fiona (1946), F218; Doreen (1959), F2930; Glynis (1952), G2089; Glenys (1941), G226; Gwen (1953), G2640; Glenda (1950), G2883; Heather (1948), H1703; Jane (1951), H1745; Iris (1940), H2637; Jayne (1941), H2639; Kay (1951), K798; Maxine (1944), N2058; Phyllis (1947), P1796; Rebecca (1943), R1025; Penelope (1948), R2247; Suzanne (1945), S1983; Sarah (1952), S2207; Tina (1949), T1843; Sylvia (1948), T1961; Marlene (1952), T534; Veronica (1951), W1813; Yvonne (1941), W2107.
9 Amanda (1947), MOP, 'Courting and Dating', A1706. See also Marlene (1952), MOP, 'Courting and Dating', T534.
10 Eileen (1951), MOP, 'Courting and Dating', E743.
11 Glenys (1941), MOP, 'Courting and Dating', G226. See also Sarah (1952), MOP, 'Courting and Dating', S2207.
12 On early twentieth-century cultures of courtship see Langhamer, 'Love and Courtship'; Ward, 'Drifting into Manhood and Womanhood'.
13 Hilary (1956), OH-15-01-01.
14 Maureen (1949), OH-15-05-04.
15 Julie (1960), OH-15-02-09.
16 Maureen (1949), OH-15-05-04.
17 Pauline (1944), OH-14-01-03.
18 Daisy (1946), MOP, 'Close Relationships' Directive (1990), B2304.
19 Maureen (1949), OH-15-05-04.
20 Julie (1960), OH-15-02-09.
21 Linda (1952), OH-15-01-03.
22 Maureen (1949), OH-15-05-04.
23 Fleeting references to fancying boys and crushes were made by: Diana (1947), OH-15-01-05; Elsie (1947), MOP, 'Close Relationships', D2123; Sarah (1952), MOP, 'Close Relationships', S2207; Shirley (1949), MOP, 'Courting and Dating', S1399.
24 Joyce (1950), OH-15-03-02.
25 Audrey (1952), OH-15-01-02.

26 Sally (1946), OH-15-05-02; Tina, MOP, 'Sex' Directive (2005), T1843.
27 Hilary (1956), OH-15-01-01.
28 Joyce (1950), OH-15-03-02.
29 Sandra (1949), OH-14-01-02.
30 Janice (1952), OH-15-03-01.
31 Kathleen (1948), OH-15-04-06; Helen (1950), OH-15-03-07; Tracy (1962), OH-14-02-01.
32 Linda (1952), OH-15-01-03; Kathleen (1948), OH-15-04-06; Deborah (1950), MOP, 'Sex', D826; Evelyn (1947), MOP, 'Sex', F3409; Vera (1942), MOP, 'Sex', W632; Dorothy (1951), MOP, 'Courting and Dating', E2538; Marjorie (1952), MOP, 'Courting and Dating', N1552.
33 Tinkler, 'Going Places or out of Place?'.
34 Jacqueline (1945), OH-15-04-03.
35 Doris (1945), OH-15-04-02.
36 Hazel (1947), OH-15-04-05; Kathleen (1948), OH-15-04-06; Helen (1950), OH-15-03-07; Cheryl (1944), MOP, 'Sex', C2078; Harriet (1951), MOP, 'Sex', H1705.
37 Barbara (1952), OH-15-02-03.
38 Rosemary (1958), OH-15-04-04.
39 Ruth (1960), OH-15-02-01.
40 Langhamer, *English in Love*; Dyhouse, *Love Lives*.
41 Judith (1946), MOP, 'Courting and Dating', J931.
42 Theresa (1954), OH-14-01-05; Barbara (1952), OH-15-02-03.
43 'When Does the Kissing Start?', *Jackie*, 5 September 1964. For discussions of the 'right' time to kiss see 'The Cathy and Claire Page', *Jackie*, 14 November 1964; 'The Cathy and Claire Page', *Jackie*, 1 February 1971; 'The Cathy and Claire Page', *Jackie*, 20 February 1971; 'The Cathy and Claire Page', *Jackie*, 25 September 1971; 'Are You Afraid of Boys? Part 2: Who's Afraid of the Big, Bad Wolf?', *Jackie*, 3 June 1976; 'The Dos and Don'ts of Dating', *Jackie*, 11 September 1976.
44 'The Cathy and Claire Page', *Jackie*, 29 February 1964; 'Got You On My Mind', *Jackie*, 11 April 1964; 'The Cathy and Claire Page', *Jackie*, 16 May 1964; 'The Cathy and Claire Page', *Jackie*, 10 October 1964; 'The Cathy and Claire Page', *Jackie*, 31 October 1964; 'The Cathy and Claire Page', *Jackie*, 16 January 1965; 'X Marks the Spot', *Jackie*, 28 August 1976.
45 Denise (1943), MOP, 'Courting and Dating', D2585.
46 Amanda (1947), MOP, 'Courting and Dating', A1706.
47 Langhamer, *English in Love*.
48 Penelope (1948), MOP, 'Courting and Dating', R2247.

49 Marion (1956), MOP, 'Courting and Dating', M2900.
50 Anna E. Ward, 'Sex and the Me Decade: Sex and Dating Advice Literature of the 1970s', *Women's Studies Quarterly* 43, no. 3/4 (2015); Jessamyn Neuhaus, 'The Importance of Being Orgasmic: Sexuality, Gender, and Marital Sex Manuals in the United States, 1920–1963', *Journal of the History of Sexuality* 9, no. 4 (2000).
51 Neuhaus, 'Importance of Being Orgasmic'.
52 On the place of relationships in constructions of adolescent sexuality see Charnock, 'How Far Should We Go?'.
53 Geraldine (1959), MOP, 'Sex', G3395. See also Harriet (1951), MOP, 'Sex', H1705.
54 Carole (1949), MOP, 'Courting and Dating', C1713.
55 Out of the individuals studied (where their pre-marital sexual status is known) approximately 30 per cent engaged in penetrative intercourse only within the context of marriage or engagement; 13 per cent were 'virgin brides'. Oral history interviewees who were virgins on their wedding night included: Vivienne (1944), OH-15-05-05; Mary (1959), OH-15-05-08. Mass Observers responding to the 2005 'Sex' Directive who were virgin brides included: Carole (1949), C1713; Gloria (1950), G3417; Iris (1940), H2637; Jayne (1941), H2639; Lorraine (1951), L3253; Mabel (1946), M3408; Paula (1955), P1009; Pamela (1947), R860; Sherri (1943), S481; Sylvia (1948), T1961; Yvonne (1941), W2107.
56 Heather (1948), MOP, 'Sex', H1703.
57 Veronica (1951), MOP, 'Courting and Dating', W1813.
58 Maria (1956), MOP, 'Sex', M2986.
59 Glenys (1941), MOP, 'Courting and Dating', G226. See also Julie (1960), OH-15-02-09.
60 Anne (1964), OH-14-01-06.
61 Tracy (1962), OH-14-02-01.
62 Judith (1946), MOP, 'Courting and Dating', J931.
63 Jane (1951), MOP, 'Courting and Dating', H1745.
64 Alan Hunt and Bruce Curtis, 'A Genealogy of the Genital Kiss: Oral Sex in the Twentieth Century', *The Canadian Journal of Human Sexuality* 15, no. 2 (2006): 70. See also Szreter and Fisher, *Sex before the Sexual Revolution*, pp. 340–41, 57–58.
65 Tracy (1962), OH-14-02-01.
66 Mabel (1946), MOP, 'Sex', M3408.
67 Theresa (1954), OH-14-01-05 and Kathleen (1948), OH-15-04-06.
68 John H. Gagnon and William Simon, 'The Sexual Scripting of Oral Genital Contacts', *Archives of Sexual Behavior* 16, no. 1 (1987): Fig. IX.

69 Lilian (1946), MOP, 'Sex', L1002, emphasis in original. On changing oral sex practices in the late twentieth century see B. A. Evans, S. M. McCormack, P. D. Kell, J. V. Parry, R. A. Bond, and K. D. Macrae, 'Trends in Female Sexual Behaviour and Sexually Transmitted Diseases in London, 1982–1992', *Sexually Transmitted Infections* 71, no. 5 (1995).

70 Susan Brownmiller, *Against Our Will: Men, Women and Rape* (Harmondsworth: Penguin, 1976); Joanna Bourke, *Rape: A History from 1860 to the Present* (London: Virago Press, 2008); Lucy Delap, '"Disgusting Details Which Are Best Forgotten": Disclosures of Child Sexual Abuse in Twentieth-Century Britain', *Journal of British Studies* 57, no. 1 (2018); Laura Fenton and Penny Tinkler, 'Me Too? Re-Encountering Youth Experiences of Sexual Violence in Post-War England from the Vantage Point of Later Life', *Contemporary British History* 37, no. 3 (2023).

71 Hazel (1947), OH-15-04-05; Theresa (1954), OH-14-01-05; Dawn (1952), MOP, 'Sex', D156.

72 Havelock Ellis, *Studies in the Psychology of Sex Vol. VI: Sex in Relation to Society* (Philadelphia: F. A. Davis Company, 1925), p. 530; Marie Stopes, *Married Love: A New Contribution to the Solution of Sex Difficulties* (London: A. C. Fifield, 1919); Theodoor H. Van de Velde, *Ideal Marriage: Its Physiology and Technique*, trans. Stella Browne (London: William Heinemann, 1928). See also Ettie A. Rout, *The Morality of Birth Control* (London: John Lane, 1925), pp. 30–31, 63–65; William Arbuthnot Lane, *Every Woman's Book of Health and Beauty* (London: Thornton Butterworth, 1936), pp. 49–51.

73 Collins, *Modern Love*.

74 *The Transmission of Life*, p. 15.

75 Le P. Warner, *L for Learner*, p. 14

76 Greet, *Facts of Life*.

77 'Growing Up – Your Questions Answered', *Jackie*, 26 August 1972.

78 'Margot Murray', *Honey*, November 1969.

79 Susan K. Freeman, 'Postwar Sex Education and the Roots of White Male Sexual Entitlement', *NOTCHES: (Re)Marks on the History of Sexuality*, 2016, http://notchesblog.com/2016/10/13/postwar-sex-education-and-the-roots-of-while-male-sexual-entitlement/ [accessed: 25 September 2024].

80 Norma (1943), MOP, 'Sex', P3392. See also Caroline (1944), OH-15-02-05.

81 Jacqueline (1945), OH-15-04-03.

82 Hilary (1956), OH-15-01-01.

83 Oral history interviewees who recalled incidences of sexual harassment, assault, or rape included: Theresa (1954), OH-14-01-05; Linda (1952), OH-15-01-03; Caroline (1944), OH-15-02-05; Helen (1950), OH-15-03-07; Jacqueline (1945), OH-15-04-03; Hazel (1947), OH-15-04-05; Kathleen (1948), OH-15-04-06; Sally (1946), OH-15-05-02; Cynthia (1944), OH-15-05-07. Respondents to the 2005 MOP Directive on 'Sex' who described having experienced some form of sexual assault included: Carole (1949), C1713; Dawn (1952), D156; Debbie (1964), D3289; Deborah (1950), D826; Grace (1954), G1846; Gail (1958), G3042; Gloria (1950), G3417; Heather (1948), H1703; Jane (1951), H1745; Kay (1951), K798; Lesley (1958), L3298; Mandy (1939), M1979; Marian (1964), M3401; Norma (1943), P3392; Pamela (1948), R860; Sarah (1952), S2207; Tina (1949), T1843.
84 Caroline (1944), OH-15-02-05.
85 Eileen (1951), MOP, 'Courting and Dating', E743.
86 Tina (1949), MOP, 'Sex', T1843.
87 Jane (1951), MOP, 'Sex', H1745; Doris (1945), OH-15-04-02.
88 Gloria (1950), MOP, 'Sex', G3417; Marian (1964), MOP, 'Sex', M3401; Rachel (1959), MOP, 'Sex', R2826.
89 Eileen (1951), MOP, 'Courting and Dating', E743.
90 Gloria (1950), MOP, 'Sex', G3417.
91 Amanda (1947), MOP, 'Sex', A1706.
92 George (1941), MOP, 'Sex', G3126.
93 Sarah (1952), MOP, 'Sex', S2207.
94 Glynis (1952), MOP, 'Courting and Dating', G2089.
95 Gwen (1953), MOP, 'Sex', G2640.
96 Mandy (1939), MOP, 'Courting and Dating', M1979; Eileen (1951), MOP, 'Sex', E743; Gail (1958), MOP, 'Sex', G3042.
97 Barbara (1952), OH-15-02-03.
98 On the gender differences in the experience of gender stimulation/apposition see Schofield, *The Sexual Behaviour of Young People*, pp. 76–83.
99 Heather (1948), MOP, 'Courting and Dating', H1703.
100 Hazel (1947), OH-15-04-05. See also Amanda (1947), MOP, 'Sex', A1706.
101 Ten out of fifty-two Observers responded positively to this question, six said they had no experience of this, the remaining thirty-six made no reference to this question. Those who responded positively were: Charlotte (1943), C2654; Deborah (1950), D826; Gwen (1953), G2640; Glenda (1950), G2883; Michele (1956), N2912;

Phyllis (1947), P1796; Pamela (1948), R860; Suzanne (1945), S1983; Sarah (1952), S2207; Yvette (1959), Y2926.
102 Hazel (1947), OH-15-04-05.
103 Joy (1954), OH-15-04-01.
104 Linda (1952), OH-15-01-03.
105 Diana (1947), OH-15-01-05.
106 This mirrors the findings of research into earlier periods. See Szreter and Fisher, *Sex before the Sexual Revolution*, pp. 131–40.
107 Norma (1943), MOP, 'Sex', P3392.
108 Charlotte (1943), MOP, 'Courting and Dating', C2654.
109 Sarah (1952), MOP, 'Courting and Dating', S2207; Yvette (1959), MOP, 'Courting and Dating', Y2926.
110 Helen (1950), OH-15-03-07; Stephanie (1960), OH-15-05-01. See also in MOP 'Courting and Dating' Directive: Charlotte (1943), C2654; Deborah (1950), D826; Gwen (1953), G2640; Glenda (1950), G2883; Phyllis (1947), P1796; Pamela (1948), R860; Suzanne (1945), S1983; Sarah (1952), S2207; Yvette (1959), Y2926.
111 Dorothy (1951), MOP, 'Courting and Dating', E2836.
112 Sarah (1952), MOP, 'Sex', S2207.
113 Penelope (1948), MOP, 'Courting and Dating', R2247.
114 Emma Wallhead, 'A Political Sexual Revolution: Sexual Autonomy in the British Women's Liberation Movement in the 1970s and 1980s', *Twentieth Century British History* 34, no. 2 (2023); Hera Cook, 'Nova 1965–1970: Love, Masculinity and Feminism, but Not as We Know It', in *Love and Romance in Britain, 1918–1970*, ed. Alana Harris and Timothy Jones (Basingstoke: Palgrave Macmillan, 2015); Zoe Strimpel, 'Heterosexual Love in the British Women's Liberation Movement: Reflections from the Sisterhood and After Archive', *Women's History Review* 25, no. 6 (2016).
115 Lynne Segal, *Straight Sex: Rethinking the Politics of Pleasure* (Berkeley: University of California Press, 1994); Carole S. Vance, *Pleasure and Danger: Exploring Female Sexuality* (London: Pandora Press, 1992); Sheila Jeffries, *Anticlimax: A Feminist Perspective on the Sexual Revolution* (London: The Women's Press, 1990); Beatrix Campbell, 'A Feminist Sexual Politics: Now You See It, Now You Don't', *Feminist Review* 5 (1980).
116 Helen (1950), OH-15-03-07.
117 Kathleen (1948), OH-15-04-06.
118 For discussions of urban anonymity see Matt Houlbrook, 'Cities', in *Palgrave Advances in the Modern History of Sexuality*, ed. H. G. Cocks and Matt Houlbrook (Basingstoke: Palgrave Macmillan,

2006), p. 135; Robert Aldrich, 'Homosexuality and the City: An Historical Overview', *Urban Studies* 41, no. 9 (2004).
119 Kathleen (1945), OH-15-04-06.
120 Dawn (1952), MOP, 'Sex', D156.
121 Gwen (1953), MOP, 'Courting and Dating', G2640.
122 Yvette (1959), MOP, 'Courting and Dating', Y2926. See also Shirley (1949), MOP, 'Courting and Dating', S1399.
123 Szreter and Fisher, *Sex before the Sexual Revolution*, pp. 128–31.

4

Friends and peers

Across the post-war decades, girls' relationships with boys had a special status within their social lives. As we saw in the previous chapter, intimate relationships existed in something of a bubble; central to the establishment and deepening of intimacy was the experience of being a couple, separate from others and who saw otherwise-hidden parts of one another. Yet, there was never any way to completely detach romantic lives or shelter intimate relationships from the wider world. Not only were such relationships subject to intense cultural influence through the romance tropes that dominated female-oriented popular culture of this period but the day-to-day reality of young people's existence meant that their romantic relationships were woven into the broader social tapestry of their lives.[1]

This chapter considers outward-facing elements of teenage sexuality to explore the roles that peer networks and friendship groups played in structuring and giving meaning to young women's sexual activity. It argues that cultures of homosociability were central to practices of heterosexuality in the mid-twentieth century. Young women may have been having sex with young men but the meaning of these relationships and this activity was shaped by girls' friendship groups and their broader peer communities. Not only did girls often learn about sex from their friends but girls' attitudes towards sex and their sexual conduct also informed how they related to one another: shared experience could form the basis of female friendships while perceived promiscuity or frigidity could radically alter a girl's place in the social hierarchy.

Situating teenage sexuality in its broader social context makes visible an often underacknowledged dynamic underpinning sexual culture and changing sexual practices in the second half of the twentieth century. From the post-war period onwards, teenage sexuality was characterised by a tension between the imperatives of intimacy and respectability that associated sex with privacy and emerging demands of social status that were based upon young women's sexuality being outward-facing and, to some extent, public. Young women's social networks, particularly when at school, were complex and hierarchical, and the playground politics and politics of popularity that occupied much of girls' time had important sexual elements. Though young women remained invested in notions of 'promiscuity' and were wary of the social sanction that was associated with going 'too far', for girls growing up between 1950 and 1980, sexual knowledge, sexual experience, and proven sexual attractiveness were prized qualities that often raised girls' standing within their peer-based social hierarchies. For girls of the post-war generation, active and visible sexuality could be an asset. These new dynamics and imperatives were key factors in changing cultures of sexual practice and in moving heterosexuality beyond the rigid confines of formal courtship into more nebulous and elastic formations.

Sexuality and social currency

Attempting to get a handle on the demographic changes associated with the post-war baby boom, mid-century sociologists, psychologists, public health professionals, and education researchers committed significant amounts of time to studying the social dynamics of adolescents. At a time when the sheer volume of young people in society made their existence and behaviour more visible, anxieties regarding delinquency and the broader challenges of raising functional citizens for a modern world became a preoccupation for many adults.[2] It was widely accepted that the 'growing up' of adolescence involved a transformation in social behaviour and that the social dynamics of youth represented a marked departure from those of childhood while also being distinct from the social norms and structures of adulthood. As we'll see in the final chapter, young people's relationships with their parents remained important but it was widely held that during adolescence family may be superseded by friends and peers in terms of the influences consciously informing young people's social experiences.

Commentators were keen to stress that this was a universal, developmental process. It was natural for young people to prioritise their relationships with their peers as they became increasingly preoccupied with courtship and more aware of generation 'gaps' that distinguished their experiences from those of their parents.[3] Alongside these universalist explanations, however, this process was understood to take on new dimensions in the post-war period as the 'baby boom' and transformations in society since the Second World War created a distinctive youth culture; in particular, affluence and the rise of mass consumerism worked to set apart the experience of post-war teenagers from that of previous generations.[4] As one lead editorial in the *British Medical Journal* expressed in 1960:

> It seems that modern children are distinguished at play from their predecessors by an urge to read adult periodicals, to dance, to listen to records, and to talk with children of their own age in clubs, cafés and other places where they feel relatively free from the restrictive influence of adults. This urge to be independent ... is encouraged by the higher standard of living which has given young people a purchasing power unimagined by their predecessors ten years ago.[5]

Mark Abrams similarly summarised these developments in his pioneering study of teenage consumption: 'the quite large amount of money at the disposal of Britain's average teenager is spent mainly on dressing up in order to impress other teenagers and on goods which form the nexus of teenage gregariousness outside the home'.[6] British youth were understood to have new, 'modern' values and priorities and were far more concerned with how they viewed one another than how they were seen by adults or authorities.

Peer groups and social status

In adolescence it was not simply girls' emotionally close relationships that shaped their worldviews. Though girls may have prioritised particular friends or friendship groups, their values, understandings of the world around them, and their behaviour were often informed by classmates, social acquaintances, and other peers in their social circles. Peer group identities and collective dynamics were understood to underpin fashion and consumer trends as well as delinquency and were an increasing site of interest for commentators observing changes in sexual mores.[7] Not only was there growing anxiety that, due to a dearth of readily available information about sex, young people were becoming one another's primary source of sex education but, by the 1970s, journalists, doctors, and educators were widely expressing concern at the fact that more and more young people were engaging in pre-marital intercourse out of a desire to keep up with their peers.[8] As the teacher and educational psychologist E. M. Chandler wrote in 1980, 'Everyone else was doing it so I thought I'd better', was now the rationale that many young women used to justify having sex. She went on: ' "Everyone else" is in fact their only guideline as to how to behave ... As everyone else is also an immature adolescent this seems very shaky support for young people undertaking one of the most momentous decisions of their lives.'[9]

Contemporaries such as Chandler understood themselves to be living in the midst of a significant social upheaval and from the vantage point of the twenty-first century this diagnosis rings true. While sex and social reputation have long been interconnected, in the decades after the Second World War this dynamic shifted. Where sexual knowledge and experience had previously had negative value and represented a threat to girls' social standing, in the post-war decades a new economy of social currency emerged that placed great value on sexual knowledge.[10] Though girls had to be careful not to go too far, associations of sex with glamour, attractiveness, and, most of all, maturity, meant that girls with sexual experience could use this to raise their social status. Arguably, this shift represented one of the most profound transformations in modern British social history. Acknowledging that sex had value and served functions beyond reflecting intimacy within couples is essential to explaining not only why the average age at first intercourse fell across the second half of the twentieth century but it is also key to understanding why new forms of heterosexuality emerged in this period, breaking away from traditions of marriage-facing courtship.[11]

Turning to the testimonies, it is clear that for girls growing up in post-war England heterosexuality was not just a matter of romantic desire and/or attraction to a particular individual. Instead, it was deeply entwined with girls' sense of social standing and status among their peers. Women such as Gladys recalled how, during their school years, 'having a boyfriend, preferably from the year above was important'.[12] To an extent, the imperative to find and keep a boyfriend was one cemented by romance culture and advice literature which repeatedly presented the 'heterosexual career' as the central pillar of adolescent femininity.[13] Strikingly, however, women often offered few details about the boyfriends of their teenage years in their testimonies. Instead, interviewees and Mass Observers' testimonies emphasised what these relationships meant for their friendships with girls and social life more broadly. The impulse to have a boyfriend was not solely motivated by romantic interest but was rooted in girls' social networks and reinforced through the everyday interactions that girls had with classmates, peers, and friends.

A teenager in the 1970s, Ruth characterised her time at an all-girls school 'as a constant battle to be with boyfriends ... socially it was all about boys'.[14] Having a boyfriend and engaging in heterosexual culture were central to feelings of belonging when women were teenagers. As Valerie put it, 'It's dreadful but I think we all have it to a greater or lesser extent, we have this need to belong. And I felt that I didn't belong until I had this boyfriend, you know.'[15] Similarly, Andrea remembered '[feeling] the lack of a boyfriend because I was worried about being different from other girls my age, many of whom had boyfriends'.[16] The link between sex and maturity also coloured these feelings – girls' feelings of isolation were intensified by the sense that others were moving ahead without them. In contrast to 'the girls in the playground who were more aware of their surroundings and boys', Caroline 'always felt like [she] was way behind everybody else'.[17] Lynne's teenage anxieties echoed Caroline's as she felt that not having a boyfriend until she went to university set her apart from her friends: 'I was relatively old when I started dating (& concerned & embarrassed that I was obviously left behind in this important activity).'[18] Part of what fuelled the stress of puberty and adolescence was the feeling that this process was happening in public and that it was possible for others to see and track how much growing up girls had left to do.

The desire to have a boyfriend was therefore often as much social as it was romantic. Stephanie's first boyfriend was a boy she spent time with at school. As she recalled though: 'I had no feelings, it was just "Oh, somebody's asked me out! I'll go with him 'cos that means I've got a boyfriend".'[19] Sarah portrayed her teenage self's quest for a boyfriend as fairly undignified: 'I wasn't proud or choosy then just desperate. Oh the joy of being able to boast at school that I was going out with a boy! I definitely felt I was now on a higher plane of existence.'[20] Acquiring a boyfriend was seen as an almost essential component of feminine adolescence and served as a way of establishing social status. This was so pronounced that some girls felt the need to invent boyfriends so as not to lose face. Jill told of how, once the more 'physically mature' girls in her class started going out with boys from outside school, '[t]he rest of us made up fictitious boyfriends who we met at places never frequented by other girls we knew'.[21] From a social standpoint, the impression of having a boyfriend could be more important than the reality of actually having one.

Performing heterosexuality and claiming social status mattered to young women as it fed into the social hierarchies that structured girls' everyday social lives. As psychologists such as J. A. Hadfield explained to contemporaries, in puberty and adolescence it was common for young people to join and form homosocial 'gangs' and 'cliques'.[22] These were often based upon shared interests or experiences (as well as proximity) and, especially within schools, created substructures within peer cohorts. Not only did classmates separate into groups but these different groups were often perceived in hierarchical terms. Though this language was not always deployed by young people themselves, notions of 'popularity' often underpinned these hierarchies and groups which embodied key values enjoyed heightened status and were seen to be at the top of the social hierarchy. As one teenage girl reported to a survey on 'Generation X' in 1963/64, 'Sheila at school slept with her boyfriend and everyone looked up to her, there's a sort of mystique about it'.[23] Interviewees and Mass Observers similarly implied that having boyfriends was closely associated with notions of popularity and being 'cool'.

The daughter of an English academic running a research lab in Jamaica, Alison spent most of her youth in the Caribbean. Her parents decided to move back to England in the mid-1970s when Alison was sixteen in order for her to complete her education in the English system. She did not remember her final years at school particularly fondly – she noted the isolation she felt at being a newcomer in a small community and how her ambitions to go on to university set her apart from her peers. She suggested that she made few female friends but stressed that this did not prevent her from being perceived as being 'popular'. Despite lacking female intimacy, she attracted a lot of male attention and this was enough to give her a degree of social standing:

> I was 16 and I had a succession of boyfriends in [small Midlands town], very quick succession of lots of different boyfriends. I was kind of a little bit exotic so I … y'know, and I, I guess I was … reasonably pretty and everything that might be popular from the boys point of view … Um, and that was sort of how I had human contact and I had friendships and I … was popular.[24]

As Alison's testimony suggests, perceived (and ideally proven) attractiveness to the opposite sex acted as an organising principle in young women's social systems. To be wanted by boys was prized by girls and offered girls opportunities for social standing if not friendship.

Social status was not just determined by the fact of having a boyfriend and 'proving' one's desirability. Rather, social kudos and currency was also linked to the possession of sexual knowledge and experience. As such, aspirations to higher social status could be incorporated into girls' decisions to engage in sexual activity. Asked what had motivated her decision to have sex at sixteen in the late 1960s, Linda replied: 'I knew that other girls in my class had, not that many, but some had. It seemed what people did.'[25] Mirroring Andrea's feelings about boyfriends in general, Marjorie recalled the immense anxiety she felt at remaining a virgin once other girls she knew became sexually active:

> At school, it seemed that sex was the sole topic of conversation. … A bunch of girls in my year talked about little else – on the bus, in class, at break. Increasingly I felt left out, as though I was one of the few virgins left in the world. Although these girls were not my particular friends, nevertheless, they had quite an influence on my friends and me. It was all talk of course, but how was I to know that? I became obsessed by the thought of losing my virginity.[26]

Girls like Marjorie did not primarily think about sex in terms of desire for erotic pleasure or to build intimacy in their romantic relationships. Instead, they saw their virginity as holding them back; without personal experience there was a limit to how much they could engage with the sexual discourse around them. In contrast to the intimacy imperative that drove sexual activity within couples (as discussed in Chapter 3), testimonies such as these reveal how young women's sexual decision-making could be informed by their female-centric social life.

The centrality of sexuality to adolescent frameworks of social status relied upon teenagers' romantic and sexual lives being visible to one another. Some of this visibility was metaphorical, stemming from cultures of boy and sex talk in which young men and women shared details of their relationships and activities with one another. In many contexts, though, this visibility was more literal with teenagers physically witnessing the relationships and heterosexual encounters of those around them. In part, this reflected modern cultures of youth sociability which saw increased mixing of the sexes. Though single-sex organisations persisted across the postwar period,[27] increasing amounts of organised leisure for young people at this time (including but not limited to Young Farmers Clubs, youth wings of political parties, and both religious and secular youth groups) aimed to better socialise boys and girls with one another.[28] At the same time, co-educational schooling was becoming more common.[29] This meant that teenagers' romantic relationships often played out within the context of their broader friendship groups. Cynthia described how her first relationships developed within a pre-existing friendship group. She stressed that these were not usually particularly emotionally involved relationships ('going out with somebody just meant that you kissed them and held hands') and that the group was somewhat 'incestuous' with the couple formations in the group being 'a bit interchangeable'.[30] This account sits neatly alongside Sally's description of her first relationships. Her first boyfriend was one of her 'gang of friends' and when that relationship fizzled out she went out with his best friend.[31]

As Sally made clear, beginning romantic relationships from existing friendship groups did not mean that teenage couples cut themselves off from the group. Instead, couples continued to spend time with the group and made additional friends through one another. Janice often spent time with her boyfriends at youth club while

Rosemary remembered discos as events which brought together friends and partners.[32] She went to discos 'quite a bit' because her boyfriend liked them. She explained, though, that these excursions were not necessarily couple-focused dates: 'I don't think I often went with just him. In fact, possibly never.'[33] Beyond commercial and organised leisure, many couples also spent a lot of time simply 'hanging out' with friends.[34] This was cheap and, though not necessarily romantic, couples enjoyed being together, developing intimacy through mundane proximity. Where previous studies, particularly of young women's social lives, have often presented girls' romantic lives and friendships as antagonistic, this was not necessarily the case.[35] Not only could the two co-exist but they were often integrated. Not all elements of a young couple's relationship may have been visible to friends but the fact of girls' relationships was often public knowledge.

Politics of display

For girls attending same-sex schools, girls could claim social status by displaying their boyfriends, therein ensuring the visibility of their heterosexual success. The school gates, in particular, were key sites for performative sexuality. Joyce attended a prestigious private school in Oxford in the 1960s. She described how her and her friends' boyfriends 'used to meet us at the school gate and you swapped scarves. That was the big thing. You to, you had to wear an MCS [Magdalen College School] scarf and they wore the High School scarf'.[36] Having a boyfriend collect them from school was also a common way of asserting social capital. Reading Kay's testimony, you can sense her younger self's satisfaction as she recalled how 'envious' her friends were when her boyfriend picked her up from school.[37]

Cultures of visibility not only mattered to those wishing to seek social status through having boyfriends. They were also pivotal in the surveillance and judgement of other people's activity. Teenagers did not generally engage in penetrative intercourse or 'higher level' sex acts in public but there was something of a casualisation of physical displays of affection and sexuality across the post-war period, and it was common for school playing fields, corridors, bus shelters, youth clubs, beaches, house parties, the doorways of halls of residence, and other public spaces to be sites of physical intimacies. Where a 1949 Mass Observation report had revealed a general distaste for 'love-making in public', young people of the post-war decades could tolerate, and at times even encourage, others' amorous activities within public spaces, though this did subject such activity to oversight, commentary, and judgement.[38]

To a certain extent, engaging in sexual interactions and activity in public space was an issue of logistics. For some girls, places such as dance halls, nightclubs and cinemas were the only spaces in which they met and/or spent time with boys. Judith, who was fourteen in 1960, described how she used to go looking for boys at the cinema and met her first boyfriend there:

> I went to a girls grammar school, it was very difficult to meet boys ... with 2 friends I used to go to the cinema on a Friday night (on the edge of the council estate). It was obvious that 3 14yr olds would welcome boys talking to them and that is how I met my first boy friend. Everyone at the cinema were either young couples or groups looking to meet the opposite sex (or so it seemed to me).[39]

Although her mother was deeply disapproving of this behaviour (mostly, Judith suggested, because the cinema was at the edge of a council estate and, therefore, Judith 'would only meet boys from the secondary modern there'), the cinema was a social space that was central in facilitating Judith's first experiences of different-sex relationships.

Even more common was the experience of meeting potential romantic interests at dances (much to the chagrin of an Exeter magistrate who could 'scarcely imagine a less suitable place for the engendering of what should be a lifelong affection and devotion').[40] Audrey, for example, described local dances that she attended as a teenager as '[a] bit like clubs now but much more innocent!', and described having her first kiss at a dance at the village hall with a boy that she had met that evening.[41] Similarly, Barbara (who was the same age as Audrey) recalled dances in her local village where the usual pattern was for her to go with a group of girlfriends: 'we'd dance around our handbags, eyeing up the boys who were eying up us'. Eventually the groups would mix and the dance would end with 'a lot of us fumbling'.[42] With few alternative opportunities for interaction with boys, girls such as Audrey seized the moment when it appeared.

Many young people engaged in sex acts in spaces such as cinemas and dance halls because these offered a degree of privacy and comfort that they felt unable to acquire elsewhere. Not wanting their parents to see or know about their activity, and without spaces of their own, many teenage couples took to public spaces that were seen as being free from adult surveillance. Looking back on her experiences of going out to clubs with her friends Tracy described the ubiquity of dancefloor kissing: 'I don't remember there'd be much dancing going on, more sitting on chairs snogging, sucking face and that sort of thing.' She went on: 'in a club, in the dark and then you'd sit on their lap in y'know, club, and it would be it would be a lot of [puts on a funny voice] fondling going on inside your clothes'.[43] This sense that the darkness and distraction of clubs created opportunities for sexual activity was similarly articulated in Eileen's Mass Observation testimony:

> Anyway, back to the first boyfriend. He was at the boys' grammar school, but worked as a DJ at the dance hall in town on Monday nights. When he had a break, we would disappear down one of the backstage corridors for a snog. One night, not too far into the relationship, he put his hand in my knickers and pushed his finger in me. At least, I hoped it was his finger! Being so naïve I did wonder.[44]

Whilst the 'dance' or 'film' were the excuses to go out for the evening, the lack of surveillance in these spaces offered unique opportunities for amorous couples.

That kissing and petting took place in spaces such as cinemas and dance halls is evidence of the ways in which definitions of 'public' and 'private' and their status as prerequisites of sexual activity were elastic, relative, and dependent upon one's imagined audience. Where young women might not have been prepared to 'get off' with their boyfriends in front of their parents, many had fewer qualms about doing so in rooms full of people their own age. Importantly, it was not just the case that teenagers could 'get away with' more in front of their peers. As the successful performance of heterosexuality conferred social status, there were also active incentives for young people to engage in sexual activity in public.

While darkness provided a form of sensory cover to prevent sexual activity and states of undress from being directly visible, a politics of space operated that allowed young people to wield the blurry lines between public and private in their favour. Barbara used the word 'Chummy!' to characterise the sexual culture of her adolescence. She described how 'everybody knew the places' where couples went to engage in physical intimacy on the way home from dances. These places were always dark and Barbara indicated that 'you just had to make sure nobody was in one when you got there'.[45] Barbara and her peers may not have wanted to be watched but when 'everybody knew' what certain spaces were for, a reputation could be built by association. This was similarly true of the infamous back row of the cinema. Across the country, the back row was notorious for being the place where couples more interested in one another than the film would sit.[46] Part of the appeal of the back row was that it was seen to be more private than the other seats in so far as no one could be sat behind, watching what couples were doing.[47] Yet, there was a certain pride and status in being seen on the back row or emerging from the back row and having one's coupled-up status imprinted onto the collective consciousness.

Outside of formal leisure spaces, mixed-sex group gatherings in people's homes facilitated heterosexual interactions and groups demonstrated a high degree of tolerance towards young couples engaging in kissing and petting in their vicinity. House parties were associated with public displays of heterosexuality. Asked what her and her friends did at such parties in the early 1970s, Rosemary replied, 'Well, I think really sitting around drinking and getting off with someone.'[48] Similarly, Joyce's dominant memories of parties were 'talking, sitting on each others' laps and kissing and playing loud music'.[49] Sally was the daughter of a tailor and told of how, when her parents went out to Bridge club on Sunday evenings in the early 1960s, her friends would come over to play cards and listen to music. It was not uncommon for these occasions to become group petting sessions: 'We'd have snogging sessions ... we used to, in the living room and there'd be about 4 or 5 couples all lying on the floor snogging.'[50] Parties such as these offered much sought-after privacy and comfort in so far as they took place inside, in domestic space, and often featured no adult oversight. Both Doris and Phyllis had penetrative sex for the first time at parties, experiences driven at least in part by the rare opportunity to make use of a bed.[51] But these spaces were also public. Other party-goers would see when a couple snuck off upstairs or outside. Girls were often hawkish in keeping track of who was with who and girls' observations would form the basis of party 'debriefs' the morning after.

One consequence of the rising value of sexual experience were rising expectations of heterosexual performance. Discussions of normal teenage heterosexuality incorporated increasingly sexual interactions. Mass Observer Anita did not recall the group dates and parties of her mid-teenage years with much fondness: 'By about 15 I was going out on group dates with girls and boys from my school. Apart from sweaty, soggy fumblings at gatherings in each other's houses, nothing much came of these outings, and I can't say they were very enjoyable.'[52] Rather than seeing 'fumblings' as an expression of desire, girls like Anita were simply going through the motions, feeling that it was easier to play along than risk creating an awkward situation by resisting boys' advances and finding themselves the odd one out.

Cultures of expectation could also characterise the dynamics of dances and discos. Theresa, for example, described how as a teenager in the 1970s she used to judge the 'success' of a dance on whether or not she got a 'snog':

> So, so, y'know, going to, going to dances and youth club and standing on the side and wondering if somebody's going to pick you up y'know, and whether you're going to have a snog or not and sort of writing in a sort of diary that I didn't really keep but y'know a sort of symbol for whether you'd been snogged or not.[53]

Her resounding memory of such dances was not of the music or dancing or of the fun she had there but her teenage self's preoccupation with whether or not a boy would 'pick [her] up'. Christine represented another side of these dynamics of social currency and heterosexual display. She described how she was made to feel that her more platonic interactions with a boy were unusual:

> I think just to prove that I could be street cred, have as much street cred as the rest of them, I think I probably joined the couples … We went to this dance, I suppose I was about 18 and we were dancing and talking and of course he was quite chatty at the time … and we were talking and talking and I overheard in the school cloakroom the following week, one of the friends saying, my nickname at school was C, 'C and B were talking all the time, you know, they were the only ones who were talking to each other, everybody else

was wrapped around, they were all necking, I couldn't understand what they were talking to each other about!'[54]

By the 1960s, when Christine was in her late teens, going to dances with boys and being seen kissing were crucial components in girls' social and sexual lives and young women were expected to be participating in such rituals. In contrast to a spatial politics of privacy that are often assumed to have been central to cultures of sexuality, certain elements of youthful sexuality were designed to be public and on display. Practices of observation and surveillance were used not only to identify transgressive behaviour but also functioned as the basis of positive social currency.

Nice girls

While post-war teenagers were developing their own values and priorities, these did not entirely supplant longer-standing cultures of sexual practice and respectability. One of the things that made the post-war period a particularly challenging time to be a teenager was that numerous discourses of sexuality co-existed and young people had to navigate a path through these, juggling the expectations of different groups. The emerging framework of social currency was certainly influential and new value was placed on sexual knowledge and experience but there remained such a thing as 'too much' experience. There were new incentives to engage in heterosexual coupling but boundaries were drawn around what kinds of heterosexuality were acceptable. Those delineations were rooted in historic traditions of respectability and morality. Adults, particularly parents, worked to establish these values but young people themselves did much of the informal policing of these limits. Though teenagers pushed back against older generations' exhortations to chastity, the logics underpinning these traditions were used to redefine acceptable conduct in the mid-century and justify the sanction of those who transgressed this.

As we saw in Chapter 2, there were material reasons for girls to approach sex with caution; getting pregnant was a threat to the futures of work, marriage, and motherhood to which young women aspired. Yet, what was at stake in warnings about sexuality was not always practical or future-facing. Instead, discourses were often rooted in moral concerns as well as more visceral feelings of distaste. Where teenagers' social hierarchies drew on a currency of popularity, notions of respectability were central to how adults regarded those around them. While teenagers encountered new codes of sexual conduct at school and in youth clubs, it is clear that girls also inherited certain ideas about sexual morality and respectable behaviour from their parents and subsequently drew upon these when considering their peers.

This dynamic was most evident in the construct of the 'nice girl'.[55] For teenage girls in post-war Britain, the 'nice girl' was a potent figure. Women such as Mandy described how, throughout their youth, the expression 'nice girls didn't' was used to promote codes of chastity and sexual restraint.[56] As Mass Observer Carolyn summarised from her experience as a teenager in the early 1960s:

> One of the things that stopped a lot of girls getting into trouble in other words getting pregnant was the concept of the Nice Girl. The older generation passed this down to our generation, you were a nice girl if you didn't run around with lots of different boys, and in other words you were nice and well behaved and most important of all you didn't get pregnant.[57]

Undoubtedly, parents' expectations for their daughters to be 'good' preceded puberty, but as girls entered adolescence these moved beyond expectations of politeness and respect of authority. Upon becoming teenagers girls' status as 'good' was perceived as being under threat from their emerging sexuality.[58]

Exactly what niceness entailed and what was at stake when not being 'nice' was not always clear: Carolyn's testimony suggests that both unplanned pregnancy and being seen to have multiple partners were problematic and it is unclear whether penetrative sex itself was the threshold or a lack of monogamy. Veronica noted similar vagueness in her testimony: 'According to my mother, girls were divided into two categories: "nice" girls and the rest. Those who did. And those who didn't. Unfortunately, she failed to define what exactly it was that they did or didn't do.'[59] Girls could deduce, however, that 'niceness' related to sexual conduct and that it was tightly bound up with notions of moral virtue and social respectability.

Much of the potency of this model stemmed from the fact that, unlike abstract moral lessons about chastity guaranteeing virtue, the idea of the 'nice girl' seemed rooted in the reality of modern society. The nice girl framework did not deny that unmarried people could have sex or that girls might enjoy it. This was a framework of sexual morality that tacitly acknowledged that there were girls who had sex and the model appreciated that young women may be aware of the fact that couples could have sex outside of marriage. Rather than denying or ignoring this, the 'nice girl' framework encouraged girls to refrain from sex on the basis that chastity was the only way to secure their future happiness through marriage. Importantly, although this framework promoted sexual restraint in order to promote individual girls' future happiness, the nice girl model was inherently comparative and encouraged girls to position themselves in relation to their peers. As Mabel stated: 'Girls were divided into nice and not nice (forward) in the sixties.'[60] Although girls were socialised into this belief system by their parents, young women themselves ensured its survival as they judged and policed one another against these codes.

This inheritance and interplay was noted by Glenys, who stressed that this framework was instilled in girls by their parents but was perpetuated by teenage girls who actively used it themselves: 'Contemporaries (female) who were considered "fast" by our parents, and ourselves, tended to flit from one boy to another and leave the area after they left school.'[61] Standing in contrast to the ideal of the chaste 'nice girl', girls could be scathing of open promiscuity which was understood as going 'too far' through the hierarchy of sex acts or sleeping with 'too many' boys/men. The archetype of the 'nice girl' was set against the 'slag', 'slut', or 'slapper' and young women actively used these constructs to judge and condemn the (perceived) behaviours and attitudes of their peers. As Rosemary described: 'it was a general stigma anyway that if you'd had sex with someone you were a bit of a slag'.[62] Similarly, Tracy recalled that, among her convent school community in the 1970s, unless you had 'a serious, serious boyfriend', going beyond 'poking' meant 'you were a right old slapper'.[63] Linda was friends with some of the so-called 'scrubbers' at her school but stressed that 'there was judgement, definitely judgement'.[64] Theresa was particularly candid about having been judgemental of other girls' sexuality:

> There were two groups of girls really. There were those that do and those that don't. Um, and I was quite, um, what's the word? I looked down on the ones that did and made it known to everybody. Y'know, the ones that come home, I mean to school after the weekend, telling everybody how much they'd been at it and that their backs were aching because they'd done so, y'know, I mean it was, it was annoying. Um, and I was sort of scornful.[65]

This oppositional framing saw girls dismiss other young women as cheap, dirty, and beneath them.

The parameters of 'acceptable' behaviour were highly elastic, however, and girls' perspectives often shifted over time, in line with their own experiences. When they themselves became sexually active, girls continued to differentiate their sexual activity from the behaviour of their peers, creating new distinctions that condoned their behaviour but which made others' illicit. After having sex herself at seventeen, Theresa still distanced herself from her 'annoying' peers. What made Theresa's behaviour acceptable in her own eyes was that she kept her sex life 'private' whereas these other girls openly discussed and bragged about their exploits:

> And for some reason I thought, when I started to have sex I thought that my sexual relationship was better and different because I wasn't doing it in the same way. I kept it y'know, I didn't tell people at school. I didn't brag about it. ... Y'know, it was, to them it was a sort of status symbol. And it wasn't to me. ... I wanted to keep, um, keep it a secret somehow. I don't know. I mean I think I still had this slight moral thing about 'Was it right? Was it wrong?' sort of thing. A bit of guilt.

A teenager in the late 1960s, the fact that her peers were having sex was of less concern to Theresa than the fact that they made their sexual exploits public and felt that their sexual experience was something to lord over other classmates. As someone who herself had some trouble reconciling her own sexual activity with her sense of guilt, she was disturbed by her peers' apparent lack of shame. For Theresa, discretion functioned not only as a way of preventing outside moral judgement but became a separate measure of integrity through which sexually active girls could alleviate some of their anxiety around their own behaviour. In this way, 'nice girl' rhetoric was divisive, creating and then perpetuating divisions and hierarchies between girls.

Solidarity and friendship

Cultures of observation, surveillance, and judgement underpinned the figure of the 'nice girl' who worked to create distinctions between girls and was often used as a way of distancing and othering individuals or groups within a social cohort. At the same time, however, discussion about sex could also be the basis of intimacy and shared identity among groups of like-minded and/or similarly experienced girls. As mentioned above, having a 'gang' or 'group' was important to teenagers and many women recalled having strong friendships in their youth. These relationships were often at the heart of girls' social worlds and were the source of much comfort and joy. Perceptions of sexual experience certainly contributed to social hierarchies that distinguished groups but shared sexual values also served to bring girls together.

Friendship groups and collective identity

While some testimonies indicated a certain porousness to group dynamics and the possibility of girls having multiple friendship groups, others described much more closed systems in which friend groups were clearly demarcated.[66] Interviewees and Mass Observers such as Lisa and Julie were quick to stress that they were set apart from their 'cooler' counterparts:

> Even in the Sixth Form, I and my little clique of friends stuck together – none of us had the self confidence of the prettier, more outgoing girls – and competition was fierce as we only had a small Sixth Form.[67]

> I wasn't in the group that were trying to get boyfriends. I was never in the cool group … I was never in the group that, kind of, did that kind of thing … I was still into making sure I did good grades and got my homework done.[68]

While their own groups were characterised in terms of shyness and bookishness, girls at the top of the social hierarchy were notably 'prettier', often more physically developed (in other words, had breasts), and more actively pursued relationships and interactions with boys and men.[69]

In this context, 'nice girl' rhetoric and judgements of other girls' behaviour could function as expressions of moral difference but they also represented a reaction and defence mechanism against social hierarchies based upon sexual experience. Women suggested that speculating about and judging the sex lives of other girls was a group activity. As Evelyn recalled: 'My school friends and I used to compare notes, guessing which other girls "did" with their boyfriends, and which didn't; there's no doubt that we looked down on girls whom we thought "did".'[70] Defining themselves against sexually active 'others', girls such as Evelyn bonded over their 'conventional attitudes', building a collective identity and an important sense of solidarity through their derision of other girls' perceived deviance.

Definitions of 'nice girls' had distinct class dimensions and middle-class girls at private and/or religious schools often perceived sexual values as a key differentiator between them and other girls in their local area. As she explained the boundaries of sexual acceptability among her social group, Joyce made such a comparison:

> I think you, if you went for anything further than the top of, the top score [on the scale of non-penetrative sex acts] then you'd be considered a slut. That was just amongst us, I'm sure. It's just my school, so I'm sure the, the, at the comp at the bottom of the playing field, they had totally different set of ten because I think a lot more of them used to get pregnant as I remember than we did.[71]

Tracy suggested that her and her friends drew similar distinctions when they were teenagers. Tracy was relatively unusual among interviewees in so far as she self-identified as having been one of the 'naughty' girls at her convent school (as opposed to being one of the 'swots'). Although her and her friends were among those that 'did', she was keen to point out that, compared to the other girls in the area who she knew through youth clubs, her sexual activity was relatively tame:

> I remember there was a school down here called Bishop Blackall, they used to call it Bishop Brothel 'cos all the girls that went to the clubs were there [at youth club] you'd always see them out behind the bins with the boys.[72]

Tracy and her friends may have been 'naughty' and sexually active, but they saw themselves as different to the girls at the local comprehensive school whose visible sexuality they viewed as seedy and desperate. Even among girls who were having sex themselves, there was often a group whose behaviour was deemed to be more problematic and who could be used as a point of reference and positive comparison.

Judging the sexual behaviours and reputations of others could serve to reinforce group identities but feelings of cohesion could be disrupted and undermined when girls within a single group came to embody different sexual practices and attitudes. Discussing cultures of sex talk in her school, Linda described how talking about sex and boys recalibrated young women's relationships with one another: 'there was definitely a virginal crowd and they were often quite religious as well … And although they might have been your best friends when you were fourteen, fifteen, suddenly they weren't anymore because you had different values'.[73] In a similar vein, Diana described herself as having been one of the sexual vanguard at her school. Having suggested that her working-class background had always distinguished her from her grammar school friends, Diana positioned her early sexual activity as yet another marker of her difference.

So did you talk about [sex]?

Yeah, yeah. And they all thought I was, I mean, these were girls who were going out with the local grammar school boys and maybe having the odd fumble now and again. I remember once when I thought I was pregnant, because my period was late, actually sitting in the changing rooms at school, completely and utterly distraught and somebody said, 'What on earth's the matter with you?', I said, 'I think I might be pregnant' and the whole place went totally silent. And I think now people, girls would deal with it totally differently but then, it was like just complete and utter shock.[74]

Though she did not suggest that she was ostracised by her peers because of her known sexual activity, this experience reinforced Diana's sense that her life and experience were beyond the comprehension of her peers.

These differences were even more unsettling when they became visible within existing friendship circles. Joy recalled the shock she felt when her friends discussed their sexual exploits:

My friends though were more, I don't know, they were more I s'pose worldly wise and they started going out with boys a lot younger and knew a lot of things … they used to talk about what they got up to and um, to me, I was quite shocked, although I never showed it or said I was shocked, inside I felt shocked at what they were doing.[75]

In describing the evolution of her friendship across her teenage years, Julie recalled how several of her closest friendships disintegrated when her friends began to take an interest in having boyfriends and having sex, interests which she did not share.[76] Marian described being 'surprised shock [sic] and scared' when her best friend revealed that she was having sex: 'I knew that some girls did like that but they had reputations and got pregnant. I hadn't thought G was like that. I thought she was like me.'[77] The anxiety of being 'left behind' was felt even more acutely when it was girls' closest friends who were doing the leaving. When they were focused upon other groups of girls, discussions about sexual morality helped to consolidate friendships and delineate social boundaries. When this discourse was directed inward, however, it had the potential to be destabilising, making visible differences between individuals that were invisible when conversation focused on those 'outside'. Significantly, though, whilst these internal rifts were unsettling to girls such as Andrea and Joy, within groups of friends individuals were not 'vilified' to the same extent as those viewed from a distance.

That girls responded differently to the same sex acts depending on who had done them highlights how assessments of appropriateness and respectability were contingent and contextually defined. Unsurprisingly, girls were more likely to be forgiving of the sexual exploits of their close peers than of girls they barely knew or disliked. Though loyalty played a part, this can also be explained by girls' greater awareness and better understanding of the contexts shaping their close friends' experiences. Rather than observing these relationships from afar and through second-hand gossip, girls had often seen the couple interacting, been involved in the deliberations over whether to have sex and in turn received much fuller retellings of friends' experiences.

Though the codes of intimacy surrounding emotionally committed relationships often demanded a degree of discretion, 'boy talk' and later sex talk were understood to be central pillars of young women's friendships in the post-war decades. Girls talked about who they liked and fancied and they would often debrief after dates and parties.[78] Rosemary, who described parties as a staple of her adolescence, presented the post-party gossip as an extension of the party itself: 'So you'd come in on the Monday at the school gates and "Did you get off with?" or "Did you hear so and so got off with", something and something else. [Laughing] That kind of thing. Yeah. We did talk about that.'[79]

Among their close friends girls often discussed 'how far' along the spectrum of sex acts they had gone with their partners. For some this discussion was a form of one-upmanship related to their ability to attract men ('It was boasting about, "Oh well he must really like me 'cos we've done so and so"'[80]), but for others this reflected genuine curiosity and interest in each other's lives. As Hazel explained:

And would you talk to your friends about sex?

Oh yes, yes, yes.

In what kind of context?

Well, you'd um ... what would you do? Well, you'd sort of talk about, 'Oh, did you kiss? Did you have a grope?' [Both laugh] 'Have you done it yet?'[81]

In her testimony, Audrey conveyed the sense that her and her friends, at high school in the mid-1960s, were deeply curious about sex, lapping up any information and gossip they could. There was much excited chatter when one of her classmates lost their virginity:

Was that quite a scandal?

Oh yes! [Laughing] [whispered tone] 'Oh goodness me, have you heard about?!' Yes, yes. It was quite, it was a mixture of shocking and, 'Oh my goodness, really, gosh!', 'How exciting!!'[82]

Close friendships allowed girls like Audrey to pursue their curiosity by creating opportunities to ask questions about other girls' sex lives ('there wasn't talking in lessons so we'd write notes and we used to write, "How far did you get with him last night?" and that sort of thing, "Oh really, gosh!!"'). As explored in Chapter 1, sex talk became an important site of sex education.

Linda explained that girls such as herself 'talked to people you knew who were doing similar things' to them.[83] These conversations served not only as a way of passing the time whilst at school but created intimacy between friends. These exchanges of experience created meaning in two ways. First, talking about their experiences with friends provided girls with an opportunity to process and make sense of what they had been doing and how they felt about it. These conversations gave girls the chance to step back from the heady intensity of sexual encounters to consider what they meant in the light of day. Second, because sex was seen as something taboo, sacred, and/or secret, including other girls within the experience became a way of demonstrating trust and fostering intimacy within those friendships.[84]

Intimacy and emotional support

This intimacy mattered because it fostered trust and care, which in turn guaranteed that girls could turn to their friends for comfort and support when faced with crisis. Numerous women recalled how discussions of sexual activity were prompted by other girls' unfortunate experiences, including unexpected pregnancy. Marilyn suggested that a classmate's pregnancy was something of a turning point for her and her friends: 'Sex didn't really form part of our conversation at school until one of the girls in my class at school had a termination.'[85] Hilary remembered that in her school days she spent 'a lot of time with weeping, distraught friends' who were 'having unprotected sex and then worrying desperately whether [they were] pregnant'.[86] Girls turned to each other to work through their feelings. The reassurance girls sought from one another often bought into and perpetuated the 'Nice Girl' binaries: girls sought to comfort themselves by pointing out the deviancy and difference of those who got pregnant. Joyce recalled the scorn she and her peer expressed for one of their classmates who became pregnant in her mid-teens in the mid-1960s: 'We weren't sympathetic, or some people were, but most of us weren't sympathetic and just thought "how simple can you get?!"'[87] Amongst other groups, however, there was a sense of solidarity. As Tracy recalled:

> We were all quite shocked when my friend got pregnant ... I told you we had these older sisters, my friend had older sisters, and her friend got pregnant and this was private school and it was all very 'Oh, er.' And I think we were all quite shocked by that, I think it scared us a bit um, that she, she had got pregnant.[88]

Teenage girls did not simply revel in the misfortune of others – they could be genuinely unsettled by others' situations and often turned to each other to help make sense of these events.

This was particularly apparent when interviewees discussed their own experiences of crises. When romantic relationships ended, girls' friends were a source of comfort. Although she believed that, as a teenager, she and her friends were less emotionally articulate than contemporary youth, Audrey showed great emotional vulnerability to her school friends when she broke up with her first serious boyfriend:

So had you talked to your friends about this relationship at all?

Yes, yes I had, yes, yes. And I did actually, I remember, I would've told them and other close friends, where I used to live there were a couple that I used to write to a lot, I told them that it'd happened and the, the little group I was friendly with at [school] I told. Yeah. And then I sobbed with them when he finished it ...

Were they quite supportive?

Yes, yes. Yeah, they were. [89]

Audrey had a difficult family situation growing up and left home to attend a prestigious private school in her teenage years in the mid-1960s. Away from home, Audrey's friends functioned as her primary support network. As her case demonstrates, not only did social networks confer meaning upon sexual experience but her travails in heterosexuality provided a basis upon which her female friendships were deepened. Having a boyfriend gave her something to talk about with her friends and, when the relationship ended, her friendships were deepened through the support they could offer at this time of grief.

Girls' peers were also mentioned as pillars of support in discussions of other problems. Given the stigma of pregnancy outside of marriage and the fact that the 'Bad Girl' model of sexual morality was one many girls associated with their parents, girls who became pregnant often attempted to conceal this from their families. Jacqueline got pregnant at twenty-one and her parents encouraged her to get an abortion. When she became pregnant again a year later she decided not to tell her parents and had to find the money to acquire an abortion herself. Keeping the secret from her parents out of shame, Jacqueline nevertheless felt able to ask her friends for help: 'Asking my own generation was perfectly alright because everybody's getting pregnant, right, left and centre.'[90]

Sally also had a 'backstreet' abortion and recalled how a close friend was the only person she felt she could talk to: 'And I can remember the misery of it, I couldn't tell my parents ... I was absolutely desperate and I remember talking to this girlfriend, this older one who I'd stayed with for a while who was a nurse, she put me in touch with a backstreet abortionist.'[91] Sally described her distress as she found herself caught in an abusive relationship and living away from home: 'It was dreadful. I was 18 didn't know what to do. Couldn't tell my parents 'cos they hated him in the first place, didn't know about the abortion.' Friends were a valued source of emotional help and support for young women in crisis though, as Sally explained, there were limits to this support: 'My girlfriends were only 18 themselves and didn't know what to do.' While young women displayed an immense capacity for compassion for their friends, at times they lacked the power or material resources to offer tangible help for those in need. Peer support in response to unplanned pregnancy and domestic abuse was an invaluable resource for young women but it could not always bear the weight required.

Beyond crises, conversations with peers were also helpful to young women in lower-stakes contexts as they tried to make sense of their own sexual feelings and experiences. In addition to being a vital source of sexual knowledge, talking about sex helped girls to navigate the 'new' discourses of female pleasure and sexual empowerment that were circulating in the post-war period. As numerous historians have noted, from the late 1960s and throughout the 1970s, popular culture promoted the notion that female pleasure should be a crucial component of sex.[92] Sex-positive guidance literature such as Alex Comfort's *The Joy of Sex* and magazines like *Cosmopolitan* utilised notions of sexual selfhood, arguing that women had a right to sexual pleasure and that sexual satisfaction was essential to their wider happiness.[93] Jacqueline suggested that living in London in the late 1960s, she was aware of these new discourses of sexual liberation, but that they did not necessarily translate into the reality of sexual practice: 'Um, *Cosmo* came along and taught us how to have an orgasm, but it wasn't sort of, "My God, this is the thing I must do with my life! I must spend every Saturday night having orgasms". It was, "Oh, that's interesting".'[94]

Thinking back on the sexual experiences of their youth, many Mass Observers and interviewees suggested that the sexual encounters of their youth offered them little in the way of sexual pleasure. Alison, Barbara, Doris, Kathleen, and a number of others made a point of mentioning that their early sexual experiences did not involve them having orgasms.[95] Theresa explained that the idealised image of sex that she had encountered in novels and films had created expectations of romance and pleasure that her early sexual experiences did not live up to:

> So with those expectations of sex, how did you find the real thing?
>
> Well, it was, y'know, it's much, it's much less romantic isn't it? Y-y'know, you're not being wooed in a caravan by a, by a beautiful man. I s'pose, um ... What do I remember? I remember it not being um, not being that satisfactory in terms of my own pleasure for quite a while.[96]

This disjuncture between what girls were reading and what they were experiencing could be disorientating. Jacqueline suggested, however, that talking to her friends and peers about sex was important in helping her to negotiate the differences between what she was doing and feeling and what didactic literature was suggesting:

> There was an expectation it was going to be all bells and lightening and the whole world's going to rock and you're going to change. ... Not in my twenties, in my early, in my teens, yeah, yeah. And that was a disappointment. And then you met girls where it did and you thought, 'Oh my God, there's something wrong with me!' And then you met girls who didn't, you thought, 'No, I'm okay'. But we all talked, you know, as women do, talked and talked about things like this.[97]

This experience was echoed by Barbara:

> There was a belief when you were starting out that you should have [an orgasm] every time. I was quite worried because I wasn't having one every time. You know but then I had friends, girlfriends, and I talked to them and neither were they. And not only that, they weren't having them very often at all. [*Right*.] ... So I didn't feel

particularly hard done by or unusual because I checked out with my friends and they were having the same experiences as me ... I understood the difference between reality and what people thought should be going on.[98]

Though young women did not necessarily feel empowered to demand more considerate sex from their partner, young women's cultures of sex talk were important in demystifying sex and, in particular, in helping women to realise that there was nothing 'wrong' with them.[99] For women of the post-war generation, there could be immense comfort in finding one's self to be part of a crowd.

Conclusion

Recognising the central role of friendship groups and peers in young people's lives is essential to understanding why increasing numbers of teenagers were engaging in sexual activity as well as why young people managed their intimate lives in the ways they did in the post-war decades. Far from simply being the backdrop against which young people's intimate lives played out, peer groups and social networks were key characters in women's accounts of adolescence and played an important role in shaping the meaning of romantic interactions and sexual activity. The potential outcomes of sex now included increased standing among one's peers. Though the limits of these encouragements had their roots in the sexual cultures of chastity and restraint articulated by adults, these were given new life and were internally policed by young women themselves.

At the same time that the post-war period saw an evolution in how sex functioned within respectability politics, as sexual practice became increasingly common among young people, it also came to feature more prominently within cultures of female friendship. Beyond the realms of reputation management, within close friendships girls were able to articulate their anxieties and concerns about sex, to celebrate the joys and heartbreaks of courtship, and share the wisdom they'd learnt on the 'front line' of experience. Often feeling adrift from the perceived 'safety' of childhood and the self-assuredness of adulthood, young women embraced having company and shoulders to cry on. Whilst publicly performed sexual experience was a volatile social currency at this time, girls often gained a lot in terms of collective identity, reassurance, condolence, and support by sharing their experiences with friends.

In these ways, girls of the post-war generations did not simply respond to changing sexual mores in the 1950s, 1960s, and 1970s but were themselves responsible for recalibrating imperatives of sexuality. Through their words and actions they were creating a new social landscape in which sexual activity was both prized and punished. They were establishing new incentives and imperatives for intimate relationships and youthful sexuality. All this change was not, however, entirely immune to more conservative elements. Girls were forging new paths and building hierarchies that spoke to their own desires and expectations but modern sexual cultures did not divorce itself completely from long-standing traditions that were uneasy with 'promiscuity' and, as the next chapter explores, older generations' rules and values were something that young women had to negotiate and manage.

Notes

1 Dyhouse, *Love Lives*; Stephen Brooke, '"A Certain Amount of Mush": Love, Romance, Celluloid and Wax in the Mid-Twentieth Century', in *Love and Romance in Britain, 1918–1970*, ed. Alana Harris and Timothy Willem Jones (Basingstoke: Palgrave Macmillan, 2015).
2 For overviews see Bill Osgerby, *Youth in Britain since 1945* (Oxford: Blackwell, 1998); John Davis, *Youth and the Condition of Britain: Images of Adolescent Conflict* (London and Atlantic Highlands: The Athlone Press, 1990).
3 J. A. Hadfield, *Childhood and Adolescence* (Harmondsworth: Pelican Books, 1962); C. I. Sandström, *The Psychology of Childhood and Adolescence*, trans. Albert Read (Harmondsworth: Pelican Books, 1966); E. H. Erikson, *Childhood and Society*, revised edn (St Albans: Triad, 1977).
4 John Barron Mays, *The Young Pretenders: A Study of Teenage Culture in Contemporary Society* (London: Michael Joseph, 1965); Peter Laurie, *Teenage Revolution* (London: Anthony Blond, 1965). For an American perspective see John Janeway Conger, 'A World They Never Knew: The Family and Social Change', *Daedalus* 100, no. 4 (1971).

5 'Adolescence', *British Medical Journal*, 23 July 1960, pp. 281–82. This was a fairly common subject of comment in the medical press. See, for example, 'Youth in Modern Society', *The Lancet*, 17 October 1959, p. 607; 'Growing Up Today', *The Lancet*, 16 July 1960; 'Adolescent, Teenager, or Human Being?', *The Lancet*, 8 April 1961, p. 757.
6 Abrams, *Teenage Consumer*, p. 10.
7 Abrams, *Teenage Consumer*; T. R. Fyvel, *The Insecure Offenders: Rebellious Youth in the Welfare State* (Harmondsworth: Pelican Books, 1963); Mary Morse, *The Unattached* (Harmondsworth: Pelican Books, 1965). On adolescent social life see Peter Willmott, *Adolescent Boys of East London*, revised edn (Harmondsworth: Pelican Books, 1969).
8 On peer-led sex education see Farrell, *My Mother Said*. Fears about sex for kudos are typified in the furore that erupted when a doctor claimed that some schoolgirls wore badges to signify that they had lost their virginity. 'Their Badge of Shame', *Daily Mirror*, 18 July 1961; 'Golliwog Sign of Girls' Dishonour', *The Daily Telegraph*, 18 July 1961; 'V.D. Among the Young Worries Doctors', *The Times*, 18 July 1961; 'Yellow Badge of Shame', *Daily Mail*, 18 July 1961; 'Wanted … a Badge of Purity', *Daily Mail*, 1 November 1961; Monica Furlong, 'Before You Pin White Doves on YOUR Daughter', *Daily Mail*, 2 November 1961.
9 E. M. Chandler, *Educating Adolescent Girls* (London: Unwin Education Books, 1980), pp. 122–23.
10 Szreter and Fisher, *Sex before the Sexual Revolution*; Roberts, *Women and Families*.
11 Wellings et al., *Sexual Behaviour in Britain*. On older forms of courtship see Langhamer, 'Love and Courtship'; Ward, 'Drifting into Manhood and Womanhood'.
12 Glenys (1941), MOP, 'Sex' Directive (2005), G226.
13 Melanie Tebbutt, 'From "Marriage Bureau" to "Points of View": Changing Patterns of Advice in Teenage Magazines: *Mirabelle*, 1956–1977', in *People, Places and Identities: Themes in British Social and Cultural History, 1700s–1980s*, ed. Alan Kidd and Melanie Tebbutt (Manchester: Manchester University Press, 2017); Penny Tinkler, *Constructing Girlhood: Popular Magazines for Girls Growing up in England, 1920–1950* (London: Taylor & Francis, 1995).
14 Ruth (1960), OH-15-02-01.
15 Valerie (1947), OH-15-05-06.
16 Andrea (1957), MOP, 'Sex', A2212.
17 Caroline (1944), OH-15-02-05.
18 Lynne (1949), MOP, 'Courting and Dating' Directive (2001), T2003.

19 Stephanie (1960), OH-15-05-01.
20 Sarah (1952), MOP, 'Courting and Dating', S2207.
21 Jill (1959), MOP, 'Sex' (2005), H3459.
22 J. A. Hadfield, *Childhood and Adolescence* (Harmondsworth: Pelican Books, 1962), pp. 206–15; Roy Nash, 'Clique Formation among Primary and Secondary School Children', *British Journal of Sociology* 24, no. 3 (1973).
23 Charles Hamblett and Jane Deverson, *Generation X* (New York: Fawcett Publications, 1964).
24 Alison (1960), OH-14-02-02.
25 Linda (1952), OH-15-01-03.
26 Marjorie (1952), MOP, 'Courting and Dating', N1552.
27 On the girl guiding movement in the post-war period, for example, see Jim Gledhill, 'White Heat, Guide Blue: The Girl Guide Movement in the 1960s', *Contemporary British History* 27, no. 1 (2013).
28 Collins, *Modern Love*; Lawrence Black, 'The Lost World of Young Conservatism', *The Historical Journal* 51, no. 4 (2008); Sian Edwards, '"Nothing Gets Her Goat!" The Farmer's Wife and the Duality of Rural Femininity in the Young Farmers' Club Movement in 1950s Britain', *Women's History Review* 26, no. 1 (2017). On the benefits of mixing see Pearl Jephcott, *Girls Growing Up* (London: Faber & Faber, 1943), chapter VI.
29 Margaret B. Sutherland, 'Whatever Happened about Coeducation?', *British Journal of Educational Studies* 33, no. 2 (1985).
30 Cynthia (1944), OH-15-05-07.
31 Sally (1946), OH-15-05-02.
32 Janice (1952), OH-15-03-01.
33 Rosemary (1958), OH-15-04-04.
34 Audrey (1952), OH-15-01-02; Beverley (1960), MOP, 'Courting and Dating', B2031.
35 Christine Griffin, *Typical Girls? Young Women from School to the Job Market* (London: Routledge and Kegan Paul, 1985). On representations of friendship and romance as antagonistic, see Angela McRobbie, *Feminism and Youth Culture: From Jackie to Just Seventeen* (London: Macmillan, 1991), pp. 100–2.
36 Joyce (1950), OH-15-03-02.
37 Kay (1951), MOP, 'Courting and Dating', K798.
38 Mass Observation, 'Love-Making in Public', MOA, file report 3086, February 1949, p. 13.
39 Judith (1946), MOP, 'Courting and Dating', J931.
40 'Why Pick on the Palais?', *Daily Mirror*, 24 January 1955. A survey by the Population Investigation Committee found that over a quarter

of British couples who married between 1950 and 1959 had met at a dance or dance hall. Rachel M. Pierce, 'Marriage in the Fifties', *Sociological Review* 11 (1963): 219.
41 Audrey (1952), OH-15-01-02.
42 Barbara (1952), OH-15-02-03.
43 Tracy (1962), OH-14-02-01.
44 Eileen (1951), MOP, 'Sex', E743.
45 Barbara (1952), OH-15-02-03.
46 Ruth (1960), OH-15-02-01; Muriel (1940), MOP, 'Sex', P1009. From MOP, 'Courting and Dating': Glynis (1952), G2089; Penelope (1948), R2247.
47 Anita (1954), MOP, 'Courting and Dating', C2053.
48 Rosemary (1958), OH-15-04-04.
49 Joyce (1950), OH-15-03-02. See also Evelyn (1947), MOP, 'Sex', F3409.
50 Sally (1946), OH-15-05-02.
51 Doris (1945), OH-15-04-02; Phyllis (1947), MOP, 'Sex', P1796. Yvette (1958), MOP, 'Sex', Y2926 also comments on others having sex at parties.
52 Anita (1954), MOP, 'Courting and Dating', C2053.
53 Theresa (1954), OH-14-01-05.
54 Christine (1947), OH-15-03-03.
55 The concept of the 'nice girl' and its use as a form of social control was theorised by feminist scholar Greer Litton Fox in the late 1970s, Greer Litton Fox, '"Nice Girl": Social Control of Women through a Value Construct', *Signs* 2, no. 4 (1977).
56 Mandy (1939), MOP, 'Courting and Dating', M1979. See also Doris (1945), OH-15-04-02. See also in MOP, 'Sex': Dawn (1952), D156; Deborah (1950), D826; Mabel (1946), M3408; Norma (1943), P3392.
57 Carolyn (1947), MOP, 'Sex', C1832. For additional examples see Chapter 5.
58 Abrams, 'Mothers and Daughters'.
59 Veronica (1951), MOP, 'Courting', W1813.
60 Mabel (1946), MOP, 'Sex', M3408.
61 Glenys (1941), MOP, 'Sex', G226.
62 Rosemary (1958), OH-15-15-04.
63 Tracy (1962), OH-14-02-01.
64 Linda (1952), OH-15-01-02.
65 Theresa (1954), OH-14-01-05.
66 Joyce (1950), OH-15-03-02.
67 Lisa (1957), MOP, 'Sex', L3037.
68 Julie (1960), OH-15-02-09. See also Mary (1958), OH-15-05-08.
69 Pauline (1944), OH-14-01-03.

70 Evelyn (1947), MOP, 'Sex', F3409.
71 Joyce (1950), OH-15-03-02.
72 Tracy (1960), OH-14-02-01.
73 Linda (1952), OH-15-01-03.
74 Diana (1947), OH-15-01-05.
75 Joy (1954), OH-15-04-01. See also Andrea (1957), MOP, 'Sex', A2212.
76 Julie (1960), OH-15-02-09.
77 Marian (1964), MOP, 'Sex', M3401.
78 Barbara (1952), OH-15-02-03; Janice (1952), OH-15-03-01.
79 Rosemary (1958), OH-15-04-04.
80 Tracy (1962), OH-14-02-01.
81 Hazel (1947), OH-15-04-05.
82 Audrey (1952), OH-15-01-02.
83 Linda (1952), OH-15-01-03.
84 On cultures of women's talk earlier in the twentieth century, see Melanie Tebbutt, *Women's Talk? A Social History of 'Gossip' in Working-Class Neighbourhoods, 1880–1960* (Aldershot: Scolar Press, 1995).
85 Marilyn (1955), MOP, 'Sex', M3476. See also Audrey (1952), OH-15-01-02.
86 Hilary (1956), OH-15-01-01.
87 Joyce (1950), OH-15-03-02.
88 Tracy (1962), OH-14-02-01.
89 Audrey (1952), OH-15-01-02.
90 Jacqueline (1945), OH-15-04-03.
91 Sally (1946), OH-15-05-02.
92 Ward, 'Sex and the Me Decade'; Steven Seidman, 'Constructing Sex as a Domain of Pleasure and Self-Expression: Sexual Ideology in the Sixties', *Theory, Culture & Society* 6, no. 2 (1989); Wallhead, 'A Political Sexual Revolution'.
93 Alex Comfort, *The Joy of Sex: A Gourmet Guide to Lovemaking* (London: Simon & Schuster UK, 1972); 'The Good Sex Guide', *Cosmopolitan*, December 1972; 'The Myth of the Sexual Revolution', *Cosmopolitan*, December 1974; 'Female Orgasms: What It Is and What It Isn't', *Cosmopolitan*, September 1972.
94 Jacqueline (1945), OH-15-04-03.
95 Alison (1960), OH-14-02-02; Barbara (1952), OH-15-02-03; Doris (1945), OH-15-04-02; Jacqueline (1945), OH-15-04-03; Kathleen (1948), OH-15-04-06. See also Gail (1958), MOP, 'Sex', G3042; Geraldine (1959), MOP, 'Sex', G3395.
96 Theresa (1954), OH-14-01-05.
97 Jacqueline (1945), OH-15-04-03.
98 Barbara (1952), OH-15-02-03.
99 Alison (1960), OH-14-02-02; Doris (1945), OH-15-04-02.

5

Parents and family

In January 1965, an article headline in *Honey* magazine proclaimed that, 'Parents are People Too'.[1] Acknowledging the important presence of parents in young people's lives as well as parents' potential to be 'a handicap' on teenagers' dating careers, the article offered a series of tips for managing parents. In so far as the article suggested strategies based on increasing communication between girls and their parents ('Talk to them', 'Ask their advice', 'Spend time with them.'), the piece conformed to much of the conventional wisdom of agony aunts of this period that prescribed an approach of rational engagement and compromise to bring daughters and their parents closer together. But 'Parents are People Too' had a sting in its tail. For all that the article recognised parents' anxieties and insecurities about their daughters' social lives and was, to a certain extent, sympathetic to these, the piece was fundamentally a guide on manipulating parents. The piece was not in fact recommending emotionally authentic intergenerational communication but instead offered strategies to subvert this to help teenage girls get their own way. Girls were advised to overshare the boring details of their dates, to selectively represent their boyfriends, and to ask advice on issues they did not really care about in order to 'neutralise' and pacify their parents so that they could get on with the more controversial aspects of their social lives without parental interference. The tone of the article was not unkind – in fact, it was paternalistic in its characterisation of parental worries – but the piece flipped the usual dynamics associated with parent–child relationships. Faced with parents who could not accept teenagers' lives and desires, young people were advised not to confront authority figures but work around them.

The post-war period has long been associated with intergenerational conflict. In the 1950s, 1960s, and 1970s, the violence linked to Teddy Boys, Mods, Rockers, and Punks, the disruption of student protests, and the explicit anti-establishment ethos of the counter-culture were used as examples of social breakdown and fraying relations between adult society and young people.[2] In the decades since, a continued academic focus on youth delinquency and movements of resistance has magnified this characterisation.[3] More recently, however, a turn to consider the everyday aspects of youth cultures and to study 'unspectacular' youth has begun to push back on straightforward understandings of a generation gap and the association of youth with rebellion. Through his study of student protest in the 1960s, Nick Thomas has shown that youth protest was not necessarily about destroying adult-led institutions but about young people wanting a greater stake in them.[4] At the same time, in showing that older generations liked rock 'n' roll of acts such as Bill Haley in the 1950s, Gillian A. M. Mitchell has called into question the assumption that 'new' and 'modern' tastes were exclusively the preserve of young people.[5]

'Parents are People Too' and the testimonies explored in this chapter suggest a different, though not incompatible, dynamic within adult–youth relations in the twentieth century. They indicate that when it came to the matters of social life, intimate relationships and sexuality, the attitudes of teenage girls often diverged from those of their parents. While girls may have been prepared to comply with their parents' rules (at least to a point), in many cases they were not prepared to sacrifice their relationships with boys. At the same time, though, girls were not necessarily willing to have these intimate relationships disrupt or destroy their home lives. Although many girls were comfortable defying their parents' rules and values, they often wanted to avoid outright conflict. Girls cared about their relationships with boys, but they also cared about their relationships with their parents. Balancing the two of these was an important dynamic shaping teenage girls' sexual lives. As 'Parents are People Too' suggested, the key to achieving this balance lay not in open communication and compromise but instead in lies, subterfuge, and maintaining the *illusion* of compliance.

Gatekeeping and validation

In the post-war period, most teenage girls lived at home. Older girls were certainly more mobile at this time than they had been in previous generations – increasing numbers of girls left home upon finishing school to go to university, pursue professional training (such as nursing college or teacher training), or to get work elsewhere – but the majority of young women of the post-war generation lived with their families until they got married.[6] The average age of marriage fell across this period but the proportion of couples who lived together before marriage remained low: of those marrying for the first time between 1971 and 1975, only 9 per cent cohabited before getting married.[7] The family home and the influence of parents was therefore a notable presence in young people's day-to-day lives. As the sociologist Diana Barker noted in 1972, this had 'important effects' on young people's heterosexuality as it affected 'who one meets, the extent to which one shows commitment, the social pressures to continue or discontinue a relationship, [and] the amount of privacy possible for the development of emotional and sexual intimacy'.[8]

As minors and dependents, teenage girls were subject not only to the laws of the land but also to the rules and expectations set out by their parents and guardians. Within oral histories, women often characterised their teenage years as a time when their relationships with their parents shifted. Testimonies often contrasted accounts of relatively 'free' childhoods with more fractious youths when parents' involvement in their lives became more troublesome. As explored later, these tensions were, in part, a generation-specific problem but they were also seen as part of the universal experience of adolescence. As Hazel reflected, 'inevitably, in your teenage years you have clashes [with your parents] I think that's part of growing up'. These flashes were fleeting though, and Hazel very clearly asserted that these did not get in the way of her having a good relationship with her parents.[9]

Parental rules and curfews

When it came to girls' interactions and relationships with boys, it was common for parents to set curfew, to police what girls wore, and to clearly set the limits of 'acceptable' behaviour. Asked directly about this kind of control in the 2001 Directive on Courting and Dating, Mass Observers presented a varied picture of post-war parenting with some parents portrayed as having been much stricter than others.[10] But while parental interventions into girls' social lives were often portrayed as having been frustrating and embarrassing for the teenagers involved, the majority of Mass Observers suggested that they usually complied with the direction of their parents. They may not have liked the rules, but they obeyed them.

Some women indicated that this compliance simply reflected the universally accepted status of children at this time. According to Wendy, 'Parents, in those days, had far more control over where one went, with whom & what time one had to be home. If they said no, that was it.'[11] Directly contrasting her childhood with those of her children and grandchildren, Daphne insisted that her generation was kept 'on a far tighter rein' than contemporary youth and that young people in the 1950s, 1960s, and 1970s had neither the capacity nor the inclination to defy their parents.[12] For other interviewees and Mass Observers, the dynamic was less authoritarian. Claiming that she 'didn't go as mad as some people did', in her teenage years, Joyce explained: 'I came from quite a traditional family with very happy parents and a good atmosphere, and I went to a really academically challenging school ... and had a lot of moral behaviour and good middle class values in inverted commas "drilled into me".'[13] Maureen, who grew up in a devout Catholic household, stressed that 'it never occurred to' her to disrespect her parents: 'You know, it's like that kind of Catholic thing, "Honour thy father and thy mother," which was ingrained.' Beyond religion, however, she indicated that her compliance came from a place of recognition: 'I knew that whatever they did, they did for the very best. Their motivation was very caring.'[14] Girls conformed to their parents' rules because they shared, or at least acknowledged, their underlying logic. Teenagers may have found certain boundaries frustrating but they did not entirely dismiss their validity.

As explored in Chapter 2, aspirations for bright girls to go to university increased significantly over the twentieth century and, as such, many middle-class parents were uneasy about their daughters beginning relationships in case they should interfere with girls' schooling and future prospects.[15] Gwen understood this logic to be at the heart of her parents' blunt and restrictive approach to her emerging social life as she was growing up in the late 1960s and early 1970s:

> My parents (especially my mother) had a <u>very</u> good try at controlling when I dated and where I could go. My school work had to come first. ...
>
> When I fell in love with a fellow student at university, my parents would not allow me to become engaged to him. They alleged an engagement ring would distract me from my studies and said I was too young.[16]

Although she resented their intervention in so far as it 'led to the collapse' of her romantic relationship, Gwen did not reject the importance of her education. Many girls embraced the futures that their education would give them and were prepared to sacrifice heterosexual relationships to pursue their studies or work.[17] Having been raised by parents who expected and encouraged academic excellence, girls bought in to their parents' faith that education would provide them with greater future prospects. Even if they rankled with the fact that they could not have everything they might want, many girls complied with their parents' restrictions, seeing them as part of a longer-term investment in their futures.

Girls' faith that their parents had their best interests at heart similarly explains adherence to parents' rules regarding the logistics of dating. Curfews were a common feature of women's stories of teenage romance and sexuality. Parents set strict limits on when girls needed to return home from dates and nights out. Yvette 'was not allowed out much in the week and had to be in on time'.[18] Similarly, Beryl remembered having 'a lovely courtship' with her future husband although her father 'laid down the law' about what time she had to be home at night: 'It was 10 o'clock during the week and on Sunday and 11 o'clock on Friday and Saturday nights.'[19] Many teenagers simply accepted this aspect of their social lives; 'it was understood that [they] would be home at a reasonable time'.[20] Girls recognised that their parents set restrictions like these out of care and concern for their safety and well-being and so they simply organised their evenings in a way that accommodated their parents' rules. Young people who relied upon public transport to access leisure activities structured their dates around their curfew and the bus timetable.

> [My mother] insisted that I got home by 10.30 which meant missing the end of the film but I always did as she said and any time I was late it was by misjudgement of the bus times.[21]
>
> There was nothing open late at night then, so a date was either a coffee bar, or meeting in a pub or going to the cinema, and then legging it to the station or bus stop to get the last ride home at 11 o'clock ... It was a military operation to time to the last second how long it would take you to get to the transport from wherever you were having fun.[22]

Curfews meant that girls had to carefully manage their leisure activity but Judith and Amanda were prepared to suffer these minor inconveniences if it meant being allowed out in the first place. Curfew was even less of an issue for those who did not have access to public transport. Teenagers living in rural and other isolated areas, for example, often needed their parents to drive them to locations such as the cinema or dance hall.[23] Relying on their parents for practical access to their social life, girls in these situations accepted a degree of parental intervention as an inevitable cost of the process.

Of course, some young women were more critical of rules such as curfew and it was only with hindsight that they appreciated their parents' choices. For Yvette, learning more about her parents' history explained a lot about their parenting style. She described her father as having been 'very strict about boys': 'he threatened to make me leave my A level college course when he picked up and "read" my copy of the Millers Tale. He also would not let us wear "revealing" clothes, saying they would attract the "wrong sort" of boy'.[24] However, she went on justify his position: 'Now I realise he was trying to protect us, he had had to marry my mother because she was pregnant with me and they were totally unsuited.' Learning more about her parents' relationship and their family history helped explain Yvette's father's overbearing parenting style and made Yvette more sympathetic to his approach.

Elsewhere, the process of becoming mothers themselves had shifted women's perspective. Deborah was a teenager in the mid-1960s and in the decades since then she had come to feel differently about her parents' reactions to her younger self's sexuality:

> The only time I remember them interfering in an embarrassing way – and as a parent now I consider it to be quite restrained and

> reasonable – was when I missed the last train home and had to spend the night in my boyfriend's family home. I was 20, but we were chaste I slept in his bed and he slept in his sleeping bag on the floor. I had phoned my parents, but the phone was downstairs, and they did not hear. In the morning we were awakened by his Father storming in to say my Father had just to phoned to ask if I was there.[25]

Over time, Deborah's indignation at having been accused of wrong-doing had been replaced with a sympathy for her parents' concern. Unlike those girls who adhered to parental boundaries on the basis of shared interests, women such as Deborah and Charlotte had 'come to learn' that parental concern for whom their daughters dated and where they went 'is probably true of most parents at any time in history'.[26] Stressing the timelessness of this experience, these testimonies presented both perspectives as natural and validated both their teenage selves' behaviour and the instincts of their parents.

Even among those who did find their parents' interventions infuriating, much of their frustration stemmed from the fact that they could not see any alternative but to obey the rules. The bittersweet tone of Glenys' testimony neatly illustrates how frustration was a product of compliance rather than rebellion. Glenys presented her parents' insistence on accompanying her home as embarrassing and uncomfortable but she did not reject the intention behind her parents' concerns, conceding that her home's location would have left her 'vulnerable' without them:

> I was 14 before I was allowed to start dating. We lived in a suburb of Liverpool but a 40 minute bus ride from the city centre. Our house was at the end of a dark, tree-lined road lit only by gas lamps. (It was an unadopted road). It was a good seven to ten minutes walk to the main road bus stop. My somewhat elderly parents were very strict with me, their only child, and living in such a dark and vulnerable place meant that my father would insist that the boy would see me home or my father would (embarrassingly) meet the bus. It was a very unhappy time for a teenager who only wanted to keep up with her schoolfriends who mostly lived in a more urban environment. At the time I longed to live somewhere with a bus stop outside the door![27]

Glenys, who was fourteen in 1955, used this example to demonstrate her parents' strictness and 'elderly' values and to highlight her difference from her friends. But while she 'longed' for a less embarrassing situation and described this as a 'very unhappy time', she did not present this as a source of outright conflict.

Meeting the parents

Curfews were an important way in which parents attempted to have some oversight of their daughters' social lives. Conceding that they could not exert a huge amount of control over teenagers' behaviour outside the home, curfews offered mothers and fathers a means of structuring their daughters' time. But girls' social and home lives did not run on entirely parallel tracks. Young people's teenage worlds were not completely isolated from their family life. In fact, many girls were committed to integrating the two. Girls could resent parents trying to set them up with potential partners and family dynamics could be strained when parents interfered too directly in girls' relationships but girls often brought their partners home and hoped that their boyfriends would be welcomed by their families.

Looking back on their teenage years from middle age and with children of their own, many women were sympathetic to their parents' desires to see them paired off with a 'nice' boy.[28] Their teenage selves, however, had less patience for their parents' matchmaking and parents' attempts to set girls up with 'suitable' boys were often firmly rejected. In her oral history interview, Kathleen told of how she rarely brought boyfriends into her parental home but that her parents were unusually approving of visits by a friend of the family:

> There was a boy who visited me at home but he was the son of their best friend, best friends. And I think he was the one that my mother would've liked me to marry. He was a nice boy, 'Why don't you go and see Richard? He's a nice boy.' 'I don't want to see Richard!!!' [Both laugh] Anyone but Richard![29]

Other girls were at least prepared to go on the dates forged through family connections. Pamela's mother tried to set her up with the son of a friend. The mothers arranged the date and decided where the couple would go and what Pamela would wear. In spite of their hopes and plans, however, the date was not a success. Pamela described the date itself as a disaster: 'I missed the last bus, he told me we'd have to walk 12 miles back, no way, I phoned for a taxi – when he came round to ask me out again I refused to go out of my bedroom till he'd left.'[30] Likewise, Sally was scathing of her parents' approval of a boy she found repulsive:

> I remember going [to a Summer Ball] with a friend of my brother, my mother thought he was wonderful 'cos he came, he was tall, dark and handsome, and he came from a very well-to-do family in Exeter and she thought this was great and I found him extremely boring and also, he … this sounds terrible, he was one of these young men who used to get all excited and pant and sweaty and he'd put his hand up my skirt and I didn't fancy him at all and I hated it.[31]

Girls like Sally and Pamela were prepared to appease their parents by going out with these boys but they were not willing to have relationships (or even second dates) with them; parental approval and a 'respectable' match were not worth enduring these boys' passivity and lechery.

The act of parents 'inspecting' potential partners has a long history within British courtship and this tradition continued into the mid-twentieth century.[32] Maxine noted that throughout her teenage years, '[b]oyfriends would call for girls, be seen and almost vetted before leaving to go out on a date. Even if I met a boy for a date, my parents would follow things up, to find out if he was a nice boy'.[33] Similarly, Gwen described how when she and her first boyfriend started dating, 'he and my father got together to negotiate where I could go and when'.[34] Parents were concerned that their daughters were going out with the right 'type' of boy. Age difference, class, religion, and race were all qualities that could prompt parental anxiety and parents often expressed their concern openly.[35] For Maxine this meant extra parental interrogation: 'One or two of my boyfriends in the 1960's were quite a bit older than me, and were given a hard time by my mother.'[36] For others, disapproval was outright. When Irene brought home a Black boyfriend, 'there was disapproval from my father and my mother was at pains to express that casualness was OK but inter racial marriage was not a good thing'.[37] Joyce similarly recalled that her parents 'weren't terribly comfortable' with some of her boyfriends: 'they weren't prejudiced against, against people from foreign countries as long as they didn't marry their daughter'.[38]

Some parents, however, were willing to be 'won over'. Glenys recalled:

> My mother always wanted to know what the boyfriend's parents did for a living. I remember one whose parents ran a wet fish shop of which she certainly didn't approve. However, D got round her by bringing her chocolates when he came to pick me up! (She took them into the kitchen to sniff them, but fortunately they didn't smell of fish!!).[39]

Definitions of what made an acceptable date or boyfriend were elastic and parents' initial reservations could be overcome.[40] Flattery and charm as well as the assurance of 'solid values' could be enough to convince parents of boys' respectability. Crucially though, parents had to meet (or at least know of) boyfriends to disapprove of them and as these testimonies make clear, the ritual of 'meeting the parents' was one loaded with meaning for teenage girls. Far from understanding their parents solely as gatekeepers to social life and obstructions to romance that girls had to work around, many girls invited their parents to interact with their romantic partners and saw the family home as a space for bringing together their family and romantic lives.

Magazines of this era frequently offered guidance on how to manage interactions between parents and boyfriends.[41] Much of this advice centred on using face-to-face interactions to reassure parents. Girls who had strict parents who did not approve of them dating, as well as girls who were nervous about the reputations of their boyfriends, were encouraged to introduce boys to their parents to dissolve some of the mystery-induced anxiety felt by parents.[42] Allowing parents to meet their boyfriends was a way of conferring legitimacy on a relationship. Not only were parents more likely to accept a relationship if they knew the boy involved but the introduction itself could serve as a rite of passage that confirmed the seriousness of the relationship.

As such, a lot could be at stake in the act of 'meeting the parents' and girls often approached the moment of meeting with a degree of trepidation. Although Clare had a couple of romantic interests in her very early teens, she did not have an 'official' boyfriend until she was fifteen. Having met this boy at youth club she recalled her nerves at introducing him to her parents: 'He was the first boy I brought home to meet mum and dad and I remember they shook hands very formally – I was so nervous.'[43] At the same time that magazines were advising girls to be open about their relationships, they simultaneously suggested that a degree of artifice was likely to be necessary to help smooth over these interactions. A 1971 feature in *Jackie* recommended the following:

> Give your boy a few hints about the things your dad likes to talk about – that should help to break the ice. And when you're giving your boyfriend a bit of a build-up before Dad meets him, DON'T tell Dad what a raver he is, and the amusing way he did 90 down the M1 with his hands off the steering wheel. Instead, make sure Dad gets to hear what a sensible, reliable, down-to-earth chap your new boyfriend is. Sounds deadly dull ... but it's JUST what dads love to hear![44]

Here and elsewhere, girls were warned against being entirely forthcoming when describing their partners and were advised to prepare their boyfriends with conversation starters and 'safe' topics of discussion. Similar advice applied when girls were being introduced to their boyfriends' parents.[45] Responding to a reader who had written to *Honey* asking for hints about how to behave when staying with her boyfriend's parents for the first time, the agony aunt insisted that this was the girl's 'chance to make friends with his family' and that the best way to do this was to 'relax and enjoy yourself' but also to 'offer to help with some of the chores' in order to ingratiate herself with his mother.[46] Teenagers managed these interactions to ensure that they were allowed to continue the relationships – girls did not want their parents to prevent them from seeing their boyfriends. But these meetings also had an important emotional component. 'Meeting the parents' could also function as an important test for young people's relationships. Fostering relationships between boyfriends and parents, or simply inviting boys into the family home and allowing them to participate in family rituals was seen as an important milestone within romantic life.

Domestic romance

Teenagers' romantic lives were certainly made much easier when their relationships were accepted by their parents. In addition to the public boy–girl interactions discussed in the previous chapter, home-based activities were also a core feature of many teenagers' romantic relationships.[47] Marjorie and her boyfriend, for example, would go to each other's houses to 'listen to records and talk'.[48] For some couples, these home-based activities allowed young people to have the relationships they desired, whilst conforming to house rules. Although many parents stipulated that girls could not go out during week-nights, many were prepared to host boyfriends in the house on those evenings.[49] Others preferred to stay at home and watch television because it was cheap. Their parents' homes represented a space where teenagers could 'sit and talk, play music and study' together without spending any money.[50] Watching television was also a low-maintenance alternative to going out; against the backdrop of schoolwork for some and full-time employment for others, watching television with company was deemed an easy, mutually enjoyable activity that required no prior arrangement or preparation.

Especially for those in longer-term relationships, the mundane domesticity of these interactions could also be read as a distinctive form of intimacy. Not only did home-based activities confer legitimacy on the relationship in so far as they reflected parental approval but the unfussiness and ordinariness of these interactions was a sign of stability and being settled. Girls were not having to publicly perform in an attempt to win over their partners; the relationship was understood to have developed beyond artifice to a natural authenticity. Judith described having had a couple of relationships in her mid-teenage years that largely consisted of going to each other's houses to do homework, 'just talking and watching TV'. Judith and her boyfriends did go out to the cinema and to dances, but the home-based activities were important in building 'real' friendship within these relationships.[51]

Maintaining good relationships between themselves and both sets of parents not only ensured that teenage couples maintained 'access' to each other but was also a matter of deep personal concern. Some of the strongest expressions of the importance of parents' engagement with and approval of girls' relationships came when these were not achieved or broke down. It was distressing for girls when their parents refused to engage with their boyfriends or when it became apparent that they themselves were disapproved of by their partner's parents.[52] Marjorie 'couldn't forgive' her father for throwing her partner out of the house 'for no apparent reason' and this was very damaging for their relationship.[53] Parents were known to resist interaction on the grounds that they didn't want a stranger in the house[54] or, more plainly, that they '[couldn't] be bothered' to engage with their daughters' partners.[55] That girls felt compelled to write to magazines to seek advice in these situations is testament to their hope that their parents would have an interest in their lives and, ideally, that they would want a relationship with their daughter's paramour. While teenagers complained to magazines when their parents were over-bearing and embarrassing, many still held meeting the parents to be an important rite of passage and a means of validating their romantic relationships.[56] Girls were invested in these relationships with their families and cared about what their parents thought. As the lines between romance and sexuality blurred, however, these dynamics could operate quite differently.

The code of silence

During the 1950s and 1960s, it was widely believed that the social and cultural transformations of the post-war period had fundamentally altered the experience of adolescence. Evidence gathered by the Labour Party's Youth Commission in the late 1950s led them to believe 'that the gap which always exists between the generations is, at the present time, wider than it has been and ought to be'.[57] Commentators from across the social and political spectrum explained and interpreted the widening gap differently – the effects of the Second World War and introduction of the welfare state were hotly debated – but many highlighted how post-war affluence (in particular better nutrition, readily available employment, and increased amounts of disposable income) contrasted to the struggles of previous generations growing up during the depression of the 1930s or the austerity of the 1940s.[58] This sense of change was not simply felt by adult society, however. Teenagers of the post-war generation also believed that their generation was breaking new ground and inhabiting a world that their parents could not understand. As Kathleen expressed at the beginning of her oral history interview:

And the music, you know, the Bob Dylan and that sort of thing, you know, 'The Times They Are A'Changing', they really, that all felt very relevant, that, it was changing. It was, 'we are part of a new world' and, you know, 'they don't understand', that was parents and that whole world, you know. The- they don't understand, we're on a different trajectory.[59]

This gap between different generations' worldviews could be particularly acute when it came to matters of intimate relationships and sex. As discussed in previous chapters, many young people growing up in the 1950s, 1960s, and 1970s felt compelled to engage in sexual behaviour (including penetrative intercourse) for a variety of personal and social reasons. Yet, this often stood in direct opposition to the attitudes and expectations of adult society and within the family home matters of sexuality were very differently charged. Writing about the early twentieth century, the historian Simon Szreter has described the persistence of 'Victorianism' within British sexual culture in 'the popular code, among all classes, of euphemism, silence, ignorance and confusions of matters of sex'.[60] Oral history and Mass Observation testimonies suggest that cultures of sexual silence within the home persisted well into the 1960s and 1970s. Girls interpreted their parents' words and actions (or, more often, their *lack* of words and actions) to mean that sex was not something to be discussed within the home or among family members. However, parents' silence on sexual matters could not prevent girls from discovering sex and as girls started to learn about sex from other sources they realised that this was something their parents had kept from them, thus perpetuating the feeling that sex was a subject meant to stay secret. Many teenage girls had good relationships with their parents in other aspects of their lives but the code of silence they inherited in relation to sex created new family dynamics during adolescence and came to play a significant role in how young people managed their sexual behaviour.

Unspeakables

The idea that there were some aspects of human life that were 'unspeakable' was instilled in children from a very young age. Mass Observers responding to the 2005 Directive on Sex were prompted to reflect on their experiences of sex in their 'early years'. Most took this to mean their life prior to attending secondary school and as part of these sexual life stories many recalled instances of looking at and touching their own and other children's genitalia. Women such as Geraldine described incidents that left them in no doubt that their genitalia were not to be touched or discussed in public.

> An early memory is my sister and I aged about 2 and 4 lying on the bedroom floor getting dressed. We were looking at each other's 'bottoms' – the word vagina was unknown to me till I was about 11 and discovered that there was a space or an entry. Before we could go any further with these explorations a furious mother descended on us and we were given to understand that we must never, ever do such a thing again.[61]

Georgina was not caught, but she was aware, even when very young, that her genitalia were 'rude' and that there was something wrong with letting somebody else see or touch them:

> The only vivid sexual experience I recall as a child occurred when an older, female cousin of mine came to visit. I can't even remember how old we might have been but I suppose I was quite small – maybe 4 or 5 – and she was 9 or 10. She was at the 'experimenting' age and always tried to spirit me upstairs to my bedroom so we could inspect each others' private parts ... why, I wasn't remotely aware, but I went along with it. I do quite clearly recall feeling that it was somehow 'wrong', probably because her furtiveness communicated itself to me, and eventually she lost interest and it stopped.[62]

Reflecting on their past selves, most Observers presented their experiences as perfectly natural manifestations of youthful curiosity. But these stories indicate that an association of their bodies and interpersonal touching with secrecy was absorbed long before young people were aware of sex itself. Having been explicitly told or made to feel that this sort of behaviour was bad did not prevent children from engaging in this type of touching or exploration – games of 'I'll show you mine if you show me yours' were reported in the testimonies.[63] It did, however, influence how and where girls did it – they 'knew' it had to be done in private and was not to be discussed with their parents.

Unsurprisingly, these feelings were echoed in many women's accounts of their early experiences of masturbation. In contrast to men's sexual life stories, in which discovering masturbation was often presented as a rite of passage and a key milestone in their sexual development, within women's stories, the role of masturbation was more ambiguous. In Lillian's words: 'Masturbation, something we all do, but something we don't really want to admit to?'[64] Mass Observers stressed that there 'certainly wasn't a word for this special activity – it just wasn't verbalised by anyone' and presented masturbation as a practice that girls 'discovered' through self-experimentation.[65] As women's memories of masturbating in bed late at night and/or at home when no one else was around suggest, crucial to these practices what not just a sense that they needed not only to be conducted in private but that they needed to stay secret.[66] Although it was never discussed, '[s]omehow', Glenys 'knew it was "wrong" by [her] parents' standards and there was often a fear of getting caught'.[67] Masturbation was not just hidden from view, it needed to be unknown.

This sense that bodies and their processes were embarrassing, shameful, and to be kept hidden was heightened further by how girls' parents, usually mothers, handled the matter of menstruation.[68] Menarche came as a surprise to several participants.[69] Kathleen recalled the confusing feelings that shrouded this experience: 'I don't remember ever being told about them and I remember when I got my first period being very frightened and hiding it. There was something shameful about it and I didn't know why.'[70] This was echoed by Julie who 'thought [she] was dying' the first time she got her period and presented her ignorance and her mother's handling of the situation as something of a betrayal: 'I inherited that kind of "Oh, don't mention it", you know, "don't talk about it, it's not something you discuss" … when I brought my daughter up I did exactly the opposite … I didn't want her to not know, I didn't want her to be scared.'[71]

Some mothers used their daughters' first periods as a convenient catalyst for discussions about sex itself; having a reason to discuss female anatomy and how it related to child-bearing created a space for discussing reproduction and sex more broadly.[72] Yet even when there was a 'natural' context for this conversation, the discussion could be shrouded in awkwardness and obfuscation. The initial discussion about menstruation (regardless of whether it occurred before or after menarche itself) was often constructed as a special conversation that should involve only a girl and her mother (and maybe a sister or cousin of roughly the same age). Especially in houses full of siblings and other family members, this insistence on discretion was unusual. Irene was born in 1952 and had her first period when she was 11: 'I was very confused by the bleeding. I came home from school and my mum told me to go upstairs and she'd come up and see me. We lived in a small busy house so I guess this was why.'[73] That their mothers set aside not only time but space to have these conversations highlighted to girls that there was something not quite normal about discussing sex and bodies.

Even among the women of the house discussing periods could be awkward as was the case for Maureen, her sister, and her mother: 'I remember my mother telling us what was going to happen and being, being absolutely horrified but I think it was probably the embarrassed way she told us. And and it was a one off that she told us.' Although her sister was eighteen months older than her, Maureen began menstruating first which was its own source of anxiety:

> I just thought I was some kind of freak. ... So for me it caused a big trauma and I actually didn't dare tell my mother. ... I was rehearsing telling her and I couldn't, I couldn't quite bring myself to, it took me ages to tell her, in the end I thought I better. And she was, you know, she was fine about it, but it was, I just felt, I felt the whole thing was very embarrassing.[74]

Despite being 'close', it was not easy for Maureen's family to discuss their bodies and bodily functions.

In other families this dynamic was more extreme as parents suggested that menstruation was not to be spoken of at all. Once Dawn had been given a basic sense of what menstruation was and how to deal with it, exchanges between her and her mother on the subject were entirely non-verbal:

> I was told by my mum that I would have a period and that I would bleed 'from down there'. And when I did I was to leave her a note and she would get me something. She was right I did bleed so I left her a note and a parcel appeared on my bed. But nothing was said.[75]

Similarly Barbara remembered: 'I started my periods relatively early, maybe on the cusp of twelve, something like that. They were not discussed. You were given your supplies and you were, you just had to get rid of these thick, thick things, and it was all kept quite hush hush.'[76] This secret created new dynamics within the family: menstruation was to be kept between a mother and daughter with fathers and siblings portrayed as best-ignorant 'others'. Some mothers explicitly communicated that menstruation was to be kept a secret, especially from men within the family:

> I remember feeling that there was something exciting and mysterious about <u>sanitary towels</u>, it was all so secretive. My mother told me where to dispose of them and on no account to let my father know when I was having a period, it was 'private'![77]

> My mother curtly told me that girls of a certain age have periods happen once month. ... And she gave me a pack of her sanitary towels which looked like nappies with strings on, and told me I had to dispose of them afterwards, not in the toilet, and to be discreet around my dad and brother. I was left bemused.[78]

Girls were raised to understand their bodies as something that would embarrass their fathers and brothers. Starting their periods required girls to actively participate in a culture of secrecy and subterfuge that was built upon the notion that women's bodies and reproductive functions transgressed boundaries of what could be addressed in respectable conversation.

Knowing what's not being said

Although many interviewees and Mass Observers repeated the sentiment that 'sex was not something that anyone spoke about', as we saw in Chapter 1, very few young people of the post-war generation made it out of their teenage years totally ignorant of sex.[79] Rather, it was precisely because they had been made aware of sex in other contexts that they came to realise that their home lives were characterised by silence on the subject. Post-war families may not have been openly discussing sex but this did not mean that there was no sexual culture within the home. Silence was the culture.

Mid-twentieth-century sociological studies suggested that middle-class parents were more inclined to discuss puberty and sex with their children than working-class parents. Testimonies suggest that this was not always the case. Valerie went so far as to argue that, in this aspect of child-rearing, 'my mother failed completely'. In her middle-class home, 'we never had any maternal discussions about relationships with boys or about sex or about anything actually'.[80] Many women who had been told the 'facts of life' by their parents portrayed these lessons as having been unsatisfactory.[81] From the testimonies it appears that many parents understood their role to be answering fundamental questions about the biological aspects of sex and reproduction. Catherine and Debbie suggested that their mothers gave them one-off lessons in biology and medicine in which 'nothing was mentioned about love or feelings' and that left them 'incredibly naïve and inexperienced in a practical sense'.[82] Although their mothers were proactive in teaching them about the facts of life, both women suggested that they were left with unanswered questions. Elsewhere, the hostile or dismissive responses that some parents gave put girls off asking questions on the topic. Jacqueline, for example, characterised her upbringing as having been 'strict' and suggested that the sex education that she was given by her mother was confined to the biological aspects of sex:

> When our next door neighbour who was the same age as I was she said, 'What happens on the wedding night?' and I said, 'I don't know'. She said, 'Ask your mother' and I asked my mother and she wouldn't speak to me! [J laughs] She wouldn't even speak to me, she was cross with me and I couldn't think why and she said, 'You mustn't speak to that girl again, you mustn't speak to that girl'.[83]

Jacqueline suggested that her mother's early dismissal of her question about the wedding night created an atmosphere in which discussion of the interpersonal and emotional aspects of sexuality was rendered impossible.

In other families, parents attempted to avoid having explicit discussions about sex altogether and instead offered sex education through reading material. When it became apparent that girls were 'ready', parents (usually mothers) would subtly give girls books or pamphlets that discussed the 'facts of life'.[84] Parents made different judgements about when their daughters needed to know this information but it usually occurred between the ages of nine and fourteen, once girls started asking questions and/or were visibly on the cusp of puberty. Reflecting on these experiences, women recognised their parents' efforts to ensure that they were not ignorant of what was to come, but portrayed this form of sex education as profoundly limited. Gloria suggested that this reading material could be lacking in detail ('I still did not know much about sex') and Lorraine explained how her parents deemed the provision of reading material to be 'job done', providing no time or space for their daughters to ask questions.[85]

Children and young women were sensitive to the cues communicated through parents' words and actions. They did not need to be told that sex was private before they could sense these subjects were not to be openly discussed. As children and teenagers, girls discovered reading material about sex (ranging from novels such as *Lady Chatterley's Lover* and sex manuals like the *Kama Sutra* or Alex Comfort's *The Joy of Sex*, to men's magazines such as *Penthouse* and *Playboy*) within their homes and realised that looking at this was 'dirty' or 'naughty' precisely because it had been hidden.[86] Finding these books was often narrated as some kind of clandestine adventure.[87] Heather recalled hunting for her older brother's copy of *Lady Chatterley's Lover* one evening when she was babysitting:

> I remember how nervous I became as it got nearer to the time that they left to go out, leaving me behind to babysit. The nerves were only because I knew I was going to try and find it and see what was written in it. After quarter of an hour or so I found it. All the juicy bits were marked by turned down corners! I read quite a bit but at the same time was so frightened in case they returned early that I soon put it back and took myself to bed early so as not to have to look them in the face.[88]

As girls got older and discovered new avenues for finding sexual knowledge, knowing about sex enabled them to better read their parents' behaviour and it was precisely because daughters knew about sex and knew that it was supposed to be private that led to awkwardness when the silence was disturbed.

This dynamic was showcased most clearly in the recurring trope of awkward television-watching experiences recalled by those who were teenagers in the 1970s. Television ownership expanded across the post-war decades and the gradual decline in formal censorship and the liberalisation of 'acceptable' content increased the visibility of sex on screen.[89] Television came to symbolise the increasing influence of the 'outside' upon home-based sexual culture and the code of silence was all the more evident once the television brought references to sex into the living room.[90] When asked about how she learned about sex Julie replied: 'Probably through the television I would say ... cause then you'd all sit there very embarrassed while there was funny noises going on and smooching.'[91] As Julie described, sexual imagery on television offered a particular form of sexual knowledge, but everybody in the room was 'embarrassed' to watch it together. It was not just young people who were found this type of interaction awkward. Maureen remembered that her father would promptly switch off the television if 'anything at all sort of risqué or embarrassing' came on, while Frances' father would '"rattle" the newspaper' which had the (perhaps undesired) effect of 'making [Frances] aware that something untoward was happening!'[92] Marian described a similar pattern:

> My parent's attitude to sex was a closed shop. Nothing of any sexual matter was ever talked about. When we watched telly, (and we were a BBC only family) I remember that my father always watched whilst reading the paper. Most of the time it lay on his lap and he looked at it down his nose but should David Attenborough have 'mating stick insects' on his programme, the paper went up and he became engrossed in the contents of what ever [sic]. And to show that he really wasn't watching he often cut across the programme with some fascinating quote from 'the said' article. I can recall my brother and I giving sideways looks to each other as we strained not to grin with embarrassment.[93]

Although nothing sexual was ever discussed in her family home, this did not stop Marian and her brother knowing about sex and knowing that it was something embarrassing. It was precisely because they knew this that they recognised their father's awkwardness and its source. Teenagers were aware of all that their parents were not discussing and quickly came to understand sex as a taboo subject not to be brought up. Sexual silence was itself a presence in the home, haunting teenagers and parents alike.

Moral codes and parental expectations

While parents did not talk openly about bodies and sexual practice, many did explicitly communicate their expectations of sexual morality. Regardless of whether their parents educated their daughters about the 'facts of life', many girls grew up being told that having sex before marriage was wrong. Deborah's experience of being told by her mother that 'sex before marriage was not for nice girls like me' was echoed across many households and girls were often made to feel that sex was something dirty and bad.[94] Some mothers suggested that sex was something unpleasant to be endured only within marriage ('My mother gave the impression that sex was something men did to women'[95]), but it was more common for parents to concede that sex was something teenagers might want to try, though insisting that these desires needed to be resisted.

In 1955, Geoffrey Gorer's study of the English national character suggested that 'the greatest influence making for pre-marital chastity is the practice of religion' and his later study of sex and marriage in England concluded much the same.[96] Certainly, religion was a significant presence in many girls' family lives. Lorraine suggested that it was 'because of [her] upbringing (practicing Church of England)' that she did not have penetrative sex until marriage, while Andrea described how having sex with her fiancé prior to marriage was particularly traumatic because she 'feared the wrath of God'.[97] For girls like Andrea and Lorraine, their understandings of sex were embedded in their religious faith and the teachings of the church. Their faith imbued sex with additional layers of meaning and was a potent influence preventing them from engaging in penetrative sex before marriage. Within other testimonies, the relationship between religion, family life, and girls' sexuality was more complex. Sheila, who grew up in 'a very Catholic household' in the 1960s, recalled that '[s]ex was only mentioned in negative terms' by her parents and that '[s]ex and the human body were something that was swept under the carpet' in her family. Despite having 'subconsciously picked up' from her parents 'that [sex] was something only "dirty" or "common" people did', Sheila did engage in sexual activity as a teenager. Framing her discovery of boys within the process of adolescence ('once my hormones kick in'), Sheila presented her experience within the realm of normal teenage behaviour but recalled how her religious upbringing shaped how she felt about her sexuality: 'I definitely had this thought that perhaps my early sexual experiences were shrouded in guilt and somehow I shouldn't be enjoying it as much as I did.'[98]

Other women referenced God and other aspects of faith as having informed their sexual lives but in more nebulous ways. As Callum Brown has described, the influence of Christian faith persisted across the second half of the twentieth century even though the number of people who understood themselves to be religious or practicing faith was declining.[99] Julie described herself as having had a 'very puritanical upbringing'. She and her siblings were 'sort of brought up C of E but [her parents] didn't go to church, either of them, so neither of them were practicing, but we all got Baptised and Confirmed. So yes, puritanical in the sense of … erm … sort of being beaten up, kind of, stern sense, just more in that expectational sense … what's expected of you'.[100] When Catherine's mother found out about her affair with a married man, 'she starting spouting about God (even though she wasn't religious)'.[101] This reaction spoke to a Christian-influenced understanding of morality despite a lack of formal religion. Within some families, moral codes were underpinned by aspects of religious faith or teachings even if the formal institutions of religion played little role in girls' lives.

In many testimonies, however, religion did not feature as an organising principle of sexual morality.[102] Instead, parents' morality lessons were framed in terms of personal pride and family honour. Parents' warnings revolved around the damage that teenage sex posed to a family's reputation. As we saw in Chapter 2, the need to avoid pregnancy lay partly in the material consequences that having a child would have on girls' futures but women also suggested that they were afraid that extra-marital pregnancy would damage their family relationships. Part of the reason that discussions of respectability and morality had such emotional power was because they were articulated by parents and family members that girls cared about and wanted to please.

Parents made it very clear that pregnancy outside of marriage would be devastating to their daughters. In Glenys' words: 'I was scared of sex as I was terrified of letting the family down by getting pregnant and "having" to get married, which is what things were like in the 1950's.'[103] Extra-marital pregnancy was seen as a source of immense familial shame. As one Mass Observer wrote, her family's attitude to her sexuality was 'bound up with this attitude don't let the neighbours know what is going on'.[104] Yet girls routinely heard stories of disgraced neighbours or classmates who had been kicked out of home or sent away because they became pregnant.[105] Their own responses to these stories often served as a reminder of how a girl's sexual behaviour was understood to reflect upon a family's reputation. In Jane's words, '[f]or a teenager to get pregnant in those days was still considered a sign of being "a slut", being "easy" or "having loose morals"'.[106] Especially within close-knit communities, parents worked hard to ensure that their families were not tarnished with the stigma of illegitimacy and promiscuity.

Parents associated chastity with respectability and worked hard to ensure that their daughters were 'nice'. As Jayne put it: 'The most important word in mother's talk was NO. "Nice" girls did not do it before marriage. This was continually reiterated, to me and also my friends mothers said the same words to their daughters.'[107] Even within households where discussions of sex and bodies were almost non-existent, parents 'made it clear that sex before marriage was not for nice girls like me, and spoke of the dangers of not controlling yourself'.[108] Parents expected their daughters to maintain standards of propriety (if not outright chastity).[109]

Parents of the post-war generation could be vocal in their disapproval of pre-marital sex and so-called 'promiscuity', but, as we have seen, this did not necessarily stop young women from pursuing sexual relationships and intimate activity. The majority of women whose experiences are explored in this research had sex before they got married and many of them did so outside of the context of engagement.[110] Many girls had penetrative sex in their mid to late teens and more still engaged in 'petting' before this. As girls got older, their relationships with boys became more involved and sex was 'transformed' from an abstract biological phenomenon to an activity that they were expected to engage in. Against this backdrop, home-based sexual cultures based upon silence and chaste morality became increasingly problematic. Although parents implored their daughters to remain chaste, girls' relationships with boyfriends and their friends as well as their wish to 'grow up' created new pressures and desires to become sexually active. Parents' warnings and rules of restraint were countered by the pleadings of aroused partners, the increasing social currency associated with sexual experience, and girls' own curiosity, and so were often written off as irrelevant and outdated. But even girls who were prepared to defy their parents' rules and principles by engaging in intimate activities did not wish for their sexual lives to become a battlefield that put them in direct conflict with their parents. In order to have the sex they wanted and stay on good terms with their parents, teenagers deployed strategies of evasion and secrecy, themselves becoming complicit in the code of silence within family homes as they organised their social and sexual lives in ways that avoided parental interference and dialogue.

Some women understood the clandestine nature of their teenage social lives as a timeless and natural phenomenon. Janice was a teenager in the mid-1960s. She had a good relationship with her mother but this did not mean that they talked openly about Janice's romantic or sex life.

> *And were you close with your mum? I know that you said she was at home a lot.*
>
> I used to talk to her a lot. I remember I used to come in at night if I'd been to youth club or something and with my dad, when my dad was away, and I'd just go and sit on her bed and talk to her and tell her what … I don't, I never got any advice from her, I never went to her with any problems, never discussed, everything was always superficial …
>
> *And so with your mum, especially when you were a teenager, was there an element of not wanting to tell her?*
>
> Oh god, yeah! There were loads of those things! [J laughs] Noooooo. No. Yeah, yes. Oh. But you don't do you? You didn't.[111]

Contemporary magazines and media also articulated the sense that miscommunication between parents and young people on the cusp of adulthood was natural. When a young woman wrote to *Jackie* in 1964 expressing concern that she felt unable to talk to her mother about boyfriends, Cathy and Claire reassured her that she wasn't 'strange' and that '[m]ost girls go through a stage like this … you'll get over it, honestly!'.[112] This dynamic was still present in the 1970s. A 1971 *Jackie* article titled 'My Mum's a Dragon' gently pointed fun at girls' interpretations of their mothers' behaviour ('The way some of you tell it, your mums breathe fire and eat young girls for breakfast!') but also acknowledged 'the odd fact that it's easier to talk over problems with a total stranger than with your own mum'.[113] This was partially attributed to how mothers' burdens of housework could make them impatient or brusque with teenagers' awkward attempts to prompt personal conversations or ask advice, but the author also recognised how discussing personal problems at home could be embarrassing.

At the same time that this 'generation gap' was understood as being a natural and inevitable part of growing up, however, it was also presented as a distinctive product of its time. Many column inches in the press were spent raising the issue of modern sexual mores, warning both parents and children of the disruption this posed to the British way of life. Across the period (and pre-dating the 'swinging sixties'), newspapers covered medical professionals' laments over the rise of venereal disease,[114] religious commentators' expressions of anxiety for declining sexual morality,[115] and teachers' concerns for how sex was diverting young people (especially girls) from aspirations of careers and families.[116] Notions that the 1960s and 1970s were witnessing a 'sexual revolution' made for excellent editorial content and while the tone was not always alarmist (a *Guardian* feature on 'The Permissive Society' that ran for several weeks in October 1967 was positively giddy about 'entering on the golden age of adult sexual equality'), there was a clear sense that the tide had turned quickly, leaving many people (mainly adults) behind.[117]

Teenagers themselves were aware of a seeming disjuncture between their own views and feelings and those of their parents. Joy described her teenage years in the late 1960s and early 1970s as witnessing 'a very strange juxtaposition':

> Because, I think it was this revolution was coming in and especially with the pill and promiscuity you were being bombarded with and I think my mum was hearing it and not liking it ... So I think that kind of led to her being really stricter as I grew older really.[118]

Joy saw her mum's strictness as a response to the altered culture in which she was growing up. Similarly, Kathleen described a sense of culture shock and adults' particular concern for what this meant for young women.

> I think uh, a lot of adults, older people, mature people, found it very worrying that their teenage children weren't under control in the same way that they had been under control when their parents you know, were sort of launching them in to their adult lives. Particularly girls.[119]

The rift between teenagers and their parents was understood in terms of an old versus young divide; teenagers in the 1960s inhabited a sexual landscape that their parents could not understand.

Teenagers were repeatedly made aware of their 'modern' moral values and the feelings of fear, anxiety, anger, and disappointment these often provoked among adults. Perhaps unsurprisingly, many young women decided to keep the details of their sexual lives a secret from their parents. Girls believed that revealing their sexual activity would result in aggravation, tension, and conflict, leading many to completely divorce their home life from their social and sexual lives. The belief that their worldviews were irreconcilable with those of their parents led young women to conceal their sexual practice. Jacqueline described having to keep her sexual activities a secret from her parents: 'I used to lie to them, I used to stay out all night, I used to go to parties, so-called "all-night" parties where I'd stay the night with my boyfriend and they didn't know.'[120] Asked why she had lied to them Jacqueline replied, 'They couldn't accept, there's no way I could've slept with a boy, you know?' Jacqueline perceived the divide between her values and those of her parents as being too wide for her to bridge and so she contrived to avoid the issue altogether. As a teenager almost twenty years later, Anne described a similar dynamic within her youthful sexuality. When she was seventeen, Anne made a very conscious decision to have penetrative sex for the first time. She carefully managed their experience and made sure that the act itself took place at her boyfriend's house so that her mother would not find out:

> I was very, uh, I'll use the word manipulative about it, in the sense that I managed it deliberately, 'cos I knew that I was making choices that were the right ones for me but weren't acceptable to my mum's idea of, of how women should be.[121]

Neither Jacqueline nor Anne wanted to hurt or anger their parents but they wanted to have sex and so chose to keep their decisions and activities a secret. Trying to ensure that their parents did not find out about it led young people to be extremely crafty in how they managed their sexual activity.

Secrecy and evasion

In 1968, the popular advice columnist Claire Rayner published *People in Love: A Modern Guide to Sex in Marriage*. As was the case with many such manuals, the book was clearly intended to be read not only by married couples but by engaged couples and young people more broadly. The book explored various aspects of sexual life from the physical, emotional, and psychological 'facts' to contraception, honeymoons, parenthood, and 'the ageing years'. In the chapter on 'The premarital period', Rayner reflected on the spatial politics of sex and insisted that 'for the vast majority of couples sexual intercourse can only be enjoyed in uninterrupted privacy'. For Rayner, couples should not expect to engage in sex before marriage as only marriage 'provide[d] adequate privacy': while parents might respect a married couple's 'right to be alone' in a bedroom, 'few mothers and fathers will willingly permit a couple sufficient privacy and time alone to enjoy intercourse'.[122]

Personal testimonies suggest that, in many homes, Rayner was right. Although Daphne always had 'a room of [her] own', she stressed that 'you would never have entertained your boyfriend up there'.[123] Tracy was a teenager twenty years after Daphne and she too was 'never allowed' boyfriends in her bedroom.[124] Even when girls grew older and entered into long-term relationships, parents often prevented unmarried couples from sharing a bedroom. When Hazel brought a boyfriend to stay at her parents' home for a weekend in the mid-1960s 'there was no question of sharing a room, that was simply not on the cards'.[125] Parents might encourage their daughters to have boyfriends and bring them home but there were limits to what they deemed appropriate and parents explicitly attempted to police young people's sexual activity through the control of domestic space.

Seizing the moment

These rules and negotiations were not ironclad, however, and teenagers often subverted their parents' attempts to monitor and separate young couples. It was possible for young people to find or create the privacy they needed for sex acts in the home. Key to this was opportunism and the result was that teenage intimacies were often characterised by a degree of furtiveness. Daphne was not allowed to take boys upstairs to her bedroom but she could 'be with' them in the sitting room:

> [Y]ou always had a sitting room and a living room and the sitting room was reserved and you were allowed to go in there and, um, be with your boyfriend. The, it wasn't as private as, you know, because,

you know you were aware that they were around but nevertheless you could be on your own. Yes. Um, uh, from a point of view of ... and you know, sort of, um, you, you, you kept your ears open for what was going on in the, could hear the television droning or whatever but, uh, there you go.[126]

Teenagers like Daphne made the most of the space they had. As Daphne notes, this behaviour did require a degree of self-policing – teenagers needed to 'keep [their] ears open' to ensure that they weren't caught – but when left alone together, young people could and did engage in intimate behaviour.

These stolen moments of domestic privacy were embedded within post-war affluence and the material circumstances of the middle classes. Like Daphne, Andrea remembered 'heavy petting' on the floor of her parents' sitting room 'when [her] parents were in the other room watching television'.[127] Owning a television was key to 'distracting' parents. Not only did the programming keep parents occupied but the sound of the television also provided a degree of audio camouflage to ensure that parents did not overhear teenagers' activities. Even more important, though, was living in a house with clearly defined rooms and multiple entertaining spaces. Not only did rooms set aside for girls to be with their partners provide the privacy teenagers needed to get intimate with one another but the fact that they had to be transitioned into (along hallways and through doors, etc.) meant that they offered young people the possibility of plausible deniability, giving them time to recompose themselves should their parents come to look in on them.

Beyond the appropriation of specific places within the home, teenage girls' opportunistic commandeering of *time* was also crucial in their creation of sexual spaces within the home. While television was a convenient parental distraction in the daytime and evening, young couples capitalised on their parents' need to sleep during overnight visits. Although parents often tried to limit sexual activity by making sleeping arrangements that separated young couples, teenagers simply reunited once everyone else was asleep.[128] As he lived some distance away from her, Heather's fiancé used to sleep on her parents' sofa when he came to visit at weekends and the living room became the site of their first experiences of penetrative intercourse:

Once we were engaged and alone at night – he slept on the settee every Saturday night – we allowed each other more physical contact but it wasn't until we had been engaged for a month or two that we went further.[129]

Jane told a similar story and used it to demonstrate her parents' complex and contradictory attitudes to teenage sexuality:

My mother never 'got moralistic' with me and fully accepted the sexual relationships she must have known I had. When one of my boyfriends came to stay for a few weeks to recover from glandular fever (I was about 21 and he was a couple of years younger) he was expected to sleep in our lounge, but I'm quite sure my mother was aware of our after-hours creeping around![130]

Jane could not say for sure that her mother knew of her activities; her tentative language ('she must've known', 'I'm quite sure') implied that the two never had explicit conversations about the subject. Both Jane and her mother perpetuated the illusion of Jane's sexual propriety at the same time that they were being mutually complicit in its deconstruction. So long as neither party rendered Jane's sexuality visible, it could be ignored and uncomfortable conversations avoided.

Other couples were less convinced of their skills of domestic deception or their parents' willingness to look the other way. Instead, they required another degree of separation between their sexual lives and their parents. Unwilling or unable to engage in sexual activity when other family members were at home, young women seized opportunities when the home was unoccupied; although their parents' home did not belong to them, they could nevertheless make the most of temporary 'ownership'. Describing her 'fling' with the paperboy, Marjorie noted that logistics were made particularly difficult as her parents did not like him so there was even more need to keep the relationship a 'secret'. Fortunately, however, they were able to make the most of his empty house: 'We went back to his house once when his family was out and went to his bedroom – I still recall it quite clearly as it was the first time I had allowed anyone to put their fingers in my vagina.'[131] While Marjorie recalled the successful capture of space, other accounts highlighted the precarity of such stolen moments. At seventeen, Barbara had penetrative sex for the first time in a Mini:

> We then went back to the house where he was living with his aunt and uncle ... His aunt and uncle were away. And we went up to his bedroom to carry on. And his aunt and uncle came back early! And I had to lie without making any noise whatsoever for about two hours until they went out again, at which point he was able to smuggle me out of the house![132]

Recalled as an amusing farce, Barbara's experience reflected teenagers' constant quest for private space.

Questions of space did not simply determine young women's access to sex but could also influence the meaning of sexual activity itself.[133] As we saw in Chapter 1, girls' experiences of having penetrative sex for the first time were often remembered as having been unsatisfactory in some way and first intercourse that took place within the family home was not immune from this characterisation. In cases like Diana's, this was partly because homes were so associated with the mundane and everyday. Although Diana and her partner managed to secure some time alone in his home and used this to have sex, he simply saw this as an interlude in his evening, jumping out of bed to watch television when they had finished: 'we were lying there, I think he was having a fag, and then he said, "Oh look at the time"! And he wanted to watch the last night at the Proms!'[134] While empty homes allowed young couples to engage in the conventions of 'normal' adult sex (namely having sex in a bed), teenagers were particularly aware that their commandeering of this space was fleeting. As such, the romantic intimacy that girls expected of sex could be tarnished by the sense of risk and their anxiety that they might get caught. Kay and her boyfriend took the opportunity of his mother going out in order to have sex for the first time but reflecting on this she suggested that the set-up did not make for a particularly satisfactory experience: 'We were cramped on his single bed, worrying that his mother might come home early ... hardly the best, most romantic setting, but maybe one that was common to many young people our age.'[135] She implied that sex was not something they would have been able to do had her boyfriend's mother been home and the sense that their occupation of this sexual space was only temporary affected how 'romantic' she found the experience.

For some girls, the need for their sexual activity to remain a secret rendered the home an inappropriate space for sexual activity.

The presence of parents (and other family members) meant that sexual activity simply could not go unobserved within domestic space. Kathleen, the daughter of a surveyor, noted that homes such as hers were unsuitable sexual spaces due to the high level of adult surveillance:

> There would usually be an adult around, in this environment that I was in, this very controlled middle-class kind of prudish atmosphere, so, yeah, there wasn't really any, I never took a boy home, ever.[136]

Kathleen simply did not see her parental home as a 'sexual resource' and many teenagers such as Kathleen suggested that their lack of sexual activity in their teens was a direct reflection of these spatial politics.[137] Others, however, similarly presented the home as an inappropriate sexual space but went on to discuss how they simply worked around this 'obstacle' in pursuit of the sex they desired.

Private acts and public spaces

From the dance halls and cinemas discussed in the previous chapter, to school corridors and building sites, teenagers could be very creative in the spaces they used for intimate behaviour. The boundary between 'acceptable' and 'unacceptable' sexual conduct was highly elastic, varying from person to person and context to context – while some couples may have been happy to kiss or pet beside the dance floor at a nightclub or party, others preferred to do so only when completely alone. However, intimacies that involved the removal of clothing, the 'comfort' of lying down, and/or which required more than a few minutes were understood to demand more 'complete' forms of privacy. Unable to pursue this at home, young couples turned to spaces which appeared to offer a degree of privacy, however fleeting. While almost any space free of adult surveillance could become a sexual space, cars and outdoor spaces such as parks and farmland featured prominently in women's accounts of their adolescent sexual lives. As Sian Edwards has demonstrated, greater mobility allowed many teenagers to travel between urban and rural space and the open landscapes of the countryside offered many young couples a different kind of privacy to that provided in the hustle and bustle of the city.[138]

In part, cars and outdoor spaces operated as sexual spaces for teenagers because they were, unlike organised leisure venues, spaces that young people occupied in the 'normal' process of spending time together. Teenagers living in suburbs, villages, or rural areas often had to be driven by boyfriends and partners to the site of any date. Alternatively, not wanting to be watched by parents or necessarily having the money to hang out in commercial leisure spaces, it was common for teenagers to go for walks or to parks to spend time with one another. Once together in these spaces, however, it was possible for young couples to get 'carried away' by their emotions and desire. This potential was widely noted by sex educators and guidance literature that suggested that girls should be wary of the overwhelming power of adolescent emotion that might lead them to behave in ways that they'd later regret. Girls were repeatedly reminded of the importance of control and not allowing themselves to be alone with boys in order to avoid letting their sexual feelings get the best of them.[139] This sense of getting caught up in the moment was certainly true of Deborah's experience. Having lost her virginity just before the end of the university term, Deborah 'longed to do it again' but she and her partner were separated as they went home for the vacation. Over the break, they agreed to meet up in a London park and there 'had sex standing up behind a tree!!! Frightful!'[140] The multiple exclamation points in her Deborah's written testimony convey a sense of amusement at her past self though her characterisation of the event as 'frightful' indicates a feeling of embarrassment that she had sex in such a public place.

Of particular concern to commentators were the new opportunities for privacy (and therefore sex) afforded by increased car ownership. Although access to a car was far from universal at this time, for teenagers the relative privacy of cars and their ability to be parked up on the way home meant that they could easily provide opportunities for sexual activity.[141] Teenage couples had 'legitimate' reasons to be in cars as these were used to go to or from the specific destination of their dates. Unlike many other spaces, cars offered a degree of comfort: they were shielded from the elements and the backseat offered a space where couples could recline, if not fully lie down. To agony aunts it was precisely this quality that made cars dangerous and advice literature often represented cars as hotbeds of overcharged teenage hormones. When a *Jackie* reader wrote to Cathy and Claire to ask whether 'necking' in a car was 'any more dangerous than necking anywhere else', the response was pointed:

> Certainly do. It's but a short step from the front seat to the back – and there it could be just too comfy! Let's face it, to keep passion manageable, there's nothing like the cold outdoors![142]

In offering teenage lovers a degree of seclusion and comfort, cars stoked the fires of temptation and too easily allowed teenagers to get 'out of control'.[143]

In contrast to adults who emphasised notions of danger, young women themselves could find this opportunism and al fresco sex highly erotic. Describing her first experience of heavy petting as 'rather delightful', Jane reflected on this experience fondly: 'He was several years older than I was, very attractive, and obviously a lot more sexually experienced. After a meal, we walked down to the river and indulged in an extremely enjoyable session.'[144] Similarly, Glenys found her first experience of sex immensely pleasurable:

> I lost my virginity – by this time I really felt I was missing out – to a manager after a Christmas office party. It was in the back of his car on the way home. I think I was the keener as he hadn't come prepared so had to withdraw but oh, it was so good.[145]

For Jane and Glenys, the outdoor setting was not 'romantic' as such but heightened the sense of eroticism and sexual excitement. Far from rendering their experiences incomplete or unsatisfactory, these young women's sexual lives were enhanced by the heightened emotions associated with expediency and secrecy.

At the same time that some adolescent sexual activity was defined by spontaneous expressions of desire and opportunism, teenagers could also be very deliberate in their negotiation of space. Sexual activity did not always 'just happen' in cars and outdoor spaces because teenagers got carried away. Rather, these spaces became sexual destinations that young couples travelled to specifically to engage in intimate behaviour. Mabel noted that her access to a car set her apart from some of her peers:

> I think a lack of privacy thwarted many couples and if my boyfriend had not been older and had a car, we would have had no opportunity to indulge in heavy petting the way we did. We would take a ride out

into the countryside and park the car in a gateway and climb into the back seat. We sank into the mud once and had to get a farmer to tow us out and were very late home. In the winter we even parked in his garage.[146]

As Mabel suggests, cars were useful in that they offered comfort and privacy of their own – couples could lie down, were shielded from the elements, and had a degree of sensory insulation – but they were also mobile, meaning that they could occupy different spaces dependent on need. Within local communities, young people used cars to create new sexual geographies. As Ruth described:

It was often the back of a car where everything was going on ... And we lived down what was called 'Lover's Lane' and when you drove down the lane, if a boyfriend was taking me home ... so I might have been 15, 16 by then ... you passed all these steamed up cars on the way down, because that was the only place where people felt that they could be undiscovered by their parents.[147]

Where the post-war press romanticised 'Lover's Lanes', for many teenagers they served a much-needed practical function as safe sites for sexual activity.[148]

Premeditation was particularly heightened when it came to having penetrative sex for the first time. Alison suggested that her parents were relatively liberal and that, had she wanted to, she probably could have had sex in her home. Yet, wishing to keep this aspect of her personal life separate from her home life, she decided to have sex elsewhere. She 'went into the woods' with her boyfriend to have sex after a date at the cinema as she 'didn't know where else to have sex ... [and] this was a way of having sex somewhere private, or hopefully private'.[149] Marjorie 'became obsessed by the thought of losing [her] virginity' when she was fifteen. 'Determined' to have sex, Marjorie 'found a willing partner in [M], a 22 year old builder working in a house nearby'. In November 1967 she took the day off school, went to the house where he was working and had sex on the floor.[150] Having sex for the first time was felt by many young women to be a significant milestone worthy of consideration and calculation. For Marjorie, having sex on the floor of a stranger's house was a pragmatic choice that made the most of the space available to her and her partner. Wanting to keep their activity a secret from their parents, Alison, Marjorie, and other girls went to great lengths to make sure that they did not raise their parents' suspicions.

In their campaigns of evasion and subterfuge, teenagers were convinced of their own cunning and took a certain amount of pride in circumventing their parents' rules and expectations. However, parents were not naive – many had themselves engaged in similar behaviour in their youth – and many were aware of the fact that their daughters were trying to escape their sights in order engage in sexual activity.[151] The testimonies also recall numerous instances of teenagers being caught by adults. For example, Sandra and a boyfriend had a backseat snogging session in a layby interrupted by a policeman while Tracy's nan (who lived with Tracy and her mum) walked in on her and a partner.[152] In some cases parents' concerns led them to clamp down on teenagers' mobility: parents might restrict access to cars or ban girls from seeing certain boys.[153] Glenys noted how her parents frowned upon her and her partner going for bicycle rides or walks as they were 'afraid of what we "might get up to" in the local countryside or in the sandhills'.[154]

Like their initial rules and restrictions, though, parents' attempts to curb their daughters' activities often came to naught. Tina and her boyfriend used the excuse of going for a 'walk' when they wanted to be intimate. Although her parents 'worried' and often came out looking for her, it did little to prevent her doing what she wanted:

> My parents never, as I remember, tried to control where we went but I do remember dad getting worried: after some 'walks' when we had in fact been having sex in my uncle's yard among the hay bales, we would meet him on the way back, coming up the road torch in hand saying he was just wondering where we were as it had got dark!! I now suspect that they worried non-stop from the moment we left the house, but they never said anything.[155]

Teenage couples demonstrated a remarkable capacity to evade parental oversight. At a time of increasing mobility, when young people had enhanced opportunities for leisure outside of the home and more excuses to be 'out', parental surveillance could not keep track of, or limit, the activities of teenagers who were set on sexual activity. Parents could manage the home in such a way as to make it an unappealing site for sexual activity but their efforts could be overwhelmed by young women's desire for sexual experimentation.

Conclusion

'Be selective. Be inventive. Protect your parents.' So advised *Honey* in 'Parents are People Too'. Teenagers of the post-war generation were encouraged to acknowledge that their parents would worry about them but this did not necessarily have to prevent young people from enjoying the social and sexual experiences they desired. As this article suggested, however, it was crucial that girls try to avoid prompting 'unhealthy' worry in their parents that would only cause emotional upset and tension at home and make their lives more difficult. The key to balancing home life and social life was pretence: '*Un*healthy worrying comes from letting your parents get exposed to life as you are actually living it.'[156]

This chapter has shown that teenage girls of the post-war generation embodied this ethos. This is not to say that teenagers lacked respect or genuine affection for their parents. Quite the opposite. Far from simply wishing to avoid superficial 'trouble', girls were genuinely invested in their relationships with their parents. Familial ties were a significant form of personal and emotional support and guidance for girls and many young women were keen for their parents to interact with their boyfriends and at least tolerated some interference in their dating lives. When it came to sex, however, girls often felt that their 'modern' sexual values and desires were incompatible with those of their parents. Those girls who did decide to indulge their sexual desires often did so in direct violation of their parents' warnings. But girls did not want their sexuality to undermine or disrupt their relationships with their parents and so conducted their sexual rebellions in ways that made them invisible to parents. Young people may have refused to obey their parents' rules but they nevertheless attempted to maintain the *illusion* of compliance. Unlike the flagrant broadcasting of generational difference inherent to post-war subcultures, adolescent sexual culture was defined by evasion and subterfuge. Teenage girls managed their sexual lives in accordance with the same philosophy that their parents used to justify limited discussions of sex at home: 'what you didn't know rather than what you did know, would protect you'.[157]

Notes

1 'Parents are People Too', *Honey*, January 1965.
2 Jonathon Green, *All Dressed Up: The Sixties and the Counterculture* (London: Jonathan Cape, 1998), pp. 7–10.
3 Louise Jackson and Angela Bartie, *Policing Youth: Britain 1945–80* (Manchester: Manchester University Press, 2014); Stuart Hall and Tony Jefferson, eds, *Resistance through Rituals: Youth Subcultures in Post-War Britain*, 2nd ed. (Abingdon: Routledge, 1993); Fowler, *Youth Culture in Modern Britain, c.1920–c.1970*.
4 Nick Thomas, 'Challenging Myths of the 1960s: The Case of Student Protest in Britain', *Twentieth Century British History* 13, no. 3 (2002).
5 Gillian A. M. Mitchell, 'Reassessing "the Generation Gap": Bill Haley's 1957 Tour of Britain, Inter-Generational Relations and Attitudes to Rock 'N' Roll in the Late 1950s', *Twentieth Century British History* 24, no. 4 (2013).
6 According to *The New Housewife Survey* conducted in the mid-1960s, 91 per cent of unmarried women between the ages of 16 and 30 were living with their parents. British Market Research Bureau Limited, *The New Housewife: Report on a Survey* (London: J. Walter Thompson, 1967), vol. II, Tables 2.20b and 2.21b.
7 Michael Murphy, 'The Evolution of Cohabitation in Britain, 1960–95', *Population Studies* 54, no. 1 (2000): 53.
8 Diana Barker, 'Young People and Their Homes: Spoiling and "Keeping Close" in a South Wales Town', *The Sociological Review* 20, no. 4 (1972).
9 Hazel (1947), OH-15-04-05.
10 The Directive asked: 'Did anybody try to control whom you could date or where you could go?' MOP, 'Courting and Dating' (2001), www.massobs.org.uk/images/Directives/Summer_2001_Directive.pdf [accessed: 25 September 2024].
11 Wendy (1943), MOP, 'Courting and Dating', W633.
12 Daphne (1941), OH-15-03-05.
13 Joyce (1950), OH-15-03-02.
14 Maureen (1949), OH-15-05-04.
15 Carol Dyhouse, 'Graduates, Mothers and Graduate Mothers: Family Investment in Higher Education in Twentieth Century England', *Gender and Education* 14, no. 4 (2002): 325–36.

16 Gwen (1953), MOP, 'Courting and Dating', G2640.
17 Sharon (1951), MOP, 'Courting and Dating', S2581; Carole (1949), MOP, 'Sex', C1713; Carolyn (1947), MOP, 'Sex', C1832; Glenys (1941), MOP, 'Courting and Dating', G226. Parents had similar hopes for boys, see MOP, 'Sex', S2207.
18 Yvette (1959), MOP, 'Courting and Dating', Y2926.
19 Beryl (1945), MOP, 'Courting and Dating', C2579.
20 Anita (1954), MOP, 'Courting and Dating', C2053.
21 Judith (1946), MOP, 'Courting and Dating', J931.
22 Amanda (1947), MOP, 'Courting and Dating', A1706.
23 Julie (1960), OH-15-02-09; Joyce (1950), OH-15-03-02; Mary (1959), OH-15-05-08.
24 Yvette (1959), MOP, 'Courting and Dating', Y2926.
25 Deborah (1950), MOP, 'Courting and Dating', D826.
26 Charlotte (1943), MOP, 'Courting and Dating', C2654.
27 Glenys (1941), MOP, 'Courting and Dating', G226.
28 See the following responses to the 2001 MOP 'Courting and Dating' Directive: Charlotte (1943), C2654; Denise (1943), D2585; Sarah (1952), S2207; Yvonne, W2107; Yvette (1959), Y2926. See also Virginia (1948), MOP, 'Close Relationships' Directive (1990), N880.
29 Kathleen (1948), OH-15-04-06.
30 Pamela (1948), MOP, 'Close Relationships', R860.
31 Sally (1946), OH-15-05-02.
32 Szreter and Fisher, *Sex before the Sexual Revolution*, pp. 184–86; Langhamer, *English in Love*, p. 123.
33 Maxine (1944), MOP, 'Courting and Dating', N2058.
34 Gwen (1953), MOP, 'Courting and Dating', G2640.
35 Shelly (1956), MOP, 'Close Relationship', Q2097. In MOP, 'Courting and Dating': Dorothy (1951), E2836; Glenys (1941), G226; Gwen (1953), G2640.
36 Maxine (1944), MOP, 'Courting and Dating', N2058.
37 Irene (1952), MOP, 'Sex', H2418. Anna Maguire, '"You Wouldn't Want Your Daughter Marrying One": Parental Intervention into Mixed-Race Relationships in Post-War Britain', *Historical Research* 92, no. 256 (2019): 349–419; Chamion Caballero and Peter J. Aspinall, *Mixed Race Britain in the Twentieth Century* (Basingstoke: Palgrave Macmillan, 2018).
38 Joyce (1950), OH-15-03-02. On the broader experiences of foreign students see Hilary Perraton, *A History of Foreign Students in Britain* (Basingstoke: Palgrave Macmillan, 2014).
39 Glenys (1941), MOP, 'Courting and Dating', G226.
40 Dorothy (1951), MOP, 'Courting and Dating', E2836.

41 'A Cathy and Claire Special on Coping with Parents', *Jackie*, 1 June 1974.
42 Select examples include: 'The Cathy and Claire Page', *Jackie*, 22 May 1965; 'The Cathy and Claire Page', *Jackie*, 2 January 1971; 'The Cathy and Claire Page', *Jackie*, 10 May 1975.
43 Clare (1956), MOP, 'Courting and Dating', C2888. Anxiety at introducing boyfriends to parents was also expressed by: Enid (1950), MOP, 'Close Relationship', D1226; Shelly (1956), MOP, 'Close Relationships', Q2097; Kay (1951), MOP, 'Courting and Dating', K798.
44 'My Mum's a Dragon', *Jackie*, 19 June 1971.
45 'Mum's the Word!', *19*, September 1969; 'A *Jackie* Special on Meeting His Parents', *Jackie*, 3 May 1975.
46 'Problems: Love and Other Things', *Honey*, October 1960.
47 Examples among responses to the 2001 MOP 'Courting and Dating' Directive include: Anita (1954), C2053; Glenys (1941), G226; Judith (1946), J931; Michele (1956), N2912; Rebecca (1943), R1025; Rita (1944), R1227; Marlene (1952), T534.
48 Marjorie (1952), MOP, 'Courting and Dating', N1552.
49 Yvette (1959), MOP, 'Courting and Dating', Y2926.
50 Michele (1956), MOP, 'Courting and Dating', N2912.
51 Judith (1946), MOP, 'Courting and Dating', J931.
52 Virginia (1948), MOP, 'Close Relationships', N880; Pamela (1948), MOP, 'Close Relationships', R860; Glenys (1941), MOP, 'Growing Up' Directive (1993), G226; Gwen (1953), MOP, 'Courting and Dating', G2640; Suzanne (1945), MOP, 'Courting and Dating', S1983.
53 Marjorie (1952), MOP, 'Courting and Dating', N1552.
54 'The Cathy and Claire Page', *Jackie*, 28 November 1964.
55 'The Cathy and Claire Page', *Jackie*, 11 July 1964.
56 'The Cathy and Claire Page', *Jackie*, 25 April 1964; 'The Cathy and Claire Page', *Jackie*, 15 February 1964.
57 The Labour Party, *The Younger Generation: Report of the Labour Party Youth Commission* (London: Labour Party, 1959).
58 The Labour Party, *The Younger Generation*; Hansard, HC Deb. Vol. 612, cols. 540–636, 30 October 1959.
59 Kathleen (1948), OH-15-04-06.
60 Simon Szreter, 'Victorian Britain, 1831–1963: Towards a Social History of Sexuality', *Journal of Victorian Culture* 1, no. 1 (1996). The legacy of so-called 'Victorianism' in sexual culture has been subject to much debate, see Frank Mort, 'Victorian Afterlives: Sexuality and Identity in the 1960s and 1970s', *History Workshop Journal* 82, no. 1 (2016); Lesley A. Hall, 'The Victorians: Our Others, Our Selves?', in *Sex, Knowledge and Receptions of the Past*, ed. Kate Fisher and Rebecca Langlands (Oxford: Oxford University Press, 2015).

61 Geraldine (1959), MOP, 'Sex' Directive, G3395. See also Marian (1964), MOP, 'Sex', M3401; Rachel (1959), MOP, 'Sex', R2862.
62 Georgina (1959), MOP, 'Sex', G3423.
63 Heather (1948), MOP, 'Sex', H1703; Vera (1942), MOP, 'Sex', W632.
64 Lillian (1946), MOP, 'Sex', L1002.
65 Tina (1949), MOP, 'Sex', T1843. See also in MOP, 'Sex': Eileen (1951), E743; Jane (1951), H1745.
66 Ruth (1960), OH-15-02-01.
67 Glenys (1961), MOP, 'Sex', G226.
68 In Spring 1996 Mass Observation circulated a Directive on the topic of 'Menstruation' which goes into more detail on menstruation throughout women's lives.
69 Janice (1952), OH-15-03-01. From MOP, 'Sex': Irene (1952), H2418; Lisa (1957), L3037; Mabel (1946), M3408; Shirley (1949), S1399.
70 Kathleen (1948), OH-15-04-06.
71 Julie (1960), OH-15-02-09.
72 Among responses to the MOP 'Sex' Directive see Evelyn (1947), F3409; Geraldine (1959), G3395; Irene (1952), H2418; Jayne (1941), H2639; Marian (1964), M3401; Muriel (1940), P1009; Yvonne (1941), W2107.
73 Irene (1952), MOP, 'Sex', H2418.
74 Maureen (1949), OH-15-05-04.
75 Dawn (1952), MOP, 'Sex', D156.
76 Barbara (1952), OH-15-02-03.
77 Glenys (1941), MOP, 'Sex', G226.
78 Marian (1964), MOP, 'Sex', M3401.
79 Lesley (1958), MOP, 'Sex', L3298.
80 Valerie (1947), OH-15-05-06.
81 Michael Schofield, 'The Sociological Contribution to Health Education', *Health Education Journal* 22 (1964): 44–48.
82 Catherine (1959), MOP, 'Sex', C3513; Debbie (1964), MOP, 'Sex', D3289.
83 Jacqueline (1945), OH-15-04-03.
84 Ruth (1960), OH-15-02-01; Angela (1961), MOP, 'Growing Up', A1783; Enid (1950), MOP, 'Close Relationships', D1226; Jill (1959), MOP, 'Sex', H3459; Lisa (1957), MOP, 'Sex', L3037; Lorraine (1951), MOP, 'Sex', L3253.
85 Gloria (1950), MOP, 'Sex', G3417; Lorraine (1951), MOP, 'Sex', L3253.
86 Jacqueline (1945), OH-15-04-03; Linda (1952), OH-15-01-03; Deborah (1950), MOP, 'Sex', D826; Heather (1948), MOP, 'Sex', H1703.

87 Catherine (1959), MOP, 'Sex', C3513; Georgina (1959), MOP, 'Sex', G3423.
88 Heather (1948), MOP, 'Sex', H1703.
89 It is estimated that 75 per cent of households in England and Wales had a television by 1961. Sue Bowden and Avner Offer, 'Household Appliances and the Use of Time: The United States and Britain Since the 1920s', *The Economic History Review* 47, no. 4 (1994). Chelsea-Anne Saxby, 'Making Love and British Telly: Watching Sex, Bodies and Intimate Lives in the Long 1970s', Unpublished PhD Thesis (University of Birmingham, 2020).
90 On the rising sexual content on television see Ben Thompson, *Ban This Filth! Mary Whitehouse and the Battle to Keep Britain Innocent* (London: Faber & Faber, 2012).
91 Julie (1960), OH-15-02-09.
92 Maureen (1949), OH-15-05-04; Frances (1961), MOP, 'Sex', F3178.
93 Marian (1964), MOP, 'Sex', M3401.
94 Anne (1964), OH-14-01-06; Stephanie (1960), OH-15-05-01. In responses to the MOP 'Close Relationships Directive': Glenys (1941), G226; Kristin (1957), K312. Responses to MOP 'Courting and Dating' Directive: Phyllis (1947), P1796; Pamela (1948), R860; Veronica (1951), W1813; Wendy (1943), W633. Responses to MOP 'Sex' Directive: Deborah (1950), D826; Jayne (1941), H2639; Mabel (1946), M3408; Muriel (1940), P1009.
95 Eileen (1951), MOP, 'Sex', E743.
96 Geoffrey Gorer, *Exploring English Character* (New York: Criterion Books, 1955), p. 116; Gorer, *Sex and Marriage in England Today*, p. 51.
97 Lorraine (1951), MOP, 'Sex', L3253; Andrea (1957), MOP, 'Sex', A2212.
98 Sheila (1958), MOP, 'Sex', S3372. Geiringer, *The Pope and the Pill*.
99 Callum G. Brown, *The Death of Christian Britain: Understanding Secularisation 1800–2000* (Oxford: Oxford University Press, 2009).
100 Julie (1960), OH-15-02-09.
101 Catherine (1959), MOP, 'Sex', C3513.
102 This is not to say that the Christian teaching had no influence whatsoever – it is difficult to understate the influence of Christianity on English codes of morality. See Peter Hennessy, *Having It So Good: Britain in the Fifties* (London: Penguin, 2007), p. 128. On the decline of religion as an influence over women's sexual decision-making, see Brown, 'Sex, Religion, and the Single Woman c.1950–75'.
103 Glenys (1941), MOP, 'Courting and Dating', G226. On illegitimacy and shame see Robinson, *In the Family Way*; Cohen, *Family Secrets*.
104 Carolyn (1947), MOP, 'Sex', C1832.

105 Kathleen (1948), OH-15-04-06 and Jill (1959), MOP, 'Sex', H3459.
106 Jane (1951), MOP, 'Sex', H1745.
107 Jayne (1941), MOP, 'Sex', H2639. See also Carolyn (1947), MOP, 'Sex', C1832.
108 Deborah (1950), MOP, 'Sex', D826.
109 Glenys (1941), MOP, 'Sex', G226.
110 Of the participants whose relationship status at first intercourse is known, 69 per cent had penetrative sex for the first time outside the context of marriage or engagement.
111 Janice (1952), OH-15-03-01.
112 'The Cathy and Claire Page', *Jackie*, 3 October 1964.
113 'My Mum's a Dragon', *Jackie*, 19 June 1971.
114 'Resurgence of Venereal Disease', *The Guardian*, 19 March 1963.
115 '"This Evil Threat to Our Family Life"', *Daily Mail*, 20 August 1954; 'The Poison of Our Morals', *Daily Mail*, 29 December 1960; 'Bishop Attacks "New Morality"', *Daily Mail*, 28 February 1964.
116 'Early Marriage Tradition: Problem for Schools', *Manchester Guardian*, 18 May 1956; 'Britain's Girl Mothers: Teen-agers in Trouble', *Manchester Guardian*, 21 March 1959.
117 Margaret Drabble, 'The Sexual Revolution', *The Guardian*, 11 October 1967. Other features in the series included: John Bird, 'But Is There Anything Left to Rebel Against', *The Guardian*, 18 October 1967; Sir Edward Boyle, MP, 'Citadels of Privacy', *The Guardian*, 20 October 1967; John Wilson, 'What Kind of Morality', *The Guardian*, 25 October 1967.
118 Joy (1954), OH-15-04-01.
119 Kathleen (1948), OH-15-04-06. See also Anne (1964), OH-14-01-06.
120 Jacqueline (1945), OH-15-04-03.
121 Anne (1964), OH-14-01-06.
122 Claire Rayner, *People in Love: A Modern Guide to Sex in Marriage* (Feltham: Paul Hamlyn, 1968), p. 35.
123 Daphne (1941), OH-15-03-05.
124 Tracy (1962), OH-14-02-01.
125 Hazel (1947), OH-15-04-05. See also Joyce (1950), OH-15-03-02.
126 Daphne (1941), OH-15-03-05.
127 Andrea (1957), MOP, 'Sex', A2212.
128 On the fraught politics of sleeping arrangements see Victoria Robinson, Jenny Hockey, and Angela Meah, '"What I Used to Do … on My Mother's Settee": Spatial and Emotional Aspects of Heterosexuality in England', *Gender, Place & Culture* 11, no. 3 (2004).
129 Heather (1948), MOP, 'Courting and Dating', H1703.
130 Jane (1951), MOP, 'Sex', H1745.

131 Marjorie (1952), MOP, 'Courting and Dating', N1552.
132 Barbara (1952), OH-15-02-03.
133 Robinson et al., 'What I Used to Do ... on My Mother's Settee', pp. 429–30.
134 Diana (1947), OH-15-01-05.
135 Kay (1951), MOP, 'Sex', K798.
136 Kathleen (1948), OH-15-04-06.
137 Robinson et al., 'What I Used to Do ... on My Mother's Settee', p. 429.
138 Sian Edwards, 'Lovers' Lanes and Haystacks: Rural Spaces and Girls' Experiences of Courtship and Sexual Intimacy in Post-War England', in *Let's Spend the Night Together: Sex, Pop Music and British Youth Culture, 1950s–1980s*, ed. The Subcultures Network (Manchester: Manchester University Press, 2023).
139 *The Transmission of Life*; Donald and Ann Hilton, *Girl Into Woman: Sex Knowledge for the Growing Girl* (Redhill: Denholm House Press, 1972), p. 29. Johnson, *Love and Sex in Plain Language*, p. 123.
140 Deborah (1950), MOP, 'Sex', D826.
141 Simon Gunn, 'People and the Car: The Expansion of Automobility in Urban Britain, c. 1955–70', *Social History* 38, no. 2 (2013).
142 'The Cathy and Claire Page', *Jackie*, 21 March 1964.
143 Gladys Denny Schulz, 'Letters to Jane', *Honey*, January 1961. Gladys Denny Schulz's book *Letters to Jane* had originally been published in the United States in 1946 and was released in Britain in 1949. *Honey* magazine serialised extracts from the book across the first half of 1961.
144 Jane (1951), MOP, 'Sex', H1745. See also MOP, 'Courting and Dating', H1745.
145 Glenys (1941), MOP, 'Sex', G226. See also this Observer's response to the 'Courting and Dating' Directive.
146 Mabel (1946), MOP, 'Sex', M3408.
147 Ruth (1960) OH-15-02-01. See also Diana (1947), OH-15-01-05.
148 Edwards, 'Lovers' Lanes and Haystacks'.
149 Alison (1960), OH-14-02-02.
150 Marjorie (1952), MOP, 'Courting and Dating', N1552.
151 Oral history testimony suggests that they may also have engaged in similar behaviours! Szreter and Fisher, *Sex before the Sexual Revolution*, chapter 2.
152 Sandra (1949), OH-14-01-02; Tracy (1962), OH-14-02-01.
153 Sarah (1952), MOP, 'Courting and Dating', S2207.
154 Glenys (1941), MOP, 'Courting and Dating', G226.
155 Tina (1949), MOP, 'Courting and Dating', T1843.
156 'Parents are People Too'.
157 Mabel (1946), MOP, 'Sex', M3408.

Conclusion

The women in this book recorded their testimonies in mid or later life. It is not surprising, therefore, that they tended to situate their accounts of adolescence in a longer-time perspective that, while focused on their own youth, made connections between this and the lives of their mothers as well as observations of their children and grandchildren.[1] Echoing earlier studies of this generation, the testimonies analysed in this book suggest that women born in the 1940s and 1950s understood their lives to have departed significantly from that of their mothers and grandmothers.[2] Women saw themselves as having benefited from the material support of the post-war welfare state and opportunities for education and employment but also described a stark break from the past in terms of the worldviews they held and femininities that they embodied. As Lynn Abrams has argued, 'the post-war generation of women is a generation visible to itself'.[3]

Yet, as well as viewing themselves as having had a radically different life experience to that of their elders, in their testimonies women also sought to distinguish their lives, and particularly their sex lives, from those of their daughters and granddaughters. Though judgements as to whether it was 'better' to have been raised in the post-war period as opposed to the late twentieth century varied, women portrayed contemporary adolescence as a foreign experience. Interviewees identified significant contrasts between their adolescent lives and 'today's standards' and often suggested that their experiences were beyond the comprehension of their children.[4] There was much in their earlier lives, they claimed, that 'young people now don't understand'.[5]

Rather than seeing these narratives of generational difference as simply an inescapable quirk of reflective testimony, we can historicise them on their own terms. This Conclusion therefore draws together themes that have emerged across the book's chapters to consider the ways in which the post-war generation's sexual lives were different from their predecessors. It then considers the forward-facing elements of women's testimonies, using these as a way of thinking about the legacies of mid-twentieth-century developments. The book ends by articulating how this study of teenage sexuality suggests new directions for the history of intimacy and offers new insights into notions of historical agency and accounts of social and cultural change in the past.

A 'breakthrough' generation?

In explaining the differences between their generation and their predecessors, women often pointed to material changes that had expanded opportunities for women of the post-war cohort; in their view, theirs was a generation of new-found freedom.[6] The expansion of co-educational schooling and organised leisure created new opportunities for young women to meet and interact with boys.[7] The post-war economic boom and raised expectations of state-provided education allowed increasing numbers of women to go into further and higher education, to pursue professions and/or to find work that supported their increasingly mobile and independent young adulthood.[8] More specifically, in the realm of sex, advances in the effectiveness of birth control, alongside the gradual relaxation of barriers to sexual health advice, lessened the risk that penetrative intercourse would lead to pregnancy.[9] At the same time, the decriminalisation of abortion in 1967 provided women with increased options should they become pregnant.[10] Though we should be wary of teleology, many of these developments were cumulative and, as such, the sexual landscapes of women growing up in the 1970s were structurally different to that faced by women born in the 1940s.

These shifts in material conditions were important but to understand sexual change we also need to acknowledge a more intangible transformation in sexual culture. Looking across the testimonies it is clear that the decades after the Second World War witnessed a profound reimagining of what sex was for. What was changing was not simply young people's capacity to engage in sexual activity but their desire to do so at all and this was rooted in changing understandings of what the function of sex was and could be. Women of the post-war generation portrayed earlier generations as having thought of sex in terms of marital duty, romantic love, and motherhood. The sexual culture of the pre-war period is characterised in their testimonies as having been tightly constrained by stifling notions of religious morality, social respectability, and patriarchal family structures.[11] Historical analyses of the earlier twentieth century suggest that such characterisations are a little simplistic but not altogether inaccurate.[12] Sex may have had a variety of functions and meanings to earlier generations but these largely remained tied to expectations of marriage and motherhood and were often defined in relation to strict notions of respectability.[13] Such expectations took on new life for the post-war generation. Attempts from the early twentieth century to use sex to shore up the institution of marriage had the unplanned effect of placing sex at the heart of heterosexual relationships that 'preceded' marriage.[14] With sexual compatibility increasingly seen as an essential feature of successful marriages, young couples in the post-war period could use the logic of 'testing' that compatibility or needing to develop their sexual skill as a justification for pre-marital sex. Believing marriage to be a life-long commitment in which they would find personal fulfilment and happiness and which required deep romantic love, women increasingly saw emotional connectedness and already-established intimacy (which they understood to be fostered through sexual activity) to be prerequisites to marriage rather than bonds that might be forged after their wedding.[15]

At the same time, the post-war generation experienced, and themselves contributed to, a sexual culture that moved sex beyond this marriage-focused frame. As we saw in Part I, sex was increasingly implicated in notions of growing up. More traditional transitions from childhood and youth to adulthood (most notably starting work and getting married) certainly remained important but in the post-war period having penetrative sex for the first time became a milestone in its own right.[16] Young people who believed themselves to be adult as well as those who were striving to achieve maturity now used sexual activity as a means of securing and asserting their adult status. The purpose of sex had, in this context, moved beyond associations with emotional commitment, family building, and romantic intimacy and was serving the processes of self-discovery and self-conscious identity building that have been linked to the psy-ification of British society in the second half of the century.[17]

In addition to its newfound purposes in relation to intimate relationships and selfhood, sex also served distinctive social functions among the post-war generation. Viewed as a marker of maturity and desirability, sexual experience was increasingly valued by young women as something which could raise their status among their peers. Where sex had been damaging to the reputations of young women in earlier periods (and legacies of this lived on across the second half of the twentieth century), managed correctly sexual experience increasingly functioned as a source of social currency.[18] This had consequences not only for young people's decisions as to whether to have sex at all but also shifted how young people managed their sexual activity as it now revolved around a complex politics of spectatorship, secrecy, and display. That sexual practice was shaped by dynamics of space was not new but young people's need to manage the (in)visibility of relationships so that they could benefit from the social kudos of sexual experience while not invoking the disapproval or censure of parents and neighbours became particularly fraught as teenage sexual practice became more common.

Shifting understandings of the function of sexual activity were therefore changing not only the day-to-day practice of sexual activity but were also creating new rationales and justifications for engaging in sexual activity. Women of the post-war generation were different to their predecessors in that they had penetrative sex earlier, with a greater number of sexual partners, and within a broader array of relationship formations, ranging from the deeply committed to the casual and fleeting. This was the case not simply because increased access to birth control removed previous constraints but also because new incentives to engage in sexual activity were emerging.

A 'transitional' generation?

While women's testimonies did much to distinguish their generation's experience from that of their predecessors, they also perceived significant differences between their teenage sex lives and those of younger generations.[19] Women pointed to a number of developments that altered the landscape of teenage sexuality across the late twentieth and early twenty-first centuries and which set their sex lives apart from those of young people in the present. Further technological developments have expanded the range of hormonal and barrier methods of birth control available to young people, arguably making it easier than ever before for couples to control their fertility.[20] Though the AIDS crisis of the 1980s occurred closer in time to the adolescences of some of the women interviewed than those of their grandchildren growing up in the 2010s, the legacies of that public health crisis continue to loom large in contemporary understandings of 'safe sex' and sexual health provision.[21] Sex acts between women were never formally criminalised but since the partial decriminalisation of sex acts between men in 1967, English society (and British society more broadly) has continued to debate the fact and status of queer sex and relationships.[22] Where the testimonies of (nominally 'straight') women of the post-war generation framed lesbianism as a hidden novelty in their youth (largely confined to rumours about games teachers and school mistresses),[23] this is not the case for young people growing up in the twenty-first century when gay, bisexual, asexual, and queer identities and relationships are discussed more openly and are visible in mainstream popular culture (though homophobia has certainly not been eradicated).[24]

When discussing what they observed in contemporary society, women were particularly adamant that the rise of the internet and social media were transforming sexual culture. These technologies have been important in offering teenagers a more expansive and inclusive sex education and have been immensely valuable to young people growing up in environments in which they feel unable to ask questions or find communities that speak to their own feelings and experience.[25] However, concerns continue to be raised about the potential harms associated with unfettered access to (increasingly violent) pornography, widespread practices of sexual image sharing, and the ways in which social media amplifies unattainable beauty standards and intensifies experiences of bullying and harassment.[26]

Although women often reflected explicitly on the changes they observed across their lifetimes, there was less recognition (or at least less overt discussion) of the significant continuities that link teenage sexuality in the post-war period to that of the present. Many of the contrasts that women drew between post-war and so-called 'Millennial' and 'Gen Z' experience, for example, spoke to changes that the former had set in motion. Discussions of teenage pregnancy represented one iteration of this dynamic. Many interviewees and Mass Observers commented on what they viewed as a 'crisis' of teenage pregnancy in the early twenty-first century. This was often used to articulate a feeling not just that individual morals had changed but that society itself had lost its way. In Annie's words: 'as a society we are going wrong somewhere as far too many of the young ruin their lives by having children before they have lived'.[27] Though many women recounted that they themselves or girls they knew had become pregnant as teenagers in the 1950s, 1960s, and 1970s (see Chapter 2), they were keen to stress that this was not like 'the society of today'.[28] As Lorraine put it: 'Things have changed vastly over the last 50 years, I think before it was much too strict and there was no compassion for pregnancy outside marriage but now it is far too lax, many couples have children and have no intention of getting married.'[29]

Lilian was particularly scathing of contemporary values, pausing her retrospective testimony to recount a conversation she had recently overheard on a bus:

> Why only a few months ago, as I waited for a bus ... I overheard two young girls in Black trousers, and school blazers – (I presume 6th formers ...) – I overheard them say, 'Do you use STRETCH MARK CREAM?' – No, I can't be arsed, my mum got me some, but I can't be arsed! ...
>
> I looked around, stretch mark cream? – I thought, No, surely not pregnant? No.
>
> But YES, from TEXTING – their blooming boyfriends – probably still in school – while these two school girls were finished early for the day – to go to their ANTE-NATAL CLASS! ...

I looked – almost aghast, was I <u>staring?</u> – (I hope <u>not.</u>) But I was amazed, shocked, disgusted. Is it me? OR have we gone crazy? 6th formers pregnant? – And easy access to THE PILL, <u>and</u> THE MORNING AFTER PILL. What's going on?[30]

There is much to unpack here (especially in relation to how educational opportunity and perceived access to contraception are informing Lilian's assessment of these girls' situations) but this outburst is all the more striking given that Lilian's own marriage had been brought forward when she became pregnant in her late teens in the mid-1960s.

Fears that the turn of the twenty-first century was witnessing a rise in teenage pregnancy were widespread and amplified by New Labour's Teenage Pregnancy Strategy, launched in 1999.[31] In reality, the conception rates for both women under sixteen and under eighteen remained relatively consistent across the final quarter of the twentieth century – the 4.5 per cent rate among under eighteens recorded in 1975 mirrored that recorded in 1999.[32] What was changing, however, was the likelihood of young women carrying pregnancies to term and the marital status of mothers. Rates of births outside of marriage were certainly higher in the 1990s and 2000s than they had been in the 1950s and 1960s – where 47.5 per cent of live births recorded in 2014 were to unmarried parents, this was true of only 5.4 per cent of births in 1960.[33] Explaining these changes requires an understanding of the different logics underpinning young people's choices as well as an awareness of the contexts in which young people made the decision to have sex and their use (or not) of birth control. These questions bring us back to the transformations in sexual culture brought about by the post-war generation. Though attitudes towards and discourses surrounding teenage pregnancy in the early twenty-first century were different to those of previous generations this was not an exclusively contemporary phenomenon and had roots in mid-century changes.[34]

Other aspects of teenage sexuality have experienced less transformation since the post-war generation's adolescence. This is not to say that certain elements of human sexuality are innate or universal, but rather is testament to how deeply rooted many aspects of English sexual culture are. The last fifteen years have seen unprecedented levels of public discussion around the issues of sexual harassment and assault. High-profile criminal investigations, the Everyday

Sexism project, the #MeToo movement and the Everyone's Invited project have been important not just in prompting conversations about contemporary sexuality but also in initiating a re-evaluation of historic practices, discourses and experience.[35] The meanings and associations of sexual 'harassment', 'assault', and 'abuse', as well as 'consent', may be different for young people in the twenty-first century and testimonies collected now may reflect differently on these issues and/or have different points of emphasis to those considered here which were captured in the 1990s, 2000s, and 2010s.[36] But for all this change, the underlying issue of how individuals make the decision to have sex and how young people negotiate one another's sexuality is one that is shared across historic and contemporary accounts. Testimonies submitted to Everyone's Invited (a project launched in 2020 to raise awareness of peer-to-peer sexual violence and sexual harassment within schools), for example, confirm that the dynamic of 'boys try, girls deny' that characterised the post-war generation's teenage sex lives is still very much alive.[37] Similarly, accounts of historic experience mirror contemporary studies which have shown how teenage girls cannot disentangle their feelings about sex from the emotional investment in their relationships, creating grey areas in sexual decision-making.[38]

The association of 'becoming sexual' with 'growing up' also persists. This is evident in contemporary 'facts of life' literature as well as in government guidance for the now-compulsory provision of Relationships and Sex Education in schools.[39] We can also observe this in the continued construction of hierarchical taxonomies of sexual activity that build towards penetrative intercourse. As discussed in Chapter 1, the precise placement of acts on the scale may have shifted over time (and in the twenty-first century taxonomies are increasingly likely to incorporate oral sex prior to penetrative sex and anal sex as a stage after it) but penetrative sex is still considered a key threshold.[40] Feminist and queer scholars and activists have critiqued this model of sexuality for its innate phallocentrism, but recognising the logic of 'development' that underpins it is essential to understanding the persistence of troubling dynamics within adolescent sexual cultures.[41]

To explain why young people continue to engage in sexual activity about which they feel ambivalent, unsure, or which they outright do not desire, we need to recognise the other imperatives motivating sexual activity. We must acknowledge that discourses of development imbue adolescent sexuality with a seemingly inescapable 'naturalness' and a forward momentum. This encourages young people to imagine their sexuality as something that is always striving forwards and crossing thresholds which make it difficult for couples and individuals to 'press pause', move 'backwards', or skip steps which do not appeal to them. Sexual activity (particularly of the pre-penetrative variety) is not necessarily understood in terms of an option or a choice but is envisaged as a preparatory step and prerequisite for the penetrative sex that comes next. While the last few decades have seen some radical transformations in English sexual culture, the logic of development that came to the fore in the mid-century persists and continues to exert a profound influence over adolescent sexual culture. For scholars and activists seeking remedies and solutions to problems in the present, tracing how historic sexual cultures have evolved over time is important to understanding the often unspoken logics and assumptions that lie at the heart of beliefs and 'knowledge' about what sex is and the purposes it serves beyond satisfying individual desire.

Intimacy, agency, and social change

Contemporary debates provide a useful justification for interrogating cultures of teenage sexuality in the past and taking this on its own terms. This history also has important ramifications for other historical narratives and our understandings of social experience in the past. The Introduction situated this study of teenage sexuality within three distinct strands of modern British social history, namely accounts of the rise of the teenager, the so-called 'sexual revolution', and the changing status of women in British history, and this research has offered significant new perspectives to scholarship in these areas. Understood as a history of youth, the book has illustrated the potential divide between adult discourses about youth and the lived experience of young people. Beyond this, it showcases the vital importance of looking beyond spectacular subcultures to historicise the 'missing middle' and the more mundane elements of young people's lives.[42] In the mid-century, change was embodied and enacted not only by young people at protest marches or those embracing the rebellious aesthetics of Mods or Punk. Entirely 'mainstream' young people, in this case young women, were subtly transforming society and were often doing so out of a desire to 'fit in', rather than stand out.

The notion that the 1960s (or any part of the post-war period) witnessed an instantaneous 'sexual revolution' is not analytically productive, but as this study has shown, changes were taking place within British sexual culture at this time. By foregrounding the lived experience of sex over its representation and by paying particular attention not just to what people said about sex but what they did, we have been able to move beyond the usual focus of histories of heterosexuality (married adults) to consider the role played by young people and the messiness of heterosexuality in this period. At the same time, in relation to both the history of sexuality and histories of gender, this work serves as an example of the potential of deploying age as a category of analysis.[43] This involves not just writing children and young people (and indeed older people) into our historical accounts but being more attentive to how historical actors structured their lives around the life cycle and the ways in which this informed how they understood and moved through the world around them.[44]

Beyond these specific subfields, the account of teenage sexuality presented here makes an important intervention into ongoing debates around historical 'agency'. Questions of agency have motivated much scholarship within the history of youth and childhood.[45] The very nature of the subject and the archives used to historicise it make considerations of power and capacity central to analyses of the representation and experience of young people in the past. Where early studies tended to approach the matter of youth agency in fairly constrained terms, locating agency in acts of rebellion and resistance (as in the case of much of the pioneering work of the Centre for Contemporary Cultural Studies in the 1970s and 1980s),[46] more recent scholarship has sought to recalibrate definitions of agency, identifying young people's capacity to shape the world around them and determine aspects of their own lives, deploying different strategies such as compliance.[47] The potential of such approaches for newly understanding teenage sexuality is evident in Chapter 5, which argued that young people's sex lives were often characterised by strategies of evasion and secrecy as teenagers attempted to circumvent their parents' rules and disapproval of their behaviour. Pushing back against narratives of 'resistance', the chapter suggested that young people did butt heads with their parents and teachers but that this did not necessarily create irreconcilable schisms within families or communities. Though the testimonies did report instances of rebellion and defiance, mutual affection, (sometimes grudging) respect, and awkward co-existence were more typical feelings defining mid-century intergenerational relations.

In their descriptions of their intimate relationship dynamics and their handling of birth control, however, the testimonies reveal the limits of such neat constructions of youth agency. As we saw most clearly in Chapters 2 and 3, young people's sexual decision-making was fraught. While some young women, in some moments (at least in the ways their later selves told their stories), very much embodied the rational, self-directed liberal selfhood typically associated with agency, others were less 'empowered'.[48] Where some were making proactive choices and following their own desires, others described their teenage sex lives in terms of compromise or coercion that remained emotionally loaded decades after the fact. Here, attempts to construct new categories or definitions of agency are not particularly productive. Instead, we are better served by stepping back from monolithic 'agency' to consider individual choices and processes of decision-making on their own terms, interrogating the contingent and specific structures, contexts and dynamics that informed individual experience. This enables us to better grasp the complexity, for example, of young people's birth control practices. These could reflect rational decision-making or a complete absence of thought; they could incorporate a sophisticated future-time perspective but might not; these could reflect a specific relationship dynamic within the couple as well as the particular circumstances in which their sexual encounter came about. The dynamics and variables here are too nebulous to be comprehensively contained under a single descriptor and are therefore best considered through an approach that aims to map and understand these different types of decision-making.

Such an approach has also proved helpful in better understanding women's decisions surrounding sexual activity. While most (though by no means all) of the sexual encounters described in testimonies were consensual, women reflected on the often troubling ways such experiences were navigated. In the negotiations that many young women conducted (both internally and with their partners) when considering sexual activity we can observe structures of patriarchy and adult authority in play, but often the core power dynamic was affective. What was in question was less young women's literal capacity to act or to resist the advances of men but instead was their willingness to do so when the emotional stake of such decisions felt so loaded. Focusing less on the binary of whether individuals in the past did or did not have agency (however broadly defined) and instead redirecting our questions to more rigorously interrogate the social contexts, relationship dynamics, and emotional regimes that framed encounters, allows for much more subtle and nuanced (though admittedly less 'conclusive') analyses of human experience in the past.

Finally, this study speaks to nascent interest in intimacy as both a historical phenomenon and an analytical category. As a subject of study, intimacy is important in so far as it allows for expansive analyses of historic social relations which cut across the typical boundaries of social, cultural, and emotional histories as well as the history of sexuality. Where other studies of heterosexual relationships have focused on individual emotions or concepts (such as Claire Langhamer's work on romantic love and Marcus Collins' examination of 'mutuality'), a focus on intimacy encourages us to think about the broader range of emotional registers that underpin close relationships and the shifting and overlapping discourses that inform how individuals navigate their circumstances.[49] At the same time, we gain a more nuanced understanding of sexual practice by situating sex acts and behaviour within an 'intimate' frame. As George Morris has suggested, part of the usefulness of intimacy as an analytic category could lie in how 'it allows us to consider the boundaries and slippages between feelings, bodies, and practices'.[50] This research takes this further by approaching intimacy from a *relational* perspective that is attentive to the *interpersonal* nature of experience. As we have seen throughout this book, intimate life often revolved around people imagining, pre-empting, and responding to the emotions and actions of others as much as around the ways that specific encounters or events provoked affective or sensory responses within individuals.

Through implementing this interpersonal understanding of intimacy, this study has shown how relationship dynamics have histories of their own. Intimacy is not a fixed historical phenomenon and it can take many forms. For example, as we have explored across the book, the relationships that girls had with their romantic partners, their friends and peers, and their parents were variously defined in terms of intimacy, be that in terms of unquestioned acceptance of its existence, awareness of its fragility, or an acknowledgement of its absence. Even where the existence of intimacy was a cornerstone of a particular relationship, these formations and the place of intimacy within them differed. Though there were some common threads – such as a sense of trust, feelings of vulnerability, and shared experience – even these operated differently in different contexts. Where the trust between friends might revolve around shared ignorance and naivety and a sense of learning together, for example, the trust a daughter felt in her parents was often rooted in a belief in their greater wisdom and commitment to their child's safety. Chapter 3 most directly explored how these chimerical facets of intimacy translated into potential differences in its function. There we explored how the association of sex with intimacy sometimes translated into girls using sex as an expression of pre-existing intimacy, while in other instances sex was used as a means of trying to create or enhance intimacy within a relationship. Elsewhere we have seen how intimacy could create a desire for young women to conform with the expectations of loved ones but there could also be instances when trust in a relationship enabled young women to forge their own path and make choices that pushed others' boundaries. Recognising these seeming contradictions in the relationship between intimacy and sex is important as it enables us to better see and explain how apparently identical experiences (such as one-night stands) or sex acts (such as engaging in penetrative sex for the first time) could carry such different meanings for individuals. Depending upon the feelings and expectations of intimacy they experienced, individuals' choices and understandings of their experiences could vary significantly. Especially in the history of sexuality where accounts of cultural discourses and representations of sex are often distinct from studies of sexual encounters and individual sexual identity and desire, considering intimacy makes clear the extent to which these were mutually constitutive and interrelated.

In addition to having differing iterations across and within relationship types, situating the findings of this research within longer histories of relationships also demonstrates how intimacy and its manifestations change over time. What is striking about the experiences of the post-war generation is the extent to which intimacy was becoming both more and less central to the practice and meaning of sexual acts. Compared to histories of marital sexuality in earlier periods in which sex was often seen by women as a 'duty',[51] the post-war generation articulated a belief that there was intimacy in the physical act of having sex and that couples became and stayed bonded through sexual acts.[52] Here, intimacy and sex were becoming more closely intertwined. As we have seen elsewhere, however, other aspects of teenage sexuality in this period suggest an increasing casualisation in sexual conduct. Where sex was previously deemed to be a 'private' matter kept between the couple, in certain post-war contexts there was value in sex lives being public and the subject of observation and discussion. Where idealised visions of heterosexuality in earlier periods located sex solely within marriage, members of the post-war generation (especially those born in the late 1950s and early 1960s) could view sex within non-committed relationships and one-off encounters as legitimate, acceptable, and sometimes even aspirational. If it existed at all in these instances, intimacy took on a very different form and function.

Looking across time, we can therefore chart the gradual evolution of intimacy as different iterations, expectations, and expressions of intimacy gain or lose prominence. I argue below that historians need to take interpersonal relationships more seriously as motors of change in the past but this does not mean assuming that human connection is static or ahistorical. Instead, we should be attentive to the evolving ways in which people in the past related to one another and how these relationships and the emotions felt and expressed within them informed people's worldviews and behaviour and consider how these dynamics themselves influenced broader changes in societies and cultures.

Intimacy can function as more than a subject of historic enquiry, however. Its value to historians, I argue, lies in its explanatory power. As this study has shown, thinking with intimacy offers new perspectives on why things happened in the past and the roles that ordinary people played in bringing about social change. More than simply presenting a new account of post-war heterosexuality, this book identifies shifting dynamics of intimacy to have been a key driver of changing sexual mores across the twentieth century. The account of social transformation offered here has very deliberately sought to move away from matters of legislation and popular culture and the macro-level structures often associated with historical change. It has considered individual subjectivities but perhaps more importantly it has foregrounded the *social* elements of sexual culture and has highlighted the pivotal role that interpersonal relationships played in shaping how historical actors understood and moved through the world around them. This is a chronically under-acknowledged aspect of historical experience. In this instance, we have seen how the potency of discourses of respectability, morality, social currency, and maturity lay less in the expertise of distant and abstract medical, political, religious, and social authorities and more in the fact that these discourses were given a voice and mobilised by people that young women cared about. Girls' relationships with authority figures such as their parents and teachers, their relationships with the siblings, family members, friends, and boyfriends that they loved and cared about deeply, as well as the relationships they had with the classmates, peers, neighbours, and acquaintances that they interacted with on a day-to-day basis were not peripheral to their sexual subjectivities and decision-making; they were central to these identities and experiences.

This kind of social history, a history of relationships, can provide a vital link between macro-level cultural and institutional change and evolutions in individual attitudes and behaviour. Transformations in social life and culture do not necessarily take place instantaneously and their architects may not be cultural icons or those who wield institutional power; this research clearly demonstrates that shifts in worldview and behaviour can occur much more gradually, in subtle stages, and without individual leaders. Crucially, social networks, community and interpersonal relationships did not simply add colour and texture to people's lives but were instrumental in shaping how people conducted themselves and thought about the world. To live is to exist within myriad social relations and to inhabit numerous social roles and it is crucial that we acknowledge the extent to which managing these relations and roles shaped the past. Though mid-century commentators dismissed the teenage girls who exchanged notes about boyfriends in history lessons, who spent their Saturday afternoons huddled over *Jackie* magazine, and who danced around their handbags together eyeing-up boys lined up on the other side of the village hall, an intimate history of relationships reveals how these girls and their friendships transformed English society.

Notes

1 On storytelling and family identity see Kristin Langellier and Eric Peterson, *Storytelling in Daily Life: Performing Narrative* (Philadelphia: Temple University Press, 2004); Richard Hall, 'Emotional Histories: Materiality, Temporality and Subjectivity in Oral History Interviews with Fathers and Sons', *Oral History* 47, no. 1 (2019); Sally Alexander, '"Do Grandmas Have Husbands?" Generational Memory and Twentieth-Century Women's Lives', *The Oral History Review* 36, no. 2 (2009). See also Judy Giles, 'Narratives of Gender, Class, and Modernity in Women's Memories of Mid-Twentieth Century Britain', *Signs: Journal of Women in Culture and Society* 28, no. 1 (2002).
2 Abrams, *Feminist Lives*; Worth, *Welfare State Generation*.
3 Abrams, *Feminist Lives*, p. 234.
4 Sally (1946), OH-15-05-02.
5 Maureen (1949), OH-15-05-04.
6 The title of this section is taken from Ingham, *Now We Are Thirty*.
7 Collins, *Modern Love*, pp. 59–89.
8 Mandler, *Crisis of Meritocracy*; Dyhouse, *Students*; Tinkler, 'Going Places or out of Place?'
9 Cook, *The Long Sexual Revolution*; Rusterholz, 'Youth Sexuality, Responsibility, and the Opening of the Brook Advisory Centres'.
10 Sheldon et al., *Abortion Act 1967*.
11 Explicit examples in MOP, 'Sex' include: Eileen (1952), E743; Geraldine (1959), G3395; Georgina (1959), G3423; Kay (1951), K798; Mabel (1946), M3408; Muriel (1940), P1009; Sheila (1958), S3372.
12 Szreter and Fisher, *Sex before the Sexual Revolution*; Roberts, *Women and Families*; Judy Giles, '"Playing Hard to Get": Working-Class Women, Sexuality and Respectability in Britain, 1918–40', *Women's History Review* 1, no. 2 (1992); Cohen, *Family Secrets*.
13 Derek Thompson, 'Courtship and Marriage in Preston between the Wars', *Oral History* 3, no. 2 (1975); Elizabeth Roberts, *A Woman's*

Place: An Oral History of Working-Class Women 1890–1940 (Oxford: Blackwell, 1984), pp. 72–124.
14 Holtzman, 'The Pursuit of Married Love'; Margaret Jackson, *The Real Facts of Life: Feminism and the Politics of Sexuality, 1850–1940* (London: Taylor & Francis, 1994); Lesley A. Hall, 'Eyes Tightly Shut, Lying Rigidly Still, and Thinking of England? British Women and Sex from Marie Stopes to Hite 2000', in *Sexual Pedagogies: Sex Education in Britain, Australia, and America, 1879–2000*, ed. Claudia Nelson and Michelle H. Martin (Basingstoke: Palgrave Macmillan, 2004).
15 Langhamer, *English in Love*.
16 On traditional milestones see Todd, *Young Women, Work, and Family*.
17 Mathew Thomson, *Psychological Subjects: Identity, Culture and Health in Twentieth-Century Britain* (Oxford: Oxford University Press, 2006); Nikolas Rose, *Governing the Soul: The Shaping of the Private Self*, 2nd ed. (London: Free Association Books, 1999).
18 Charnock, 'Teenage Girls, Female Friendship'. On sexual politics in earlier periods see Szreter and Fisher, *Sex before the Sexual Revolution*; Giles, 'Playing Hard to Get'.
19 The title of this section is taken from Jerman, *The Lively-Minded Women*, pp. 15–23.
20 The NHS currently offers advice on twelve different methods of contraception (not including sterilisation), https://www.nhs.uk/conditions/contraception/ [accessed: 25 September 2024].
21 Public Health England, *HIV in the UK: Towards Zero HIV Transmissions by 2030, 2019 Report* (London: Public Health England, 2019), GW-920, https://assets.publishing.service.gov.uk/media/603d1dcae90e07055c1404c8/HIV_in_the_UK_2019_towards_zero_HIV_transmissions_by_2030.pdf [accessed: 25 September 2024]
22 Harry Cocks, 'Conspiracy to Corrupt Public Morals and the "Unlawful" Status of Homosexuality in Britain after 1967', *Social History* 41, no. 3 (2016); Rebecca Jennings, *Tomboys and Bachelor Girls: A Lesbian History of Post-War Britain* (Manchester: Manchester University Press, 2007); Jeffrey Weeks, *Coming Out: The Emergence of LGBT Identities in Britain from the Nineteenth Century to the Present*, 3rd ed. (London: Quartet Books, 2016).
23 Sally (1946), OH-15-05-02; Geraldine (1959), MOP, 'Sex', G3395; Yvette (1958), MOP, 'Sex', Y2926.
24 On lesbianism in the mid-twentieth century see Jennings, *Tomboys and Bachelor Girls*. On bisexual politics see Martha Robinson Rhodes, 'Bisexuality, Multiple-Gender-Attraction, and Gay Liberation Politics in the 1970s', *Twentieth Century British History* 32, no. 1 (2021).

On increasing visibility and representation see Sebastian Buckle, *Homosexuality on the Small Screen: Television and LGBT Identity in Britain* (London: Bloomsbury Academic, 2018); Daniel Tomlinson-Gray, ed., *Big Gay Adventures in Education: Supporting LGBT+ Visibility and Inclusion in Schools* (London: Routledge, 2020); Lauren B. McInroy and Shelley L. Craig, 'Perspectives of LGBTQ Emerging Adults on the Depiction and Impact of LGBTQ Media Representation', *Journal of Youth Studies* 20, no. 1 (2017).

25 Daniel P. Baker, 'Growing Up Gay in a Digital World: A Double-Edged Sword for Sexual Minority Young Men in England', *Children and Youth Services Review* 128 (2021); Nicola Döring, Deevia Bhana, and Kath Albury, 'Digital Sexual Identities: Between Empowerment and Disempowerment', *Current Opinion in Psychology* 48 (2022); Mary Bryson, 'When Jill Jacks In: Queer Women and the Net', *Feminist Media Studies* 4, no. 3 (2004).

26 Faye Mishna et al., 'Unsolicited Sexts and Unwanted Requests for Sexts: Reflecting on the Online Sexual Harassment of Youth', *Youth & Society* 55, no. 4 (2021); Fiona Vera-Gray, Clare McGlynn, Ibad Kureshi, and Kate Butterby, 'Sexual Violence as a Sexual Script in Mainstream Online Pornography', *The British Journal of Criminology* 61, no. 5 (2021); Laura Vandenbosch, Jasmine Fardouly, and Marika Tiggemann, 'Social Media and Body Image: Recent Trends and Future Directions', *Current Opinion in Psychology* 45 (2022); Y. Kelly, A. Zilanawala, C. Booker, and A. Sacker, 'Social Media Use and Adolescent Mental Health: Findings From the UK Millennium Cohort Study', *EClinicalMedicine* 6 (2018).

27 Annie (1965), MOP, 'Sex', A3434.

28 Carolyn (1947), MOP, 'Sex', C1832.

29 Lorraine (1951), MOP, 'Sex', L3253. See also in MOP, 'Sex': Carole (1948), C1713; Harriet (1951), H1705; Janet (1950), J3496. There were some exceptions to this, such as Pauline (1944), OH-14-01-03 who made the point that, 'I don't think anything's changed, it's just that you had to get married in those days.'

30 Lilian (1946), MOP, 'Sex', L1002. Emphasis in original.

31 Lisa Arai, *Teenage Pregnancy: The Making and Unmaking of a Problem* (Bristol: Policy Press, 2009).

32 Office of National Statistics, 'Teenage Pregnancies: Perception versus Reality' (2016), www.ons.gov.uk/peoplepopulationandcommunity/birthsdeathsandmarriages/conceptionandfertilityrates/articles/teenagepregnanciesperceptionversusreality/2016-03-09 [accessed: 25 September 2024].

33 Office of National Statistics, 'Summary of Key Birth Statistics, 1838 to 2022', *Births in England and Wales: Summary Tables,* www.ons.gov.uk/peoplepopulationandcommunity/birthsdeathsandmarriages/livebirths/datasets/birthsummarytables [accessed: 25 September 2024].

34 Evans and Thane, *Sinners? Scroungers? Saints?*

35 Victoria Browne, 'The Persistence of Patriarchy: Operation Yewtree and the Return to 1970s Feminism', *Radical Philosophy* 188 (2014); Laura Bates, *Everyday Sexism: The Project That Inspired a Worldwide Movement* (London: Simon & Schuster, 2014); Bianca Fileborn and Rachel Loney-Howes, eds, *#MeToo and the Politics of Social Change* (Basingstoke: Palgrave Macmillan, 2019); Karen Boyle, *#MeToo, Weinstein and Feminism* (Basingstoke: Palgrave Macmillan, 2019); Sara Soma, *Everyone's Invited* (London: Simon & Schuster, 2022).

36 Fenton and Tinkler, 'Me Too?'; Hannah Charnock, 'Writing the History of Male Sexuality in the Wake of Operation Yewtree and #MeToo', in *Men and Masculinities in Modern Britain: A History for the Present*, ed. Matt Houlbook, Katie Jones, and Ben Mechen (Manchester: Manchester University Press, 2023).

37 https://www.everyonesinvited.uk/about [accessed: 25 September 2024]. Melissa Burkett and Karine Hamilton, 'Postfeminist Sexual Agency: Young Women's Negotiations of Sexual Consent', *Sexualities* 15, no. 7 (2012); Janet Holland, Caroline Ramazanoglu, Sue Sharpe, and Rachel Thomson, *The Male in the Head: Young People, Heterosexuality and Power*, 2nd ed. (London: The Tufnell Press, 2004); Maddy Coy, Liz Kelly, Fiona Elvines, Maria Garner, and Ava Kanyaeredzi, *'Sex without Consent, I Suppose That Is Rape': How Young People in England Understand Sexual Consent* (London: Office of the Children's Commissioner, 2013).

38 Christine Barter, Melanie McCarry, David Berridge, and Kathy Evans, *Partner Exploitation and Violence in Teenage Intimate Relationships* (NSPCC, 2009).

39 See, for example, Susan Meredith, *Growing Up: Adolescence, Body Changes and Sex* (London: Usborne, 1991) which was initially been published in 1985 and was updated and reissued in 1997 and again in 2004. *Statutory Guidance on Relationships and Sex Education (RSE) and Health Education* (London: Department for Education, 2021), https://www.gov.uk/government/publications/relationships-education-relationships-and-sex-education-rse-and-health-education [accessed: 25 September 2024].

40 C. Marston and R. Lewis, 'Anal Heterosex among Young People and Implications for Health Promotion: A Qualitative Study in the UK', *BMJ Open* 4, no. 8 (2014); Lewis et al., 'Bases, Stages and "Working Your Way Up"'.

41 Malachi Willis, Kristen N. Jozkowski, Wen-Juo Lo, and Stephanie A. Sanders, 'Are Women's Orgasms Hindered by Phallocentric Imperatives?', *Archives of Sexual Behavior* 47, no. 6 (2018); Jessica Valenti, *The Purity Myth: How America's Obsession with Virginity Is Hurting Young Women* (New York: Seal Press, 2009).
42 Woodman, 'Researching "Ordinary" Young People in a Changing World'.
43 Laura L. Lovett, 'Age: A Useful Category of Historical Analysis', *Journal of the History of Childhood and Youth* 1, no. 1 (2008); Steve Mintz, 'Reflections on Age as a Category of Historical Analysis', *Journal of the History of Childhood and Youth* 1, no. 1 (2008); Mary-Jo Maynes, 'Age as a Category of Historical Analysis: History, Agency, and Narratives of Childhood', *Journal of the History of Childhood and Youth* 1, no. 1 (2008).
44 Charnock, 'How Far Should We Go?'
45 Mona Gleason, 'Avoiding the Agency Trap: Caveats for Historians of Children, Youth, and Education', *History of Education* 45, no. 4 (2016); Kristin Alexander, 'Agency and Emotion Work', *Jeuness: Young People, Texts, Cultures* 7, no. 2 (2015).
46 Hall and Jefferson, *Resistance through Rituals*.
47 Maynes, 'Age as a Category of Historical Analysis'; Susan A. Miller, 'Assent as Agency in the Early Years of the Children of the American Revolution', *Journal of the History of Childhood and Youth* 9, no. 1 (2016).
48 Walter Johnson, 'On Agency', *Journal of Social History* 37, no. 1 (2003): 115.
49 Collins, *Modern Love*; Langhamer, *English in Love*.
50 Morris, 'Intimacy in Modern British History', p. 797.
51 Szreter and Fisher, *Sex before the Sexual Revolution*, pp. 326–32. In her study of working-class women's lives in the early twentieth century, Elizabeth Roberts summarised that sex was 'regarded as necessary for the procreation of children or as an activity indulged in by men for their own pleasure, but it never discussed in the evidence as something which could give mutual happiness'. Roberts, *A Woman's Place*, p. 84.
52 See also Langhamer, *English in Love*.

Bibliography

Primary material

Archive material

Oral sources

'QWMC: Changes in birth control', British Library Sound Archive, C644.

Mass Observation Archive, The Keep, University of Sussex

Mass Observation, 'Love-making in public', Mass Observation Archive, file report 3086, Feb. 1949.
Mass Observation Project Directives
    Close Relationships (1990)
    Growing Up (1993)
    Courting and Dating (2001)
    Sex (2005)

Newspapers, magazines, and periodicals

    19
    British Medical Journal
    Cosmopolitan
    Daily Mail
    Daily Mirror
    The Daily Telegraph
    The Guardian
    Honey
    Jackie
    The Lancet
    Manchester Guardian

Petticoat
Picture Post
The Spectator
Sunday Pictorial
The Times
Weekend Telegraph

Published primary sources

Abrams, Mark. *The Teenage Consumer*. London: The London Press Exchange, 1959.
Anon. *The Transmission of Life*, 6th ed. London: The Girl Guides Association, 1954.
Barnes, Kenneth. *15+ Facts of Life*. London: British Medical Association, 1961.
Barnett, Len. *Sex and Teenagers in Love*. Redhill: Denholm House Press, 1967.
Brennan, Malcolm. *Sex Education: Training in Chastity*. Catholic Truth Society: London, 1974.
Chandler, E. M. *Educating Adolescent Girls*. London: Unwin Education Books, 1980.
Chesser, Eustace. *Grow Up and Live*. Harmondsworth: Pelican Books, 1949.
———. *The Sexual, Marital and Family Relationships of the English Women*. London: Hutchinson's Medical Publications, 1956.
Comfort, Alex. *The Joy of Sex: A Gourmet Guide to Lovemaking*. London: Simon & Schuster UK, 1972.
Corner, George W. *Attaining Womanhood: A Doctor Talks to Girls About Sex*. London: George Allen & Unwin, 1953.
De la Bedoyere, Quentin and Irene. *Choices in Sex*. London: Burns & Oates, 1964.
Ellis, Havelock. *Studies in the Psychology of Sex Vol. VI: Sex in Relation to Society*. Philadelphia: F. A. Davis Company, 1925.
Erikson, E. H. *Childhood and Society*, revised edn. St Albans: Triad, 1977.
Fyvel, T. R. *The Insecure Offenders: Rebellious Youth in the Welfare State*. Harmondsworth: Pelican Books, 1963.
Greet, Cirrel. *Facts of Life*. London: Tom Stacey, 1972.
Hacker, Rose. *The Opposite Sex*. London: Pan Books, 1960.
Hadfield, J. A. *Childhood and Adolescence*. Harmondsworth: Pelican Books, 1962.
Hamblett, Charles, and Jane Deverson. *Generation X*. New York: Fawcett Publications, 1964.
Hill, Maurice and Michael Lloyd-Jones. *Sex Education: The Erroneous Zone*. London: National Secular Society, 1970.

Hilton, Donald and Ann. *Girl Into Woman: Sex Knowledge for the Growing Girl*. Redhill: Denholm House Press, 1972.
Ingleby, Alan H. B. *Learning to Love*. London: Transworld Publishers, 1962.
Jephcott, Pearl. *Girls Growing Up*. London: Faber & Faber, 1943.
John, Denys. 'In a Comprehensive School'. In National Marriage Guidance Council, *Sex Education in Perspective*, pp. 17–26. Rugby: National Marriage Guidance Council, 1972.
Johnson, Eric W. *Love and Sex in Plain Language*, revised edn. London: Andre Deutsch, 1975.
The Labour Party. *The Younger Generation: Report of the Labour Party Youth Commission*. London: Labour Party, 1959.
Lane, William Arbuthnot. *Every Woman's Book of Health and Beauty*. London: Thornton Butterworth, 1936.
Le P. Warner, Nancy. *L for Learner: Towards an Understanding of Sex*. London: The Girl Guides Association, 1962.
Meredith, Susan. *Growing Up: Adolescence, Body Changes and Sex*. London: Usborne, 1991.
Morse, Mary. *The Unattached*. Harmondsworth: Pelican Books, 1965.
Myrdal, Alva and Viola Klein. *Women's Two Roles: Home and Work*. London: Routledge, 1998 [1956].
Pascal, Julia, 'Prima Ballerina Absoluta'. In *Truth, Dare or Promise: Girls Growing Up in the Fifties*, edited by Liz Heron, pp. 27–43. London: Virago, 1985.
Pomeroy, Wardell B. *Girls and Sex*. Harmondsworth: Pelican Books, 1970.
Rayner, Claire. *People in Love: A Modern Guide to Sex in Marriage*. Feltham: Paul Hamlyn, 1968.
Rout, Ettie A. *The Morality of Birth Control*. London: John Lane, 1925.
Sandström, C. I. *The Psychology of Childhood and Adolescence*, trans. Albert Read. Harmondsworth: Pelican Books, 1966.
Sage, Lorna. *Bad Blood*. London: Fourth Estate, 2000.
Schofield, Michael. *The Sexual Behaviour of Young People*. London: Longmans, 1965.
———. 'The Sociological Contribution to Health Education'. *Health Education Journal* 22 (1964): 44–48.
Spock, Benjamin. *A Young Person's Guide to Life and Love*. London: Bodley Head, 1971.
Stopes, Marie. *Married Love: A New Contribution to the Solution of Sex Difficulties*. London: A. C. Fifield, 1919.
Van de Velde, Theodoor H. *Ideal Marriage: Its Physiology and Technique*, trans. Stella Browne. London: William Heinemann, 1928.
Willmott, Peter. *Adolescent Boys of East London*, revised edn. Harmondsworth: Pelican Books, 1969.
Wimperis, Virginia. *The Unmarried Mother and Her Child*. London: Sir Halley Stewart Trust, George Allen & Unwin, 1960.

Reports and statistics

Blunden, Ronald M. *A Survey of Adoption in Great Britain*, Home Office Research Studies 10. London: HMSO, 1971.

Board of Education. *Sex Education in Schools and Youth Organisations*. London: His Majesty's Stationery Office, 1943.

British Market Research Bureau Limited. *The New Housewife: Report on a Survey*. London: J. Walter Thompson, 1967.

Clifton, Soazig, Elizabeth Fuller, and Dan Philo on behalf of the Natsal team. *National Survey of Sexual Attitudes and Lifestyles (Natsal-3) Reference Tables*. www.natsal.ac.uk/sites/default/files/2020-11/natsal-3-reference-tables.pdf [accessed: 25 September 2024].

Department of Education. *Statutory Guidance on Relationships and Sex Education (RSE) and Health Education*. London, 2021. www.gov.uk/government/publications/relationships-education-relationships-and-sex-education-rse-and-health-education [accessed: 25 September 2024].

Department of Employment. *British Labour Statistics Historical Abstract 1886–1968*. London: Her Majesty's Stationery Office, 1971.

Dunnell, Karen. *Family Formation 1976*. London: Her Majesty's Stationery Office, 1979.

Office of National Statistics. *Births in England and Wales: Summary Tables*. www.ons.gov.uk/peoplepopulationandcommunity/birthsdeathsandmarriages/livebirths/datasets/birthsummarytables [accessed: 25 September 2024].

Office of National Statistics. *Information on Births by Parents' Characteristic Statistics*. London, 2021. www.ons.gov.uk/peoplepopulationandcommunity/birthsdeathsandmarriages/livebirths/datasets/birthsbyparentscharacteristics [accessed: 25 September 2024].

Office for National Statistics. *Marriages in England and Wales: 2017*. London: ONS, 2021. www.ons.gov.uk/peoplepopulationandcommunity/birthsdeathsandmarriages/marriagecohabitationandcivilpartnerships/bulletins/marriagesinenglandandwalesprovisional/2017 [accessed: 25 September 2024].

Office of National Statistics. 'Teenage Pregnancies: Perception versus Reality'. 2016. https://www.ons.gov.uk/peoplepopulationandcommunity/birthsdeathsandmarriages/conceptionandfertilityrates/articles/teenagepregnanciesperceptionversusreality/2016-03-09 [accessed: 25 September 2024].

Public Health England. *HIV in the UK: Towards Zero HIV Transmissions by 2030, 2019 Report*. London: Public Health England, 2019. https://assets.publishing.service.gov.uk/media/603d1dcae90e07055c1404c8/HIV_in_the_UK_2019_towards_zero_HIV_transmissions_by_2030.pdf [accessed: 25 September 2024].

Report of the Committee on the Age of Majority, Cmd. 3342. London: Her Majesty's Stationery Office, 1967.

Secondary material

Abrams, Lynn. *Feminist Lives: Women, Feelings and the Self in Post-War Britain*. Oxford: Oxford University Press, 2023.

———. 'Liberating the Female Self: Epiphanies, Conflict and Coherence in the Life Stories of Post-War British Women'. *Social History* 39, no. 1 (2014): 14–35.

———. 'Mothers and Daughters: Negotiating the Discourse on the "Good Woman" in 1950s and 1960s Britain'. In *The Sixties and Beyond: Dechristianisation in North America and Western Europe, 1945–2000*, edited by Nancy Christie and Michael Gauvreau. Toronto: University of Toronto Press, 2013.

———. 'Talking about Feminism: Reconciling Fragmented Narratives with the Feminist Research Frame'. In *Beyond Women's Words: Feminisms and the Practices of Oral History in the Twenty-First Century*, edited by Katrina Srigley, Stacey Zembrzycki and Franca Iacovetta, pp. 81–94. London: Routledge, 2018.

Adelman, Mara B. 'Sustaining Passion: Eroticism and Safe-Sex Talk'. *Archives of Sexual Behavior* 21, no. 5 (1992): 481–94.

Aldgate, Tony. '"I Am a Camera": Film and Theatre Censorship in 1950s Britain'. *Contemporary European History* 8, no. 3 (1999): 425–38.

Aldrich, Robert. 'Homosexuality and the City: An Historical Overview'. *Urban Studies* 41, no. 9 (2004): 1719–37.

Alexander, Kristin. 'Agency and Emotion Work'. *Jeuness: Young People, Texts, Cultures* 7, no. 2 (2015): 120–28.

Alexander, Sally. '"Do Grandmas Have Husbands?" Generational Memory and Twentieth-Century Women's Lives'. *The Oral History Review* 36, no. 2 (2009): 159–76.

Alexander, Sally. 'The Mysteries and Secrets of Women's Bodies: Sexual Knowledge in the First Half of the Twentieth Century'. In *Modern Times: Reflections of a Century of English Modernity*, edited by Mic Nava and Alan O'Shea. London and New York: Routledge, 1996.

Allen, Barbara. 'Re-Creating the Past: The Narrator's Perspective in Oral History'. *The Oral History Review* 12 (1984): 1–12.

Anderson, Stuart. '"The Most Important Place in the History of British Birth Control": Community Pharmacy and Sexual Health in Twentieth Century Britain'. *Pharmaceutical Journal* 266, no. 7129 (2001): 23–29.

Arai, Lisa. *Teenage Pregnancy: The Making and Unmaking of a Problem*. Bristol: Policy Press, 2009.

Baker, Daniel P. 'Growing up Gay in a Digital World: A Double-Edged Sword for Sexual Minority Young Men in England'. *Children and Youth Services Review* 128 (2021): 106119.

Barker, Diana. 'Young People and Their Homes: Spoiling and "Keeping Close" in a South Wales Town'. *The Sociological Review* 20, no. 4 (1972): 569–90.

Barter, Christine, Melanie McCarry, David Berridge, and Kathy Evans. *Partner Exploitation and Violence in Teenage Intimate Relationships*. Bristol: NSPCC, 2009.

Bates, Laura. *Everyday Sexism: The Project That Inspired a Worldwide Movement*. London: Simon & Schuster, 2014.

Bennett, Andy. 'Situating "Subculture": On the Origins and Limits of the Term for Understanding Youth Cultures'. In *Researching Subcultures, Myth and Memory*, edited by Bart van der Steen and Thierry P. F. Verburgh, pp. 19–34. Basingstoke: Palgrave Macmillan, 2020.

Bentley, Nick, Beth Johnson, and Andrzej Zieleniec, eds. *Youth Subcultures in Fiction, Film and Other Media*. Basingstoke: Palgrave Macmillan, 2018.

Bingham, Adrian. *Family Newspapers? Sex, Private Life, and the British Popular Press 1918–1978*. Oxford: Oxford University Press, 2009.

———. 'Pin-up Culture and Page 3 in the Popular Press'. In *Women and the Media: Feminism and Femininity in Britain, 1900 to Present*, edited by Maggie Andrews and Sallie McNamara, pp. 184–98. London: Routledge, 2014.

Black, Lawrence. 'The Lost World of Young Conservatism'. *The Historical Journal* 51, no. 4 (2008): 991–1024.

Borge, Jessica. *Protective Practices: A History of the London Rubber Company and the Condom Business*. Montreal: McGill-Queen's University Press, 2020.

Bourke, Joanna. *Rape: A History from 1860 to the Present*. London: Virago Press, 2008.

Bowden, Sue, and Avner Offer. 'Household Appliances and the Use of Time: The United States and Britain since the 1920s'. *The Economic History Review* 47, no. 4 (1994): 725–48.

Boyle, Karen. *#Metoo, Weinstein and Feminism*. Basingstoke: Palgrave Macmillan, 2019.

Brewitt-Taylor, Sam. 'Christianity and the Invention of the Sexual Revolution in Britain, 1963–1967'. *The Historical Journal* 60, no. 2 (2017): 519–46.

Brooke, Stephen. '"A Certain Amount of Mush": Love, Romance, Celluloid and Wax in the Mid-Twentieth Century'. In *Love and Romance in Britain, 1918–1970*, edited by Alana Harris and Timothy Willem Jones, pp. 81–99. Basingstoke: Palgrave Macmillan, 2015.

———. *Sexual Politics: Sexuality, Family Planning, and the British Left from the 1880s to the Present Day*. Oxford: Oxford University Press, 2011.

Brooks, Val. 'The Role of External Examinations in the Making of Secondary Modern Schools in England 1945–65'. *History of Education* 37, no. 3 (2008): 447–67.

Brown, Callum G. *The Death of Christian Britain: Understanding Secularisation 1800–2000*. Oxford: Oxford University Press, 2009.

———. 'Sex, Religion, and the Single Woman c.1950–75: The Importance of a "Short" Sexual Revolution to the English Religious Crisis of the Sixties'. *Twentieth Century British History* 22, no. 2 (2011): 189–215.

Browne, Victoria. 'The Persistence of Patriarchy: Operation Yewtree and the Return to 1970s Feminism'. *Radical Philosophy* 188 (2014): 9–19.

Brownmiller, Susan. *Against Our Will: Men, Women and Rape*. Harmondsworth: Penguin, 1976.
Bryson, Mary. 'When Jill Jacks In: Queer Women and the Net'. *Feminist Media Studies* 4, no. 3 (2004): 239–54.
Buckle, Sebastian. *Homosexuality on the Small Screen: Television and LGBT Identity in Britain*. London: Bloomsbury Academic, 2018.
Bugge, Christian. '"Selling Youth in the Age of Affluence": Marketing to Youth in Britain since 1959'. In *An Affluent Society: Britain's Post-War 'Golden Age' Revisited*, edited by Lawrence Black and Hugh Pemberton, pp. 185–202. Aldershot: Ashgate, 2004.
Bunkle, Phillida. 'The 1944 Education Act and Second Wave Feminism'. *Women's History Review* 25, no. 5 (2016): 791–811.
Burkett, Melissa, and Karine Hamilton. 'Postfeminist Sexual Agency: Young Women's Negotiations of Sexual Consent'. *Sexualities* 15, no. 7 (2012): 815–33.
Caballero, Chamion, and Peter J. Aspinall. *Mixed Race Britain in the Twentieth Century*. Basingstoke: Palgrave Macmillan, 2018.
Campbell, Beatrix. 'A Feminist Sexual Politics: Now You See It, Now You Don't'. *Feminist Review* 5 (1980): 1–18.
Carter, Laura. 'The Hairdresser Blues: British Women and the Secondary Modern School, 1946–72'. *Twentieth Century British History* 34, no. 4 (2023): 726–53.
Charnock, Hannah. '"How Far Should We Go?": Adolescent Sexual Activity and Understandings of the Sexual Life Cycle in Postwar Britain'. *Journal of the History of Sexuality* 32, no. 3 (2023): 245–68.
———. 'Teenage Girls, Female Friendship and the Making of the "Sexual Revolution" in England, 1950–1980'. *The Historical Journal* 63, no. 4 (2020): 1032–53.
———. 'Writing the History of Male Sexuality in the Wake of Operation Yewtree and #Metoo'. In *Men and Masculinities in Modern Britain: A History for the Present*, edited by Matt Houlbook, Katie Jones, and Ben Mechen, pp. 288–98. Manchester: Manchester University Press, 2023.
Clarke, John. 'Defending Ski-Jumpers: A Critique of Theories of Youth Subcultures'. In *On Record: Rock Pop and the Written Word*, edited by Simon Frith and A. Goodwin, pp. 81–96. London: Routledge, 1990.
Clarke, Michael. 'On the Concept of "Sub-Culture"'. *The British Journal of Sociology* 25, no. 4 (1974): 428–41.
Cocks, Harry. 'Conspiracy to Corrupt Public Morals and the "Unlawful" Status of Homosexuality in Britain after 1967'. *Social History* 41, no. 3 (2016): 267–84.
———. '"The Social Picture of Our Own Times": Reading Obscene Magazines in Mid-Twentieth-Century Britain'. *Twentieth Century British History* 27, no. 2 (2016): 171–94.
Cohen, Deborah. *Family Secrets: Living with Shame from the Victorians to the Present Day*. London: Viking, 2013.

Coleman, David. 'Population and Family'. In *Twentieth-Century British Social Trends*, edited by A. H. Halsey and Josephine Webb, pp. 27–93. Basingstoke: Macmillan, 2000.

Collins, Marcus. *Modern Love: An Intimate History of Men and Women in Twentieth-Century Britain*. London: Atlantic Books, 2003.

Conger, John Janeway. 'A World They Never Knew: The Family and Social Change'. *Daedalus* 100, no. 4 (1971): 1105–38.

Cook, Hera. *The Long Sexual Revolution: English Women, Sex and Contraception 1800–1975*. Oxford: Oxford University Press, 2004.

———. 'Nova 1965–1970: Love, Masculinity and Feminism, but Not as We Know It'. In *Love and Romance in Britain, 1918–1970*, edited by Alana Harris and Timothy Jones, pp. 225–43. Basingstoke: Palgrave Macmillan, 2015.

Cook, Matt. 'Sexual Revolution(s) in Britain'. In *Sexual Revolutions*, edited by Gert Hekma and Alain Giami, pp. 121–40. Basingstoke: Palgrave Macmillan, 2014.

Coy, Maddy, Liz Kelly, Fiona Elvines, Maria Garner, and Ava Kanyaeredzi. *'Sex without Consent, I Suppose That Is Rape': How Young People in England Understand Sexual Consent*. London: Office of the Children's Commissioner, 2013.

Davidson, Roger. *Illicit and Unnatural Practices: The Law, Sex and Society in Scotland since 1900*. Edinburgh: Edinburgh University Press, 2019.

Davidson, Roger, and Gayle Davis. *The Sexual State: Sexuality and Scottish Governance 1950–80*. Edinburgh: Edinburgh University Press, 2012.

Davies, Christie. *Permissive Britain: Social Change in the Sixties and Seventies*. London: Pitman Publishing, 1975.

Davis, John. *Youth and the Condition of Britain: Images of Adolescent Conflict*. London and Atlantic Highlands: The Athlone Press, 1990.

Dawson, Graham. *Soldier Heroes: British Adventure, Empire and the Imagining of Masculinities*. London: Routledge, 1994.

Delap, Lucy. '"Disgusting Details Which Are Best Forgotten": Disclosures of Child Sexual Abuse in Twentieth-Century Britain'. *Journal of British Studies* 57, no. 1 (2018): 79–107.

Department for Education. *Statutory Guidance on Relationships and Sex Education (Rse) and Health Education*. London, 2021. www.gov.uk/government/publications/relationships-education-relationships-and-sex-education-rse-and-health-education [accessed: 25 September 2024].

Dickens, Emma. *Immaculate Contraception: The Extraordinary Story of Birth Control from the First Fumblings to the Present Day*. London: Robson Books, 2000.

Döring, Nicola, Deevia Bhana, and Kath Albury. 'Digital Sexual Identities: Between Empowerment and Disempowerment'. *Current Opinion in Psychology* 48 (2022): 101466.

Dyhouse, Carol. *Girl Trouble: Panic and Progress in the History of Young Women*. London: Zed Books, 2013.

———. 'Graduates, Mothers and Graduate Mothers: Family Investment in Higher Education in Twentieth Century England'. *Gender and Education* 14, no. 4 (2002): 325–36.

———. *Heartthrobs: A History of Women and Desire*. Oxford: Oxford University Press, 2017.

———. *Love Lives: From 'Cinderella' to 'Frozen'*. Oxford: Oxford University Press, 2021.

———. *Students: A Gendered History*. London: Routledge, 2005.

Edwards, Sian. 'Lovers' Lanes and Haystacks: Rural Spaces and Girls' Experiences of Courtship and Sexual Intimacy in Post-War England'. In *Let's Spend the Night Together: Sex, Pop Music and British Youth Culture, 1950s–1980s*, edited by The Subcultures Network, pp. 94–112. Manchester: Manchester University Press, 2023.

———. '"Nothing Gets Her Goat!" The Farmer's Wife and the Duality of Rural Femininity in the Young Farmers' Club Movement in 1950s Britain'. *Women's History Review* 26, no. 1 (2017): 26–45.

———. *Youth Movements, Citizenship and the English Countryside: Creating Good Citizens, 1930–1960*. Basingstoke: Palgrave Macmillan, 2017.

England, L. R. 'Little Kinsey: An Outline of Sex Attitudes in Britain'. *The Public Opinion Quarterly* 13, no. 4 (1949–50): 587–600.

Evans, B. A., S. M. McCormack, P. D. Kell, J. V. Parry, R. A. Bond, and K. D. Macrae. 'Trends in Female Sexual Behaviour and Sexually Transmitted Diseases in London, 1982–1992'. *Sexually Transmitted Infections* 71, no. 5 (1995): 286–90.

Evans, Tanya, and Pat Thane. *Sinners? Scroungers? Saints? Unmarried Motherhood in Twentieth-Century England*. Oxford: Oxford University Press, 2012.

Farmer, Richard. 'The Profumo Affair in Popular Culture: *The Keeler Affair* (1963) and "the Commercial Exploitation of a Public Scandal"'. *Contemporary British History* 31, no. 3 (2017): 452–70.

Farrell, Christine. *My Mother Said…: The Way Young People Learn About Sex and Birth Control*. London: Routledge and Kegan Paul Books, 1978.

Fenton, Laura, and Penny Tinkler. 'Me Too? Re-Encountering Youth Experiences of Sexual Violence in Post-War England from the Vantage Point of Later Life'. *Contemporary British History* 37, no. 3 (2023): 339–66.

Fileborn, Bianca, and Rachel Loney-Howes, eds. *#Metoo and the Politics of Social Change*. Basingstoke: Palgrave Macmillan, 2019.

Finch, Janet, and Penny Summerfield. 'Social Reconstruction and the Emergence of Companionate Marriage, 1945–1959'. In *Marriage, Domestic Life and Social Change: Writings for Jacqueline Burgoyne, 1944–88*, edited by David Clark, pp. 7–32. London and New York: Routledge, 1991.

Fisher, Kate. *Birth Control, Sex, and Marriage in Britain 1918–1960*. Oxford: Oxford University Press, 2006.

———. 'Marriage and Companionate Ideals since 1750'. In *Routledge History of Sex and the Body 1500 to the Present*, edited by Sarah Toulalan and Kate Fisher, pp. 328–47. London and New York: Routledge, 2013.
———. 'Women's Experiences of Abortion before the 1967 Act'. In *Abortion Law and Politics Today*, edited by Ellie Lee, pp. 213–32. Manchester: Manchester University Press, 1998.
Fisher, Will. '"Wantoning with the Thighs": The Socialization of Thigh Sex in England, 1590–1730'. *Journal of the History of Sexuality* 24, no. 1 (2015): 1–24.
Fowler, David. *The First Teenagers: The Lifestyle of Young Wage-Earners in Interwar Britain*. London: Woburn Press, 1995.
———. *Youth Culture in Modern Britain, c.1920–c.1970*. Basingstoke: Palgrave Macmillan, 2008.
Fox, Greer Litton. '"Nice Girl": Social Control of Women through a Value Construct'. *Signs* 2, no. 4 (1977): 805–17.
Fraser, Derek. *The Evolution of the British Welfare State: A History of Social Policy since the Industrial Revolution*, 5th ed. London: Palgrave, 2017.
Fuhg, Felix. *London's Working-Class Youth and the Making of Post-Victorian Britain, 1958–1971*. Basingstoke: Palgrave Macmillan, 2021.
Gagnon, John H., and William Simon. 'The Sexual Scripting of Oral Genital Contacts'. *Archives of Sexual Behavior* 16, no. 1 (1987): 1–25.
Geiringer, David. *The Pope and the Pill: Sex, Catholicism and Women in Post-War England*. Manchester: Manchester University Press, 2019.
Gildart, Keith. *Images of England through Popular Music: Class, Youth and Rock 'n' Roll, 1955–1976*. Basingstoke: Palgrave Macmillan, 2013.
Giles, Judy. 'Narratives of Gender, Class, and Modernity in Women's Memories of Mid-Twentieth Century Britain'. *Signs: Journal of Women in Culture and Society* 28, no. 1 (2002): 21–41.
———. '"Playing Hard to Get": Working-Class Women, Sexuality and Respectability in Britain, 1918–40'. *Women's History Review* 1, no. 2 (1992): 239–55.
Gleason, Mona. 'Avoiding the Agency Trap: Caveats for Historians of Children, Youth, and Education'. *History of Education* 45, no. 4 (2016): 446–59.
Gledhill, Jim. 'White Heat, Guide Blue: The Girl Guide Movement in the 1960s'. *Contemporary British History* 27, no. 1 (2013): 65–84.
Glew, Helen. *Gender, Rhetoric and Regulation: Women's Work in the Civil Service and London County Council, 1900–55*. Manchester: Manchester University Press, 2016.
Goodwin, John, and Henrietta O'Connor. 'Ordinary Lives: "Typical Stories" of Girls' Transitions in the 1960s and the 1980s'. *Sociological Research Online* 18, no. 1 (2013): 191–99. http://www.socresonline.org.uk/18/1/4.html [accessed: 25 September 2024].
Gorer, Geoffrey. *Exploring English Character*. New York: Criterion Books, 1955.

———. *Sex and Marriage in England Today: A Study of the Views and Experience of the Under-45s*. London: Nelson, 1971.

Grant, Linda. *Sexing the Millenium: Women and the Sexual Revolution*. New York: Grove Press, 1993.

Green, Jonathon. *All Dressed Up: The Sixties and the Counterculture*. London: Jonathan Cape, 1998.

Griffin, Christine. *Typical Girls? Young Women from School to the Job Market*. London: Routledge and Kegan Paul, 1985.

Grimley, Matthew. 'Law, Morality and Secularisation: The Church of England and the Wolfenden Report, 1954–1967'. *The Journal of Ecclesiastical History* 60, no. 4 (2009): 725–41.

Gunn, Simon. 'People and the Car: The Expansion of Automobility in Urban Britain, c. 1955–70'. *Social History* 38, no. 2 (2013): 220–37.

Hall, Lesley A. 'Eyes Tightly Shut, Lying Rigidly Still, and Thinking of England? British Women and Sex from Marie Stopes to Hite 2000'. In *Sexual Pedagogies: Sex Education in Britain, Australia, and America, 1879–2000*, edited by Claudia Nelson and Michelle H. Martin, pp. 53–71. Basingstoke: Palgrave Macmillan, 2004.

———. *Sex, Gender and Social Change in Britain since 1880*, 2nd ed. Basingstoke: Palgrave Macmillan, 2013.

———. 'The Victorians: Our Others, Our Selves?'. In *Sex, Knowledge and Receptions of the Past*, edited by Kate Fisher and Rebecca Langlands, pp. 161–77. Oxford: Oxford University Press, 2015.

Hall, Richard. 'Emotional Histories: Materiality, Temporality and Subjectivity in Oral History Interviews with Fathers and Sons'. *Oral History* 47, no. 1 (2019): 61–70.

Hall, Stuart, and Tony Jefferson, eds. *Resistance through Rituals: Youth Subcultures in Post-War Britain*, 2nd ed. Abingdon: Routledge, 1993.

Halsey, A. H. 'Further and Higher Education'. In *British Social Trends since 1900: A Guide to the Changing Social Structure of Britain*, edited by A. H. Halsey, pp. 221–53. Houndmills: Macmillan, 2000.

Hampshire, James. 'The Politics of School Sex Education Policy in England and Wales from the 1940s to the 1960s'. *Social History of Medicine* 18, no. 1 (2005): 87–105.

Hampshire, James, and Jane Lewis. '"The Ravages of Permissiveness": Sex Education and the Permissive Society'. *Twentieth Century British History* 15, no. 3 (2004): 290–312.

Harris, Alana. '"The Writings of Querulous Women": Contraception, Conscience and Clerical Authority in 1960s Britain'. *British Catholic History* 32, no. 4 (2015): 557–85.

Harrison, Laura. *Dangerous Amusements: Leisure, the Young Working Class and Urban Space in Britain, C. 1870–1939*. Manchester: Manchester University Press, 2022.

Haste, Cate. *Rules of Desire: Sex in Britain World War I to the Present*. London: Chatto & Windus, 1992.

Hennessy, Peter. *Having It So Good: Britain in the Fifties*. London: Penguin, 2007.

Hilliard, Chris. *A Matter of Obscenity: The Politics of Censorship in Modern England*. Princeton: Princeton University Press, 2021.
Hitchcock, T. 'Sex and Gender: Redefining Sex in Eighteenth-Century England'. *History Workshop Journal* 41, no. 1 (1996): 72–90.
Hoggart, Lesley. *Feminist Campaigns for Birth Control and Abortion Rights in Britain*. Lewiston: Edwin Mellen Press, 2003.
Holland, Janet, Caroline Ramazanoglu, Sue Sharpe, and Rachel Thomson. 'Deconstructing Virginity: Young People's Accounts of First Sex'. *Sexual and Relationship Therapy* 15, no. 3 (2000): 221–32.
———. *The Male in the Head: Young People, Heterosexuality and Power*, 2nd ed. London: The Tufnell Press, 2004.
Holtzman, Ellen M. 'The Pursuit of Married Love: Women's Attitudes toward Sexuality and Marriage in Great Britain, 1918–1939'. *Journal of Social History* 16, no. 2 (1982): 39–51.
Houlbrook, Matt. 'Cities'. In *Palgrave Advances in the Modern History of Sexuality*, edited by H. G. Cocks and Matt Houlbrook, pp. 133–56. Basingstoke: Palgrave Macmillan, 2006.
Hunt, Alan, and Bruce Curtis. 'A Genealogy of the Genital Kiss: Oral Sex in the Twentieth Century'. *The Canadian Journal of Human Sexuality* 15, no. 2 (2006).
Hunter, I. Q. 'Take an Easy Ride: Sexploitation in the 1970s'. In *Seventies British Cinema*, edited by Robert Shail, pp. 3–13. Basingstoke: Palgrave Macmillan, 2008.
Ingham, Mary. *Now We Are Thirty: Women of the Breakthrough Generation*. London: Eyre Methuen, 1981.
Jackson, Louise. 'Childhood and Youth'. In *Palgrave Advances in the Modern History of Sexuality*, edited by H. G. Cocks and Matt Houlbrook, pp. 231–55. Basingstoke: Palgrave Macmillan, 2005.
Jackson, Louise, and Angela Bartie. *Policing Youth: Britain 1945–80*. Manchester: Manchester University Press, 2014.
Jackson, Margaret. *The Real Facts of Life: Feminism and the Politics of Sexuality, 1850–1940*. London: Taylor & Francis, 1994.
Jamieson, Lynn. 'Changing Intimacy in the Twentieth Century: Seeking and Forming Couple Relationships'. In *A History of Everyday Life in the Twentieth Century Scotland*, edited by Lynn Abrams and Callum G. Brown, pp. 76–102. Edinburgh: Edinburgh University Press, 2010.
Jeffries, Sheila. *Anticlimax: A Feminist Perspective on the Sexual Revolution*. London: The Women's Press, 1990.
Jennings, Rebecca. *Tomboys and Bachelor Girls: A Lesbian History of Post-War Britain*. Manchester: Manchester University Press, 2007.
Jerman, Betty. *The Lively-Minded Women: The First Twenty Years of the National Housewives Register*. London: Heinemann, 1981.
Jobling, Paul. 'Playing Safe: The Politics of Pleasure and Gender in the Promotion of Condoms in Britain, 1970–1982'. *Journal of Design History* 10, no. 1 (1997): 53–70.
Johnes, Martin. *Wales since 1939*. Manchester: Manchester University Press, 2012.

Johnson, Walter. 'On Agency'. *Journal of Social History* 37, no. 1 (2003): 113–24.
Jones, Claire L. *The Business of Birth Control: Contraception and Commerce in Britain before the Sexual Revolution*. Manchester: Manchester University Press, 2020.
Jones, Helen. *Women in British Public Life 1914–1950*. Harlow: Longman, 2000.
Keating, Jenny. *A Child for Keeps: The History of Adoption in England, 1918–45*. Basingstoke: Palgrave Macmillan, 2009.
Kelly, Y., A. Zilanawala, C. Booker, and A. Sacker. 'Social Media Use and Adolescent Mental Health: Findings from the UK Millennium Cohort Study'. *EClinicalMedicine* 6 (2018): 59–68.
Koedt, Anne. 'The Myth of the Vaginal Orgasm'. In *Notes from the Second Year*, edited by New York Radical Women, pp. 37–41. New York, 1970.
Kramer, Anne-Marie. 'The Observers and the Observed: The "Dual Vision" of the Mass Observation Project'. *Sociological Research Online* 19, no. 3 (2014): 226–36.
Langellier, Kristin, and Eric Peterson. *Storytelling in Daily Life: Performing Narrative*. Philadelphia: Temple University Press, 2004.
Langhamer, Claire. *The English in Love: The Intimate Story of an Emotional Revolution*. Oxford: Oxford University Press, 2013.
———. 'Feelings, Women and Work in the Long 1950s'. *Women's History Review* 26, no. 1 (2017): 77–92.
———. 'Love and Courtship in Mid-Twentieth-Century England'. *The Historical Journal* 50, no. 1 (2007): 173–96.
———. '"Who the Hell Are Ordinary People?": Ordinariness as a Category of Historical Analysis'. *Transactions of the Royal Historical Society* 28 (2018): 175–95.
———. *Women's Leisure in England, 1920–60*. Manchester: Manchester University Press, 2000.
Laurie, Peter. *Teenage Revolution*. London: Anthony Blond, 1965.
Lewis, Jane. *Women in England, 1870–1950: Sexual Divisions and Social Change*. Bloomington: Indiana University Press, 1984.
Lewis, Jane, and John Welshman. 'The Issue of Never-Married Motherhood in Britain, 1920–70'. *Social History of Medicine* 10, no. 3 (1997): 401–18.
Lewis, Ruth, Cicely Marston, and Kaye Wellings. 'Bases, Stages and "Working Your Way Up": Young People's Talk About Non-Coital Practices and "Normal" Sexual Trajectories'. *Sociological Research Online* 18, no. 1 (2013): 233–41.
Limond, David. 'Frequently but Naturally: William Michael Duane, Kenneth Charles Barnes and Teachers as Innovators in Sex(uality) Education in English Adolescent Schooling: C. 1945–1965'. *Sex Education* 5, no. 2 (2005): 107–18.
Lonchraine, Rebecca. 'Bosom of the Nation: Page Three in the 1970s and 1980s'. In *Rude Britannia*, edited by Mina Gorji, pp. 96–112. London and New York: Routledge, 2007.

Loughran, Thomas, Andrew Mycock, and Jonathan Tonge. 'A Coming of Age: How and Why the UK Became the First Democracy to Allow Votes for 18-Year-Olds'. *Contemporary British History* 35, no. 2 (2021): 284–313.

Lovett, Laura L. 'Age: A Useful Category of Historical Analysis'. *Journal of the History of Childhood and Youth* 1, no. 1 (2008): 89–90.

Lowe, Rodney. *The Welfare State in Britain since 1945*, 3rd ed. Basingstoke: Palgrave, 2004.

Lynch, Charlie. 'Moral Panic in the Industrial Town: Teenage "Deviancy" and Religious Crisis in Central Scotland C. 1968-9'. *Twentieth Century British History* 32, no. 3 (2021): 371–91.

Maguire, Anna. '"You Wouldn't Want Your Daughter Marrying One": Parental Intervention into Mixed-Race Relationships in Post-War Britain'. *Historical Research* 92, no. 256 (2019): 432–44.

Mandler, Peter. *The Crisis of Meritocracy: Britain's Transition to Mass Education since the Second World War*. Oxford: Oxford University Press, 2020.

———. 'Educating the Nation I: Schools'. *Transactions of the Royal Historical Society* 24 (2014): 5–28.

———. 'Educating the Nation II: Universities'. *Transactions of the Royal Historical Society* 25 (2015): 1–26.

Marston, C., and R. Lewis. 'Anal Heterosex among Young People and Implications for Health Promotion: A Qualitative Study in the UK'. *BMJ Open* 4, no. 8 (2014): e004996.

Maynes, Mary-Jo. 'Age as a Category of Historical Analysis: History, Agency, and Narratives of Childhood'. *Journal of the History of Childhood and Youth* 1, no. 1 (2008): 114–24.

Mays, John Barron. *The Young Pretenders: A Study of Teenage Culture in Contemporary Society*. London: Michael Joseph, 1965.

McCance, C., and D. J. Hall. 'Sexual Behaviour and Contraceptive Practice of Unmarried Female Undergraduates at Aberdeen University'. *The British Medical Journal* 2, no. 5815 (1972): 694–700.

McCarthy, Helen. *Double Lives: A History of Working Motherhood*. London: Bloomsbury, 2020.

———. 'Social Science and Married Women's Employment in Post-War Britain'. *Past & Present* 233, no. 1 (2016): 269–305.

———. 'Women, Marriage and Paid Work in Post-War Britain'. *Women's History Review* 26, no. 1 (2017): 46–61.

McCormick, Leanne. *Regulating Sexuality: Women in Twentieth-Century Northern Ireland*. Manchester: Manchester University Press, 2013.

McCray Beier, Lucinda. *For Their Own Good: The Transformation of English Working-Class Health Culture, 1880–1970*. Columbus: Ohio State University Press, 2008.

McInroy, Lauren B., and Shelley L. Craig. 'Perspectives of LGBTQ Emerging Adults on the Depiction and Impact of LGBTQ Media Representation'. *Journal of Youth Studies* 20, no. 1 (2017): 32–46.

McIntosh, Tania. '"An Abortionist City": Maternal Mortality, Abortion, and Birth Control in Sheffield, 1920–1940'. *Medical History* 44, no. 1 (2000): 75–96.

McLaren, Angus. *Twentieth-Century Sexuality: A History*. Oxford: Blackwell, 1999.

McLelland, Mark. '"Kissing is a Symbol of Democracy!" Dating, Democracy, and Romance in Occupied Japan, 1945–1952'. *Journal of the History of Sexuality* 19, no. 3 (2010): 508–35.

McRobbie, Angela. *Feminism and Youth Culture: From Jackie to Just Seventeen*. London: Macmillan, 1991.

———. 'Settling Accounts with Subcultures: A Feminist Critique'. In *On Record: Rock Pop and the Written Word*, edited by Simon Frith and A. Goodwin, pp. 66–80. London: Routledge, 1990.

McRobbie, Angela, and Jenny Garber. 'Girls and Subculture: An Exploration'. In *Resistance through Rituals: Youth Subcultures in Post-War Britain*, edited by Stuart Hall and Tony Jefferson, pp. 209–22. London: Hutchinson, 1976.

Mechen, Ben. '"Closer Together": Durex Condoms and Contraceptive Consumerism in 1970s Britain'. In *Perceptions of Pregnancy from the Seventeenth to the Twentieth Century*, edited by Jennifer Evans and Ciara Meehan, pp. 213–36. Basingstoke: Palgrave Macmillan, 2017.

———. '"Instamatic Living Rooms of Sin": Pornography, Participation and the Erotics of Ordinariness in the 1970s'. *Contemporary British History* 36, no. 2 (2022): 174–206.

Milcoy, Katherine. *When the Girls Come out to Play: Teenage Working-Class Girls' Leisure between the Wars*. London and New York: Bloomsbury Academic, 2017.

Miles, Joanna, Daniel Monk, and Rebecca Probert, eds. *Fifty Years of the Divorce Reform Act*. Oxford: Bloomsbury, 2022.

Miller, Susan A. 'Assent as Agency in the Early Years of the Children of the American Revolution'. *Journal of the History of Childhood and Youth* 9, no. 1 (2016): 48–65.

Mills, Helena. 'Using the Personal to Critique the Popular: Women's Memories of 1960s Youth'. *Contemporary British History* 30, no. 4 (2016): 463–83.

Mintz, Steve. 'Reflections on Age as a Category of Historical Analysis'. *Journal of the History of Childhood and Youth* 1, no. 1 (2008): 91–94.

Mishna, Faye, Elizabeth Milne, Charlene Cook, Andrea Slane, and Jessica Ringrose. 'Unsolicited Sexts and Unwanted Requests for Sexts: Reflecting on the Online Sexual Harassment of Youth'. *Youth & Society* 55, no. 4 (2021): 630–51.

Mitchell, Gillian A. M. 'Reassessing "the Generation Gap": Bill Haley's 1957 Tour of Britain, Inter-Generational Relations and Attitudes to Rock 'N' Roll in the Late 1950s'. *Twentieth Century British History* 24, no. 4 (2013): 573–605.

Morris, George. 'Intimacy in Modern British History'. *The Historical Journal* 64, no. 3 (2021): 796–811.
Mort, Frank. 'The Ben Pimlott Memorial Lecture 2010: The Permissive Society Revisited'. *Twentieth Century British History* 22, no. 2 (2011): 269–98.
———. *Capital Affairs: London and the Making of the Permissive Society.* New Haven: Yale University Press, 2010.
———. 'Victorian Afterlives: Sexuality and Identity in the 1960s and 1970s'. *History Workshop Journal* 82, no. 1 (2016): 199–212.
Mugglestone, Lynda. '"The Indefinable Something": Representing Rudeness in the English Dictionary'. In *Rude Britannia*, edited by Mina Gorji, pp. 23–34. Abingdon: Routledge, 2013.
Murphy, Kate. 'A Marriage Bar of Convenience? The BBC and Married Women's Work 1923–39'. *Twentieth Century British History* 25, no. 4 (2014): 533–61.
Murphy, Michael. 'The Evolution of Cohabitation in Britain, 1960–95'. *Population Studies* 54, no. 1 (2000): 43–56.
Murray, Gillian. 'Taking Work Home: The Private Secretary and Domestic Identities in the Long 1950s'. *Women's History Review* 26, no. 1 (2017): 62–76.
Nash, Roy. 'Clique Formation among Primary and Secondary School Children'. *British Journal of Sociology* 24, no. 3 (1973): 303–13.
Neuhaus, Jessamyn. 'The Importance of Being Orgasmic: Sexuality, Gender, and Marital Sex Manuals in the United States, 1920–1963'. *Journal of the History of Sexuality* 9, no. 4 (2000): 447–73.
O'Neill, Daniel. '"People Love Player's": Cigarette Advertising and the Teenage Consumer in Post-War Britain'. *Twentieth Century British History* 28, no. 3 (2017): 414–39.
Osgerby, Bill. '"Well, It's Saturday Night an' I Just Got Paid": Youth, Consumerism and Hegemony in Post-War Britain'. *Contemporary Record* 6, no. 2 (1992): 287–305.
———. *Youth in Britain since 1945.* Oxford: Blackwell, 1998.
Perraton, Hilary. *A History of Foreign Students in Britain.* Basingstoke: Palgrave Macmillan, 2014.
Pierce, Rachel M. 'Marriage in the Fifties'. *Sociological Review* 11 (1963): 215–40.
Pilcher, Jane. 'School Sex Education: Policy and Practice in England 1870 to 2000'. *Sex Education* 5, no. 2 (2005): 153–70.
Portelli, Alessandro. 'What Makes Oral History Different'. In *The Oral History Reader*, edited by Robert Perks and Alistair Thomson, pp. 48–58. London: Routledge, 2016.
Porter, Roy, and Lesley A. Hall. *The Facts of Life: The Creation of Sexual Knowledge in Britain, 1650–1950.* New Haven: Yale University Press, 1995.
Preston, John. *A Very English Scandal: Sex, Lies and a Murder Plot at the Heart of the Establishment.* London: Viking, 2016.

Probert, Rebecca, ed. *Cohabitation and Non-Marital Births in England and Wales, 1600–2012*. Basingstoke: Palgrave Macmillan, 2014.

Ramsay, Laura Monica. 'The Ambiguities of Christian Sexual Discourse in Post-War Britain: The British Council of Churches and Its Early Moral Welfare Work'. *Journal of Religious History* 40, no. 1 (2016): 82–103.

Reiss, Ira. 'The Scaling of Premarital Sexual Permissiveness'. *Journal of Marriage and Family* 26, no. 2 (1964): 188–98.

Richards, Martin P. M., and B. Jane Elliott. 'Sex and Marriage in the 1960s and 1970s'. In *Marriage, Domestic Life and Social Change: Writings for Jacqueline Burgoyne, 1944–88*, edited by David Clark, pp. 33–54. London and New York: Routledge, 1991.

Roberts, Elizabeth. *A Woman's Place: An Oral History of Working-Class Women 1890–1940*. Oxford: Blackwell, 1984.

———. *Women and Families: An Oral History, 1940–1970*. Oxford: Blackwell, 1995.

Robinson, Emily, Camilla Schofield, Florence Sutcliffe-Braithwaite, and Natalie Thomlinson. 'Telling Stories about Post-War Britain: Popular Individualism and the "Crisis" of the 1970s'. *Twentieth Century British History* 28, no. 2 (2017): 268–304.

Robinson, Jane. *In the Family Way: Illegitimacy between the Great War and the Swinging Sixties*. London: Viking, 2015.

Robinson, Victoria, Jenny Hockey, and Angela Meah. '"What I Used to Do ... on My Mother's Settee": Spatial and Emotional Aspects of Heterosexuality in England'. *Gender, Place & Culture* 11, no. 3 (2004): 417–35.

Robinson Rhodes, Martha. 'Bisexuality, Multiple-Gender-Attraction, and Gay Liberation Politics in the 1970s'. *Twentieth Century British History* 32, no. 1 (2021): 119–42.

Roffman, Deborah M. 'The Power of Language: Baseball as a Sexual Metaphor in American Culture'. *SIECUS Report* 19, no. 5 (1991): 1–6.

Rose, Nikolas. *Governing the Soul: The Shaping of the Private Self*, 2nd ed. London: Free Association Books, 1999.

Ruiz, Jason. 'Private Lives and Public History: On Excavating the Sexual Past in Queer Oral History Practice'. In *Bodies of Evidence: The Practice of Queer Oral History*, edited by Nan Alamilla Boyd and Horacio N. Roque Ramirez, pp. 113–29. Oxford: Oxford University Press, 2012.

Rusterholz, Caroline. 'Youth Sexuality, Responsibility, and the Opening of the Brook Advisory Centres in London and Birmingham in the 1960s'. *Journal of British Studies* 61, no. 2 (2022): 315–42.

Segal, Lynne. *Straight Sex: Rethinking the Politics of Pleasure*. Berkeley: University of California Press, 1994.

Seidman, Steven. 'Constructing Sex as a Domain of Pleasure and Self-Expression: Sexual Ideology in the Sixties'. *Theory, Culture & Society* 6, no. 2 (1989): 293–315.

Sheldon, Sally, Gayle Davis, Jane O'Neill, and Clare Porter. *The Abortion Act 1967: A Biography of a UK Law*. Cambridge: Cambridge University Press, 2023.

Sheridan, Dorothy. '"Damned Anecdotes and Dangerous Confabulations": Mass-Observation as Life History'. *Mass Observation Occasional Papers* 7 (1996). www.massobs.org.uk/images/occasional_papers/no7_sheridan.pdf [accessed: 25 September 2024].
———. 'Writing to the Archive: Mass-Observation as Autobiography'. *Sociology* 27, no. 1 (1993): 27–40.
Silies, Eva-Maria. 'Taking the Pill after the "Sexual Revolution": Female Contraceptive Decisions in England and West Germany in the 1970s'. *European Review of History: Revue européenne d'histoire* 22, no. 1 (2015): 41–59.
Silverstone, Rosalie. 'Office Work for Women: An Historical Review'. *Business History* 18, no. 1 (1976): 98–110.
Smith, Helen. 'Working-Class Ideas and Experiences of Sexuality in Twentieth-Century Britain: Regionalism as a Category of Analysis'. *Twentieth Century British History* 29, no. 1 (2018): 58–78.
Smith, Lisa. '"You're 16…You Should Probably Be on the Pill": Girls, the Non-Reproductive Body, and the Rhetoric of Self-Control'. *Studies in the Maternal* 6, no. 1 (2014). www.mamsie.bbk.ac.uk [accessed: 25 September 2024].
Soma, Sara. *Everyone's Invited*. London: Simon & Schuster, 2022.
Spencer, Stephanie. *Gender, Work and Education in Britain in the 1950s*. Basingstoke: Palgrave Macmillan, 2005.
———. 'Girls at Risk. Early School-Leaving and Early Marriage in the 1950s'. *Journal of Educational Administration and History* 41, no. 2 (2009): 179–92.
Sprecher, Susan, Anita Barbee, and Pepper Schwartz. '"Was It Good for You, Too?": Gender Differences in First Sexual Intercourse Experiences'. *The Journal of Sex Research* 32, no. 1 (1995): 3–15.
Stanley, Liz. *Sex Surveyed 1949–1994: From Mass-Observation's 'Little Kinsey' to the National Survey and the Hite Report*. London: Taylor & Francis, 1995.
Stewart, Fiona J. 'Femininities in Flux? Young Women, Heterosexuality and (Safe) Sex'. *Sexualities* 2, no. 3 (1999): 275–90.
Strange, Julie-Marie. 'The Assault on Ignorance: Teaching Menstrual Etiquette in England, C. 1920s to 1960s'. *Social History of Medicine* 14, no. 2 (2001): 247–65.
Strimpel, Zoe. 'Heterosexual Love in the British Women's Liberation Movement: Reflections from the Sisterhood and after Archive'. *Women's History Review* 25, no. 6 (2016): 903–24.
———. *Seeking Love in Modern Britain: Gender, Dating and the Rise of 'the Single'*. London: Bloomsbury Academic, 2020.
Summerfield, Penny. 'Culture and Composure: Creating Narratives of the Gendered Self in Oral History Interviews'. *Cultural and Social History* 1, no. 1 (2004): 65–93.
Sutcliffe-Braithwaite, Florence, and Natalie Thomlinson. 'Vernacular Discourses of Gender Equality in the Post-War British Working Class'. *Past & Present* 254, no. 1 (2022): 277–313.

Sutherland, Margaret B. 'Whatever Happened about Coeducation?'. *British Journal of Educational Studies* 33, no. 2 (1985): 155–63.

Swanson, Gillian. *Drunk with the Glitter: Space, Consumption and Sexual Instability in Modern Urban Culture*. London: Routledge, 2007.

Szreter, Simon. 'Victorian Britain, 1831–1963: Towards a Social History of Sexuality'. *Journal of Victorian Culture* 1, no. 1 (1996): 136–49.

Szreter, Simon, and Kate Fisher. *Sex before the Sexual Revolution: Intimate Life in England 1918–1963*. Cambridge: Cambridge University Press, 2010.

Tebbutt, Melanie. 'From "Marriage Bureau" to "Points of View". Changing Patterns of Advice in Teenage Magazines: *Mirabelle*, 1956–1977'. In *People, Places and Identities: Themes in British Social and Cultural History, 1700s–1980s*, edited by Alan Kidd and Melanie Tebbutt, pp. 180–201. Manchester: Manchester University Press, 2017.

———. *Women's Talk?: A Social History of 'Gossip' in Working-Class Neighbourhoods, 1880–1960*. Aldershot: Scolar Press, 1995.

Thom, Deborah. 'Better a Teacher Than a Hairdresser? "A Mad Passion for Equality" or, Keeping Molly and Betty Down'. In *Lessons for Life: The Schooling of Girls and Women, 1850–1950*, edited by Felicity Hunt, pp. 124–46. Oxford: Blackwell, 1987.

Thomas, Nick. 'Challenging Myths of the 1960s: The Case of Student Protest in Britain'. *Twentieth Century British History* 13, no. 3 (2002): 277–97.

———. '"To-Night's Big Talking Point Is Still That Book": Popular Responses to the Lady Chatterley Trial'. *Cultural and Social History* 10, no. 4 (2013): 619–34.

Thompson, Ben. *Ban This Filth! Mary Whitehouse and the Battle to Keep Britain Innocent*. London: Faber & Faber, 2012.

Thompson, Derek. 'Courtship and Marriage in Preston between the Wars'. *Oral History* 3, no. 2 (1975): 39–44.

Thompson, Sharon. 'Putting a Big Thing into a Little Hole: Teenage Girls' Accounts of Sexual Initiation'. *The Journal of Sex Research* 27, no. 3 (1990): 341–61.

Thomson, Mathew. *Psychological Subjects: Identity, Culture and Health in Twentieth-Century Britain*. Oxford: Oxford University Press, 2006.

Tinkler, Penny. '"Are You Really Living?" If Not, "Get with It!": The Teenage Self and Lifestyle in Young Women's Magazines, Britain 1957–70'. *Cultural and Social History* 11, no. 4 (2014): 597–619.

———. 'Cause for Concern: Young Women and Leisure, 1930–50'. *Women's History Review* 12, no. 2 (2003): 233–62.

———. *Constructing Girlhood: Popular Magazines for Girls Growing up in England, 1920–1950*. London: Taylor & Francis, 1995.

———. 'Going Places or out of Place? Representations of Mobile Girls and Young Women in Late-1950s and 1960s Britain'. *Twentieth Century British History* 32, no. 2 (2021): 212–37.

Tinkler, Penny, Laura Fenton, and Resto Cruz. 'Introducing "Resonance": Revisioning the Relationship between Youth and Later

Life in Women Born 1939–52'. *The Sociological Review* 71, no. 1 (2022): 37–57.
Tisdall, Laura. '"What a Difference It Was to Be a Woman and Not a Teenager": Adolescent Girls' Conceptions of Adulthood in 1960s and 1970s Britain'. *Gender & History* 34, no. 2 (2022): 495–513.
Todd, Selina. *Young Women, Work, and Family in England, 1918–1950*. Oxford: Oxford University Press, 2005.
———. 'Young Women, Work, and Leisure in Interwar England'. *The Historical Journal* 48, no. 3 (2005): 789–809.
Tomlinson-Gray, Daniel, ed. *Big Gay Adventures in Education: Supporting LGBT+ Visibility and Inclusion in Schools*. London: Routledge, 2020.
Tonkin, Elizabeth. *Narrating Our Pasts: The Social Construction of Oral History*. Cambridge: Cambridge University Press, 1992.
Valenti, Jessica. *The Purity Myth: How America's Obsession with Virginity Is Hurting Young Women*. New York: Seal Press, 2009.
Vance, Carole S. *Pleasure and Danger: Exploring Female Sexuality*. London: Pandora Press, 1992.
Vandenbosch, Laura, Jasmine Fardouly, and Marika Tiggemann. 'Social Media and Body Image: Recent Trends and Future Directions'. *Current Opinion in Psychology* 45 (2022): 101289.
Vera-Gray, Fiona, Clare McGlynn, Ibad Kureshi, and Kate Butterby. 'Sexual Violence as a Sexual Script in Mainstream Online Pornography'. *The British Journal of Criminology* 61, no. 5 (2021): 1243–60.
Voigt, David. 'Sex in Baseball: Reflections of Changing Taboos'. *Journal of Popular Culture* 12, no. 3 (1978): 389–403.
Wallhead, Emma. 'A Political Sexual Revolution: Sexual Autonomy in the British Women's Liberation Movement in the 1970s and 1980s'. *Twentieth Century British History* 34, no. 2 (2023): 354–76.
Ward, Anna E. 'Sex and the Me Decade: Sex and Dating Advice Literature of the 1970s'. *Women's Studies Quarterly* 43, no. 3/4 (2015): 120–36.
Ward, Stephanie. 'Drifting into Manhood and Womanhood: Courtship, Marriage and Gender among Young Adults in South Wales and the North-East of England in the 1930s'. *The Welsh History Review* 26, no. 4 (2013): 623–48.
Weeks, Jeffrey. *Coming Out: The Emergence of LGBT Identities in Britain from the Nineteenth Century to the Present*, 3rd ed. London: Quartet Books, 2016.
———. *Sexuality and Its Discontents*. London: Routledge and Kegan Paul, 1986.
———. *The World We Have Won: The Remaking of Erotic and Intimate Life*. London and New York: Routledge, 2007.
Wellings, Kay, Julia Field, Anne M. Johnson, and Jane Wadsworth. *Sexual Behaviour in Britain: The National Survey of Sexual Attitudes and Lifestyles*. London: Penguin Books, 1994.
Whyte, William. *Redbrick: A Social and Architectural History of Britain's Civic Universities*. Oxford: Oxford University Press, 2015.

Willis, Malachi, Kristen N. Jozkowski, Wen-Juo Lo, and Stephanie A. Sanders. 'Are Women's Orgasms Hindered by Phallocentric Imperatives?'. *Archives of Sexual Behavior* 47, no. 6 (2018): 1565–76.

Wilson, Dolly Smith. 'A New Look at the Affluent Worker: The Good Working Mother in Post-War Britain'. *Twentieth Century British History* 17, no. 2 (2006): 206–29.

Wilson, Elizabeth. *Only Halfway to Paradise: Women in Postwar Britain 1945–1968*. London: Tavistock, 1979.

Wilson, Guerriero R. 'Women's Work in Offices and the Preservation of Men's "Breadwinning" Jobs in Early Twentieth-Century Glasgow'. *Women's History Review* 10, no. 3 (2001): 463–82.

Wivel, Ashley. 'Abortion Policy and Politics on the Lane Committee of Enquiry, 1971–1974'. *Social History of Medicine* 11, no. 1 (1998): 109–35.

Woodman, Dan. 'Researching "Ordinary" Young People in a Changing World: The Sociology of Generations and the "Missing Middle" in Youth Research'. *Sociological Research Online* 18, no. 1 (2013): 7. http://www.socresonline.org.uk/18/1/7.html [accessed: 25 September 2024].

Worth, Eve. *The Welfare State Generation: Women, Agency and Class in Britain since 1945*. London: Bloomsbury Academic, 2022.

———. 'Women, Education and Social Mobility in Britain during the Long 1970s'. *Cultural and Social History* 16, no. 1 (2019): 67–83.

Index

#MeToo movement 150, 255
19 (magazine) 63

abortion 195–96
    pre-1968 110–13
    statistics 110
Abortion Act (1967) 7, 110, 249
Abrams, Lynn 13, 21, 90, 248
Abrams, Mark 4
adolescence 177
advice literature 41
affluence 4, 174, 216, 249
age as a category of analysis 257
age of consent 71
age of majority 4
agency
    as analytic tool 14, 258
    claims of 69
    in the history of youth 257–58
AIDS 252

baby boom 3
Barker, Diana 206
bedrooms 231
Board of Education 43
Bob Dylan 217
Borge, Jessica 104
boyfriends
    break-ups 195
    as status symbol 176–77, 180
    see also relationships
Brewitt-Taylor, Sam 9, 10

British Board of Film
    Censors 8
British Medical Journal 50, 174
Brown, Callum 9, 225

cars
    as site of sexual activity
        233, 236–38
censorship 52
Centre for Contemporary
    Cultural Studies (CCCS)
    5, 257
Chandler, E.M. 175
chastity 8, 9, 65, 187, 227
Chesser, Eustace 41
cinema 10, 181
    back row 183
Clarke, Michael 5
class identity 24
    complexity of 24–26
cohabitation 206
Collins, Marcus 7, 52, 259
Comfort, Alex 196, 223
condoms
    gender dynamics of use
        104–6
    see also contraception
consent
    ambiguity of 258
consumerism 4, 11, 174
contraception
    gendered nature of 9

contraception (*continued*)
    as shared endeavour 101
    see also condoms; oral
        contraceptive pill
Corner, George W. 41
Cosmopolitan 16, 196
courtship 133–34
    see also relationships;
        romance
crushes 136–37
curfew 208–9

Daily Mail 87
dances 139, 181, 184
desire
    gendered nature of
        151–52, 157–58
displays of affection 180
    see also kissing
divorce 97
Domestic Violence and
    Matrimonial Proceedings
    Act (1976) 12
Dyhouse, Carol 11

education
    expansion of higher
        education 11, 91, 249
    grammar school 11, 24, 92
    see also university
Education Act (1944) 11
Edwards, Sian 235
Ellis, Havelock 151
employment
    careers 12
    and freedom 93
    interwar cultures of work 11
    secretarial work 25, 93
    women's 'dual role' 12
Employment Protection Act
    (1975) 12
Everyday Sexism project 255

Family Law Reform Act (1969) 87
Family Planning Association 8
feminism 12
    ambivalence towards 12
    see also Women's Liberation
        Movement
first intercourse
    age at 8
    as choice 69
    as experiment 72
    motivated by
        curiosity 71
    as premeditated 239
    relationship at 147–48
    as talking point 193
    as transformative 72–74
    see also penetrative
        intercourse; sexual
        activity; virginity
Fisher, Kate 8, 16, 22, 104
friendship
    groups 179–80
    intimacy within 194
    rifts within 191–92
    as support system 194, 196

Garber, Jenny 5
Geiringer, David 16
generation gap 216–17, 229
generational identity
    13, 216, 248
    comparison to previous
        generations 13, 250
    comparison to younger
        generations 252–53
genitalia
    as private 218
Girl Guides Association 65
Gorer, Geoffrey 225
The Guardian 229

Hadfield, J. A. 177
heterosexuality
    romanticisation of 142
Hilliard, Chris 52
homosociability 172
    see also friendship
Honey 16, 87, 144,
    204, 214, 240

illegitimacy 87
intimacy
  as analytic tool 15
  of friendship 194
  as historical subject 14, 259–61
  as motor of social change 15, 261–62
  in the mundane 215
  of touch 144

Jackie 16, 144, 214, 228, 237, 263
Jobling, Paul 104
The Joy of Sex 196, 223

Kama Sutra 223
kissing 56, 137, 138, 143–44
  see also sexual activity
Klein, Viola 12

Labour Party Youth Commission 216
Lady Chatterley's Lover 7, 52, 223
Langhamer, Claire 5, 98, 133, 259
Latey Committee 4
Legitimacy Act (1959) 87
lesbianism 252

magazines 10, 213
  see also publications by title
marriage 85
  age at 4
  changing expectations of 96
  as marker of adulthood 4
  shotgun weddings 96, 97, 114, 115
Mass Observation 43, 181
Mass Observation Project 17
  'Close Relationships' Directive (1990) 17, 18
  'Courting and Dating' Directive (2001) 17, 96, 133, 144, 157, 207
  differences to oral history 18–20

'Growing Up' Directive (1993) 17
'Sex' Directive (2005) 17, 18, 217
masturbation 218
McRobbie, Angela 5
Mechen, Ben 104
memory
  remembering emotions 21
  shaped by contemporary attitudes 44–45, 151, 209
  see also popular memory
menstruation 219–21
Mills, Helena 90
Mitchell, Gillian A. M. 205
Morris, George 259
motherhood 116
Myrdal, Alva 12

National Survey of Sexual Attitudes and Lifestyles (NATSAL) I (1991) 62
newspapers 10
  see also publications by title
'Nice Girls' 227
  definitions of 186
novels 10, 52, 95, 197
  see also publications by title

Obscene Publications Act (1959) 7
Operation Yewtree 151
oral contraceptive pill
  as cause of sexual revolution 8, 9
  creating new expectations of sex 159
  as liberating 100
  non-use 102–3
  usage statistics 8
  use as proactive choice 100–1
  see also contraception

oral history 16
   differences to Mass Observation testimonies 18–20
   self-selection bias 22
   see also testimonies
oral sex 149–50
   see also sexual activity
orgasms 196
   see also pleasure

parents
   expectations for daughters 92, 207
   as gatekeepers 212–13
   as matchmakers 211–12
   and sex education 50, 219, 221–23
   shaping sexual values 65, 186–87
parties 139, 183, 184
Pascal, Julia 11
peer pressure 175
penetrative intercourse
   outside marriage 63
   as test of compatibility 145
   see also first intercourse; sexual activity; virginity
Penthouse 223
permissive society 6
Petticoat 16, 87
petting 56
   categories of 57–58
   as pleasurable 60–61
   as 'slippery slope' 57
   see also sexual activity
Playboy 223
pleasure 237
   absence of 59, 155
   prioritisation of male 156
   see also orgasm
popular memory 23
popularity 177, 189
   see also social currency; social status

pornography 252
pregnancy
   as talking point 194
   contemporary attitudes 253–54
   fear of 88–90, 97
   judging risk of 108
   statistics 113
   stigma of extra-marital pregnancy 87
   as talking point 194
privacy 182, 188
   defined by context 184, 235
promiscuity
   class dimension 190–91
   definitions of 187
   judgement of 187

Rayner, Claire 230
relationships
   'going out' with boys 139
   holiday romances 139
   serial monogamy 139
   see also boyfriends; sexual partners
religion
   Catholicism 65, 207, 225
   religious morality 9, 225–26
reputation
   family honour 226–27
Roberts, Elizabeth 16
romance 95

Schofield, Michael 8, 64
Sex Discrimination Act (1975) 12
sex education
   absence of 45
   adult awkwardness 48–50
   changing attitudes towards 42, 43
   contemporary comparisons 44–45, 252
   critiques of provision 44
   focus on biology 46–47
   reading material 50, 222, 230
   timing of 47–48

variability of provision 43
  see also advice;
    sexual knowledge
sexual activity
  al fresco 236, 237, 238, 239
  as deepening intimacy 157
  coercion 162
  discussions about 54, 192–94, 197–98
  gendered nature of 155
  pressure to engage in 160
  and relationship status 141, 142, 146, 187
  taxonomies of 55, 62, 72, 154, 255
  terminology 21
  value of discretion 69, 188
  see also first intercourse;
    kissing; oral sex;
    penetrative
    intercourse; petting
sexual assault 153
sexual harassment 152–53
  as commonplace 153–54
  contemporary discourses of 254–55
sexual knowledge
  acquired through reading 51, 52, 223
  experience as knowledge 54
  shared with friends 51–52, 53
  see also sex education
Sexual Offences Act (1967) 7
sexual partners
  numbers of 132
  one-night stands 140
  see also boyfriends;
    relationships
sexual revolution 6, 7, 257
  feminist critiques of 160
  post-war understandings of 229
  symbols of 2

sleeping arrangements 231, 232–33
social currency
  sex as 175, 178–79
social media 252
social mobility 24
social status
  importance in adolescence 174
  see also popularity
The Spectator 49
Stopes, Marie 151
subcultures 5, 256
The Sun 7
Sunday Pictorial 6
Swinging London 2
Szreter, Simon 8, 16, 217

television
  depictions of sex 10, 223–24
  distracting parents 232
  as leisure activity 215
testimonies
  anonymity 19
  capturing historic emotions 21
  as ego-centric 132
  as evidence of historic sexual practice 20
  as method for capturing lived experience 16
  motivations for recording 23
  willingness to discuss sex 18, 19, 22
  see also Mass Observation Project; memory; oral history
Thomas, Nick 205
The Times 7
Tinkler, Penny 5
Todd, Selina 5

university 11
  see also education

van de Velde, Theodoor 151
virginity
    association with youth 67
    value of 64–65
    see also chastity; first intercourse

welfare state 3, 11, 12
withdrawal 104

Wolfenden Report 7
Women's Liberation Movement 12
    see also feminism
Worth, Eve 24, 90

young adulthood 90–91
youth studies
    missing middle 6

EU authorised representative for GPSR:
Easy Access System Europe, Mustamäe tee 50,
10621 Tallinn, Estonia
gpsr.requests@easproject.com

www.ingramcontent.com/pod-product-compliance
Lightning Source LLC
LaVergne TN
LVHW050046200525
811683LV00004B/34